Medieval Tastes

ARTS AND TRADITIONS OF THE TABLE

ARTS AND TRADITIONS OF THE TABLE: PERSPECTIVES ON CULINARY HISTORY
Albert Sonnenfeld, Series Editor

For the list of titles in this series, see page 269.

Medieval Tastes

Food, Cooking, and the Table

———————◆———————

Massimo Montanari

TRANSLATED BY BETH ARCHER BROMBERT

COLUMBIA UNIVERSITY PRESS *NEW YORK*

Columbia University Press
Publishers Since 1893
New York   Chichester, West Sussex
Copyright © 2012 Gius, Laterza & Figli. All rights reserved.
Published by arrangement with Marco Vigevani Agenzia Letteraria
Translation copyright © 2015 Columbia University Press
All rights reserved

Library of Congress Cataloging-in-Publication Data

Montanari, Massimo, 1949- [Gusti del Medioevo. English] Medieval Tastes :
food, cooking, and the table / Massimo Montanari ;
translated by Beth Archer Brombert.
pages cm
Translation of: Gusti del Medioevo. Includes bibliographical references and index.
ISBN 978-0-231-16786-4 (cloth : alk. paper)—978-0-231-53908-1 (ebook)
1. Food—Europe—History—To 1500.
2. Food habits—Europe—History—To 1500.
3. Cooking, Medieval.
I. Title.
TX351.M6613 2015
394.1′20940902—dc23
2014023679

Columbia University Press books are printed on permanent
and durable acid-free paper.
This book is printed on paper with recycled content.
Printed in the United States of America
c 10 9 8 7 6 5 4 3 2 1

COVER ART: Bibliothèque Nationale, Paris, France/Bridgeman Images
COVER DESIGN: Milenda Nan Ok Lee

Contents

Contents

Medieval Tastes

Introduction

Invitation to the Voyage

WHEN IT COMES to food and cooking, the Middle Ages often take the starring role. This is not only because medievalists, like all historians, devote much attention nowadays to this long neglected subject of history but also because marketing strategies for food production and catering were born in the Middle Ages. In truth, *Middle Ages* in most cases is no more than a generic term used to evoke an equally generic image. But that term and that image are evidently considered useful for selling and making more appealing commercial offerings. The term *medieval* attributes an added value to products and services. History is brought into play as the locus of "birth" and "origin."

This is a concern typical of our era: to authenticate the present by recalling the past, to legitimize what we are making now by saying that it used to be made long ago. The expression "long ago," historically meaningless, indicates something of a more genuine nature than does "a time past"; "long ago" is an indistinct, mythical time when things are presumed to have come into being. Then they came down to us, after a "historical" journey, which is, in reality, without history because nothing happens then. The "tradition" invoked is not the fruit of events, experiences, encounters, changes, inventions, and compromises—history, in a word—but is static and immobile. It is the "idol of origins," about which

Marc Bloch has written, which leads us "to explain the most recent by means of the most remote."

If we look at European labels—DOP, IGP, STG—proclaiming the denomination of protected origins, protected geographic origins, and guaranteed traditional specialties, we are amazed by the vagueness of historical documentation, which, after all, is the requisite foundation for authenticating and registering a product. References, when there are any, are second- and thirdhand. History is reduced to anecdotal snippets of little interest other than fulfilling a legislative requirement to provide the pedigree of the product, placing it in a context of consolidated "tradition." That "tradition" may even be extremely recent. At present, it takes only twenty-five years for a product to acquire recognition as typical or traditional. With regard to image, however, ancient looks better than modern. To claim "medieval" or, even better, "Roman" origin is a way of enhancing the nobility of the product. The older the history and the more remote the "origin," the more the product will seem worthy of being safeguarded.

The basic assumption is to think of "continuity" as a seal of guarantee. That things are subject to continuous modifications, that the flavors of foods and the tastes of people change with time, that the social and cultural contexts determine constantly changing forms of usage, that the same objects do not always correspond to the same names—all this, which is obvious to the historian, is of no interest to the general public. They would rather believe that "tradition" all by itself is a guarantee of quality, and believing that "it has always been made this way," generation after generation, is enough for total assurance.

The presumed continuity between present and past is based on a double mechanism of reduction: leading the present back to the past by projecting onto the Middle Ages the image of what we are today, of what we produce and consume today; and leading the past to the present, interpreting the Middle Ages simply as the premise or "beginning" of today. There is no question of dating practices or products or of placing them in a time frame. Quite the contrary. Aside from a few statements genuinely based on archival documents or literary works, to evoke the Middle Ages generally *de-historicizes* the subject, making it more vague and less precise, taking it out of history and into legend, out of reality and into fiction. Medievalists can rest easy: in the common perception, the term *Middle Ages* does not signify a period of history, defined by a chronology of its own and by events that occurred during that time; it is merely an idea, a concept.* The term *Middle Ages* used in the marketing of food means tradition, origins, antiquity; it means "once upon a time."

By analyzing this imaginary construct, the language that produces it, and the rhetoric that sustains it, one thing becomes apparent. In the promotion of food products, no "discussion" under the aura of the Middle Ages is negative because of the value automatically endowed by the antiquity of "tradition," whoever its guarantors: peasants weighted with experience and inventiveness, landowners in search of new pleasures, and cooks able to benefit from available resources (or from their occasional scarcity, for which they made up with ingenious creativity), as well as clever artisans and shopkeepers and, finally, monks, the absolute warranty of gastronomic know-how.

We should pause for a moment to consider the invariably positive nature of "medieval" images related to food products, for this is a culturally anomalous factor, contradictory to the ambiguity always associated with the idea of the Middle Ages in the contemporary imagination. Such an idea is twofold: the Middle Ages are a period of glorious adventures, of amorous damsels and brave knights, of deep and noble sentiments; but they are also a time of obscurity and fear, superstition, violence, and barbarism. The two images, both of them uncertain, are not gratuitous inventions of popular fantasy but arose out of centuries of historiographic inventions, initiated by the humanists of the Renaissance, who characterized the Middle Ages as "void" of civilization. What else can the term *medieval* suggest, linked by humanists to that millennium, if not the notion of a "middle period," a lengthy pause while awaiting the return of civilization after a temporary eclipse? The obscure and irrational image of the Middle Ages was consolidated during the Protestant Reformation, which attacked the church of Rome as the depository of "medieval" corruption and superstition. To this was later added the Enlightenment polemic against "feudal" privileges and abusive powers incorrectly attributed to the Middle Ages (and, on the contrary, entirely "modern").

Alongside these gloomy Middle Ages, a shimmering Middle Ages had evolved, put forth by the Counter-Reformation and later exalted

*In case it helps the nonspecialist, medievalists typically divide the Middle Ages into three separate periods: the "early" Middle Ages, from roughly the fall of Rome in 476 CE through 1000; the "high" Middle Ages, roughly from 1001 to 1300; and the "late" Middle Ages, which end around 1500.—Trans.

by the Romantic period in the name of the very irrationality that the Enlightenment saw as unworthy, transforming it into the Romantic ideal of original purity, uncorrupted emotions, and national unity. All judgments (or rather prejudices) that slowly constructed the two contrasting images of the Middle Ages selected only partial aspects of the "real" Middle Ages, isolated from the context of the period's entirety and from the life of its people. The obscure Middle Ages and the luminous one live side by side today in the collective imagination, which has digested and assimilated both premises, blending them in an unforeseeable manner. But when it comes to food, the Middle Ages are decidedly and exclusively *good*, for they represent the nostalgic dream of a pure and uncontaminated past that guarantees authenticity and quality.

Things change when the marketing of the Middle Ages introduces theme events, festivals, and rural or municipal feasts—all very common in many European countries—offering historical processions with ladies in costume, knights in noble combat, archery contests, games in the central square[†] along with reconstructions of artisans' shops and markets and all kinds of amenities under the aegis of a Middle Ages filled with warmth and goodness, genuine humanity, and profound sentiments. During those festivals, however, even the *other* Middle Ages are revealed (and later become preponderant), reflecting the obscure and malevolent, with their classic stereotypes of black magic, witches, torture, poisoning, and exorcisms of fears and anxieties that are in us but that we prefer to relegate to a finished past.

Even gastronomy enters into this world of festivals when the tenebrous Middle Ages cohabit with the luminous Middle Ages. This would seem to be the "good" side, with its habitual trousseau of platitudes about the healthfulness, tastiness, and purity of medieval food. But beware: here, we are no longer talking about simple products, or products that boast "medieval origins." Here, we are talking about cuisine and recipes prepared *in the medieval manner*, or presumed such. The experience is less trustworthy and requires a few precautions. The journey into time, in this case, is one *we* have to make. But are we really prepared to play the game and forget—if but for a few hours—our own customs?

Here, then, is a different strategy of marketing. On one side is the proposal of the conventional image of the "traditional" Middle Ages

---

[†]Games such as the Palio in Siena, soccer in medieval costume in Florence, the game of the Saracen in Arezzo, and the medieval festival in Monteriggioni.—Trans.

and as such already part of our experience (thus nothing to fear). On the other are strange dishes and unusual menus, *exotic* food, which we are invited to sample as curiosities for an evening out of the ordinary. However, since the unknown is not excluded from our disorientation, or, hypothetically, our disgust, we are immediately reassured that the game will not be too trying, that we will limit ourselves merely to sampling this medieval *diversity*, barely intuiting it, and be quickly brought back to domestic security. In short, so long as "medieval" remains synonymous with "tradition" everybody is happy. But when "medieval" risks exposing itself, acquiring more precise contours both cultural and chronological, then it is better to keep one's distance.

For this reason, culinary dishes in festival menus tend toward the contemporary. "Tasty dishes on a medieval theme made of simple and genuine ingredients" will be served by "tavern keepers in period costumes" (quoted from the websites of various events), but this cuisine brought down from the past, as though to make it more flavorful, is kept within parameters of today. The Middle Ages thus invoked are "suspended between reality and fantasy," but fantasy is hard to insert into cooking. The fantasy of the Middle Ages peters out in costumes and performances. The recipes are, in most cases, those of today, barely disguised by an unusual ingredient or a strange name but reassuring to the diners that this foray into the past will not lead them far from home.

There are many vocabularies and many choices. The range of possibilities differs widely between those who presume to reconstruct recipes and settings of an "authentic" medieval banquet and those who stop at amusing slogans such as *"ristorante e pizzeria, Medioevo in allegria* [restaurant and pizzeria, Middle Ages in fun]"; between those who take themselves too seriously and those who toy with an invented Middle Ages. What interests us, above all, is to confirm the ambiguity on which the marketing of medieval cooking is based: at the same time that it promotes its appeal, it cautions against it. The appeal is one of adventure, "a voyage in time," yet the diffidence is the same as accompanies every traveler who undertakes an adventure to some distant land. Just as the traveler visits the many restaurants in exotic places that propose tamed versions of their own cuisine, so the traveler in time enjoys being protected from the Middle Ages (fascinating but barbaric), settling into the living room of the "tradition" and the "territory" they think they know. Or else they delude themselves—and that squares the circle—into believing that that "tradition" is "medieval." It is what an advertisement, ingenious in its way, proclaims as an Emilian "medieval inn, near to home, far in time."

If we move from the marketing of products to the marketing of cooking, things change progressively. Enthusiasm for the medieval (identified with "tradition" and therefore assuredly good) has cooled, leaving room for doubt about the quality of medieval food—and possibly the conviction that, all things considered, during the Middle Ages people ate *worse* than today. The myth of origins has given way to the myth of progress. The "obscure" Middle Ages have taken over the "luminous" Middle Ages. The paradigm of modernity—assumed to be better by definition—has won out in the end. Held at the right distance, the Middle Ages have the contours of a dream. To experience it personally (like Roberto Benigni and Massimo Troisi in the film *Non ci resta che piangere* [All we have left are tears] can become a nightmare—which is why the game of medieval cooking ends quickly, on the other side of the threshold that would really make it different. To use the language of the *Michelin Guide*, the Middle Ages "deserve a detour" but perhaps not the trip.

Personally, I think that traveling to unknown places is interesting and formative, which is why I would like to invite the reader on a voyage to the foods and cooking of the Middle Ages. In this volume, I have collected a number of works that over the years I have devoted to the history of medieval taste, in its broadest sense, in the full amplitude of the repertory of food: types of production, cooking practices and gastronomic preparation, attitudes toward consumption, table manners, rules and rituals related to food, and cultural and scientific coordinates. These are pieces that were written for various occasions, principally during the past decade but in some cases earlier. A few examine an overall picture; others look at specific products or practices. In all of them, I have tried to bring together the material as well as the symbolic dimensions of food, which seem to me inextricably related and which in turn explain and justify themselves in a relationship that I like to define as interactive. To emphasize the dynamic of historical change and to understand the elements of difference beyond continuity—this has been my constant objective.

During the course of this journey, I hope that a greater intimacy will develop between the reader and the Middle Ages and that this period will be seen no longer exclusively as the symbol of obscurity but also as the symbol of light—because shadow and light are part of every era. Let it simply be a piece of our history.

CHAPTER I

Medieval Near, Medieval Far

"MEDIEVAL" COOKING has become fashionable today. But how can one presume to reconstruct the culinary taste of six, seven, or even ten centuries ago? The question, and consequently the answer, is, in fact, based on two different dimensions of taste. The first is that of taste as *flavor*—a particular sensation of the tongue and palate that is, by definition, a subjective, fleeting, incommunicable experience. In this regard, the historical experience of food is inevitably and irretrievably lost forever.

But taste is also *knowledge*—the sensory evaluation of what is good or bad, of what pleases or displeases. It is an evaluation that comes from the mind before the tongue, for the brain, not the tongue, is the organ of gastronomic pleasure. Someone had to have taught us how to distinguish and classify flavors: good/bad, pleasing/displeasing, tasty/disgusting. Seen this way, taste is not at all a subjective and incommunicable reality, but rather one that is collective and communicated. It is a cultural experience that is transmitted from birth, linked to all the other variables that contribute to creating the "values" of a society.

A great historian of cooking, Jean-Louis Flandrin, has coined the expression "structures of taste" precisely to underscore the collective and shared character of this kind of experience.[1] It is clear that this second dimension, which does not coincide with the first, but determines it in large measure, can be investigated historically by examining the remains, the traces, the "sources" (as they are called by historians) that every society in the past has left behind.

What remains? What traces? What "sources"?

In first place are cookbooks, texts of modest literary value, to which scholars, too busy investigating "high" aspects of history, paid little or no attention for a long time. Only in the last few decades has the history of food and gastronomy been accepted, and not without fierce resistance, into the pantheon of subjects deserving of historical research. A handful of scholars launched, less timidly than before, into an examination of those texts and searched for new ones in the archives and libraries of the world, with surprising results. Innumerable cookbooks are buried in manuscript codices, either in complete form or in fragments. Whether preserved singly or mixed into other texts (for the most part on medicine and dietetics), they reveal, at least for the last centuries of the Middle Ages, the fourteenth and fifteenth, a trove of documentary material whose existence was unsuspected.[2] This flowering of cookbooks, both in Italy and in other European countries, constitutes, on the one hand, the culmination of many centuries of experience and, on the other, the starting point for successive developments of so-called Renaissance cooking, the ultimate and more elaborate phase of the medieval tradition.

But we cannot stop at cookbooks. Medieval gastronomic culture emerges from many other texts: treatises on medicine and hygiene devote much space to dietary questions and to the proper use of foods with regard to health (as already mentioned, cookbooks were often inserted into such manuscripts); treatises on agriculture delve into the alimentary use of plants and animals; treatises on etiquette are not lacking in information about the esthetics of food, the table, and convivial service; literary and poetic texts also reveal great attention to the subject of food, central to a society that not only experienced the problem of daily survival, but also, and precisely because of that, attributed to food the function of distinguishing individuals and groups, signaling their status, their rank in terms of wealth and power. All the documents reflect in some way the alimentary needs and choices of the society. To know what, how, and when things are produced or acquired and by whom (verifiable in such documents as acts of sale and purchase, property agreements, inventories, and municipal and rural statutes) is evidently integral to the consumption and customs of food. To this can be added the wealth of material provided by archeology—traces of food, human and animal remains, domestic utensils and containers—and by iconography, often decisive in terms of function and appearance. Systems and techniques of cooking, shapes and dimensions of tools, and types of behavior and table rituals can emerge from an excavation or a miniature with greater clarity and precision than from written accounts.

In short, there is no dearth of information. But what can we deduce from it regarding the modes of consumption and the "tastes of the time"? Are the Middle Ages near or far?

In the field of food and gastronomy, the distance between the Middle Ages and us is marked by two major events. The first is the conquest of the New World by Europeans, a stupendous episode, to say the least, with regard to the history of food products. In the space of a few centuries, the panorama of available resources changed on all the continents because of the rapid and often forced diffusion of New World products that took root in Europe, Africa, and Asia, thereby modifying the eating habits of millions of people. In Europe alone, one need think only of the impact of the tomato on Mediterranean cooking or the potato on the continental diet, not to mention corn, which assumed first place in the diet of the peasantry, or plants like the chili pepper, which were adopted with such conviction in certain regions of Europe (in particular, Hungary and, within Italy, Calabria) as to become in time the distinctive characteristic of the local gastronomic identity.

Let us not, however, focus too much on these new presences (or absences, if we wish to look at them from the vantage point of the Middle Ages; it would be like stressing the absence of television from the medieval home). I would point out, instead, that this revolution of products did not so much influence types of cooking as reinforce them, in the sense that it served to confirm rather than overturn millennial traditions. The potato, with a higher yield, took the place of traditional products such as the turnip and the rutabaga and was added to such traditional dishes as gnocchi, a typical medieval favorite, which had long been made only with water and flour; the potato was even tried in bread making. A similar interpretative procedure in the wake of tradition— psychologically and culturally defined as a "reduction of the unknown to the known"[3]—occurred in the case of corn, which came to replace other, inferior grains (primarily millet) that had been used for centuries to make polenta. As for the tomato, it established itself initially as a sauce, sauces being one of the foundations (an absolute *must*) of medieval cooking.

This is not to negate the importance of the new foodstuffs, but merely to say that, on the technical level, they did not significantly modify European gastronomic culture; rather, they served to confirm certain basic lines. The New World was itself exploited far and wide to produce foods, previously unknown there, that were intended for Old World consumers. Wheat, wine, oil, pork, and beef—basics of the European dietary model—appeared for the first time in the Americas, as did sugar and coffee, which the Europeans transplanted along with squadrons of African slaves sent to cultivate them. All these movements, though they overturned the economy of the world and the life of the people, served in a way to solidify, rather than modify, European culinary tastes, as they came to be defined at the beginning of the Middle Ages.

Less important on the social and economic levels, but more influential on the level of taste, was a second revolution that occurred between the seventeenth and eighteenth centuries. A retrospective examination that goes from today back to the Middle Ages immediately reveals that our notion of cooking, the system of flavors that seem to us "naturally" desirable, is significantly different from the one that for ages—not only during the Middle Ages, but even a few centuries ago as well—people considered good and looked for in foods. Contemporary cooking (in Italy and other European countries) has a primarily analytic character that tends to separate sweet, salty, bitter, sour, and spicy, reserving for each one an autonomous place, both in individual foods and in the order of the meal. This kind of practice is allied with the idea that cooking must respect, insofar as possible, the natural flavor of each food, different and particular from one time to the next, and for that reason keep each one separate from others. But these simple rules do not constitute a universal archetype of cooking that always existed and was always the same. They are the result of a minor revolution that took place in France during the seventeenth and eighteenth centuries.

"Cabbage soup has to taste of cabbage, leek of leek, turnip of turnip," Nicolas de Bonnefons recommended in his "letter to masters of the house" in the middle of the seventeenth century. This seemingly innocent affirmation is, in reality, an upheaval of modes of thinking and eating, established over centuries. Renaissance cooking, medieval cooking, and, going back even further, ancient Roman cooking had evolved a model based principally on the idea of artificiality and the mingling of flavors. The preparation of a single foodstuff, as well as its position within the meal, corresponded to a synthetic rather than an analytic logic: to keep together rather than separate.⁴ This went back to rules of dietary science that held as "equilibrated" a food containing within itself all the nutritional qualities, each perceived in turn, and made perceptible by the other flavors.⁵ The perfect food was thought to be the one in which all flavors, and therefore all benefits, were present simultaneously. The cook was thus expected to intervene, to alter the character of food products in a manner that was radical at times. Cooking was seen as an art of blending, intended to modify or transform the "natural" taste of foods into something else, something "artificial."

A typical example of this culture is the taste for sweet and sour, which combines sugar with lemon juice (reinterpreting and refining the mixture of honey and vinegar, characteristic of ancient Roman cooking, when these two products of Middle Eastern origin were brought to Europe by the Arabs). It is a taste that has not completely disappeared and is still found in more conservative European cooking, such as that of Germany, and more generally in the cooking of eastern Europe. What comes to mind are lingonberry preserves and cooked pears and apples to accompany meat (in particular, game); this is medieval cooking. Or, from Cremona, Italy, such products as *mostarda*, which combines the pungency of spices with the sweetness of sugar; this is medieval cooking. Or the pepper and sugar of *panpepato* and *pfeffernuss* along with other Christmas sweets. To go farther afield, there are the sweet and sour dishes of Chinese cuisine and bastilla, the pastry-covered pigeon with honey in the Moroccan tradition. This is medieval cooking, a cuisine of contrast that is in search of balance, the ground zero where distances between flavors are abridged. This "structure of taste"—intimately related to the science of dietetics and in a way also to a philosophy and a vision of the world—has been completely modified in Europe, beginning in France and later in Italy, during the past two centuries, and this modification is undoubtedly the major barrier to understanding a world as different as the Middle Ages. A piece of personal advice: a voyage in space to the gastronomic traditions of North Africa can serve as a visa in time to our own Middle Ages.

Another basic characteristic of medieval gastronomy that keeps it remote from us is the extreme paucity of fats. Medieval cooking is fundamentally lean, making use of such acidic ingredients for the sauces that inevitably accompanied fish and meat as wine, vinegar, citric juices, and *agresta* (the juice of sour grapes), mixed with spices and thickened with soft bread, liver, almonds, walnuts, or egg yolk.[6] The oil- or butter-based sauces that are more familiar to our tastes—mayonnaise, white and brown roux—are all modern inventions that profoundly altered the taste and appearance of food as of the eighteenth century.[7]

The tendency in medieval cooking to superimpose and amalgamate flavors, rather than keeping them separate, has its analogue in cooking techniques; they, too, were not kept rigidly apart, but were "cumulative," so to speak. Boiling, roasting, frying, and braising were obviously different methods of cooking, but in many cases, they were also different *moments* of the same procedure, planned one after the other as successive phases of the preparation. In some cases, this corresponded to practical requirements. For example, the preliminary boiling of meats—commonly practiced at least until the end of the eighteenth century—also served to preserve them while awaiting subsequent preparation. It could also be a method of tenderizing them. Like most other culinary choices, it was also, and mostly, a matter of taste.

By crossing various techniques, one could obtain special flavors and special textures. This last element was highly regarded by medieval taste, accustomed as it was to tactile contact with food far beyond ours, oral or manual, because food was more often than not directly manipulated without any intermediary, given that the use of cutlery was minimal.[8] Only the spoon was really necessary for liquid foods. The fork was seen either as a form of excessive (and long-contested) refinement in table manners or else as a necessity to take hold of such foods as pasta, boiling hot and slippery, that could not readily be negotiated with the hands. It is not by chance that the fork appeared in Italy earlier than elsewhere because it was above all in Italy, already in the latter part of the Middle Ages, that pasta assumed an importance unknown elsewhere. As for meat, the use of the fork was considered unnatural and hygienically questionable even in the later modern era, and even in Italy.

Another reason for the distance between the Middle Ages and today is the order of dishes, the manner of serving foods.[9] The fundamental difference is the absence—even long after the Middle Ages and at least until the mid-nineteenth century—of what came to be known as *service à la russe*, meaning a succession of predetermined and identical dishes served to all the guests. Today, this seems normal and even obvious.

The medieval table, however, followed a different model, similar to the one still common in China, Japan, and other contemporary societies in which many dishes are served simultaneously and each guest chooses what he likes and the order in which he likes it. In informal meals, there is a single course; in more complex and more formal ones, a series of successive courses—hot and cold, of varying numbers, and composed of various ingredients—is determined by the importance and elegance of the banquet. In either setting, the choice is up to the individual diner, in keeping with a model seen today only at the buffet table. This can produce disastrous results when guests are obliged to eat standing up while juggling plates, cutlery, and glasses, but if carefully planned logistically, it can provide guests with a maximum of autonomy and movement.

Although medieval culture was resistant to uniformity, its culinary culture was not characterized by this liberal dimension of choice, bound as it was to a somewhat contradictory idea of eating: individuals did indeed have the right to satisfy their own needs and desires, but there were also the rights and duties that came from belonging to a certain social caste.[10] In this regard, to eat certain things and not others was a sign of social distinction and discrimination. At important banquet tables, the same dishes were not served to everyone; rather, each person was served "according to the quality of his person," meaning his social status. Only then did individual options come into play. Further, because the symbolic value of a single food was as important as its nutritional and gustative properties, the duty of a specific status might mandate the consumption of foods that were not necessarily desirable on the personal level. A case in point is a fourteenth-century Florentine, a member of the Council of Priors, who, "obliged" to eat pheasant and partridge on every holy day, confessed, once he returned to private life, that he loathed the flavors of those meats.[11] The dynamic between individual taste and collective taste thus appears highly complex. Social conformism, always present when it comes to eating, was even more onerous in the Middle Ages than it is today.

It is precisely this inextricable link between the real and the imaginary, between flavors tasted and flavors conceived, that makes every gastronomic experience unrepeatable outside the cultural and psychological context in which it took place. If between us and the Middle Ages there are many points that bring us together, equally important are those that separate us. Among the ones we share are the products, many of medieval invention, that continue to be widely used in the alimentary identity of today: one need think only of pasta. Although pasta remains the leitmotif in the long history of Italian cooking, other products have also endured, such as polenta, bread, and a hundred other flour-based preparations that for centuries ensured the survival and pleasure of people. That continuity may be more important in peasant cooking, in the systems of consumption among the lower classes, but studies on this subject are too cursory and impressionistic to allow such an affirmation, which may be deductive. I would not deny that, basically, even the cooking of the poor (along with the alimentary resources of the poor) has undergone significant change over the centuries.

A question remains: Can this cuisine, however we manage to define it in all its chronological, geographic, and social variations, be reproduced? The key problem in "doing medieval cooking today" is that of determining the proper boundary between philological studies of the texts and practice in the kitchen. To put it unambiguously, that boundary is hard to identify beforehand. Only the sensibility and experience of the one who is doing the work can determine it properly, and even then the effort involves inevitable risk, given the contradiction mentioned above. If the gastronomic culture of past centuries, understood as a collective patrimony, can be studied and re-created with some measure of credibility, it is wholly unreliable on the level of personal experience (the sensations felt while eating). The object has changed: the products of today are no longer those of a thousand years ago, even if they carry the same name. More important, the subject has changed; the consumers are no longer the same, and their sensory education is vastly different. The situation is desperate, to say the least, for anyone who presumes to reach a "historically" plausible result. This is somewhat like listening to the fourteenth-century music of *Ars Nova** or the innovative melodies of Guillaume de Machaut as reconstructed by lovers of ancient music. However we may try, we cannot eradicate from our brain our experience of Bach, Mozart, and Beethoven (or Stravinsky or Schoenberg) and so can never relive the experience of someone a few centuries ago who heard *Ars Nova* as avant-garde music. On an intellectual level, "full immersion" in the past can work to some degree, but on an emotional level, it is technically impossible.

---

*The new polyphonic musical style developed in France and the Low Countries.—Trans.

With regard to subjective emotion, it is not at all the case that philological fidelity to the text is the best way to re-create the sensation of the past. The very opposite can occur; that is, the highest degree of adaptation—knowledgeably controlled—may turn out to be much more faithful than formal fidelity. To take one example, the mortar and pestle are very different from an electric blender, and the consistencies obtained from the two utensils are also very different. However, in *our* experience it is the blender that works best to "grind finely," as did the mortar during the Middle Ages. The two sensations, objectively very unlike, can coincide on a subjective level, but we will never know for sure.

And what applies to techniques is even more relevant to flavors: the over-spiced foods of the Middle Ages were not at all "over" for the people of that era. The same holds for the way food was taken: to eat with one's hands, as we would have to in order to imitate medieval usage to the fullest, no longer corresponds to our cultural experience, although it does to those of other cultures, as in the case of Moroccan couscous. Once again, North Africa serves as a kind of mirror of the medieval experience. We are unaccustomed to eating with our hands, so that if ever we do, it is an exotic curiosity. During the Middle Ages, it was "normal" for Europeans; it no longer is (despite the occasional infraction of the rule when we go to McDonald's, whose success is said to be due in part to the retrieval of repressed historical experiences).

We will have to make do with simple approximations and accept that our desire to know is destined to remain superficial, even if it is intellectually prudent and informed. This is like traveling in foreign countries and trying to understand cultures alien to our own, but being unable to *feel* them. All we can do is *play* at medieval cooking, abiding by certain rules (there is no game without rules) but not falling into the arrogance of philological reconstruction as an end in itself. Aside from resulting in inauthentic sensations, this would not even be possible in many cases, as medieval cookbooks often neglect to provide precise quantities of the ingredients—not out of carelessness, but rather because they are addressed to a readership of experts, if not always to one of professionals. To reconstruct the "authentic" recipe would moreover be a contradiction—contrary not only to the art of cooking, which is above all the art of invention ("if you have to follow to the letter the recipes in which nothing is left to chance," Jean-Louis Flandrin wrote, "you might as well give them to a machine to make"[12]), but also to the more authentic spirit of the Middle Ages that we are trying to reshape. The incredible number of variations found in medieval cookbooks for dishes of the same name is an expression of regional and local variations; to give just one example, among the dozens of recipes for "blancmange," a favored dish in medieval cooking, it is impossible to identify a single ingredient that is common to them all.[13] It is also a metaphor for the basic principle that every good cook should follow: "a qualified cook," we read in an Italian text of the fourteenth century, "will be knowledgable in all things according to the differences between regions, and will be able to vary and color foods as he sees fit."[14]

CHAPTER II

Medieval Cookbooks

THE FIRST ITALIAN manuscripts containing recipes for cooking appeared in the fourteenth and fifteenth centuries, the latter part of the Middle Ages. They reveal a culture already definable as Italian, while moving toward a broader European scope. The kind of cooking proposed by these texts is not local but rather international, a kind of *koiné* with many common aspects and recipes that recur in various regions of Europe.[1] To go beyond the "territorial" (which only recently has become a requisite in gastronomic culture) represented a prestigious objective in the Middle Ages, and, for the upper classes (the direct or indirect audience for these cookbooks), it indicated a kind of "artificial" cooking, a repertory that could be shared because it was not restricted by local boundaries.[2] Within this framework, however, "regional" and "national" characteristics were not absent. The circulation of recipes and productions did not exclude the existence of differences; in a way, it presupposed them. Neither did it exclude the possibility of singling out within a European context more circumscribed areas of cultural identity, or "regional" and "national" gastronomic models—although they, too, were defined not by their ties to the resources and traditions of a particular territory but, on the contrary, by the circulation of individual territorial experiences within a broader framework.

In other words, Italian cookbooks of the fourteenth and fifteenth centuries do not reflect any specific local culture; yet at the same time, they incorporate local usages from the entire peninsula. What emerges is a common culture within a geographic and cultural space that still today defines itself as Italy, determined by exchanges among the various regions—or, more accurately, among the cities, because in Italy it is the city that generates gastronomic culture and culture in the broader sense.[3] All this has important implications at the level of history because it shows how the sharing of a culture[4] creates the identity of a nation even more than its institutions. Politically, Italy did not exist during the Middle Ages (and would not exist before the end of the second half of the nineteenth century). But, culturally, it was a vital reality well-known to contemporaries of the period. And because cuisine is culture, it was also through the flavors and models of taste that this Italian identity manifested itself. This is what Salimbene da Parma, the thirteenth-century monk-chronicler, had in mind when he commented that "the red wines of Auxerre [Burgundy] are not as good as the red wines of Italy."[5]

Here, then, in the earliest Italian cookbooks, do we find references to dishes that evoke local customs of the peninsula.[6] The oldest among them, the *Liber de coquina* from southern Italy, offers recipes for cabbage "in the Roman style," for greens "in the style of Campania," and for beans in the style of "Marca di Treviso." Among ingredients, it mentions wheat from the Puglie and pasta from Genoa, and among products, it speaks of "Lombard compote," or what is known today as the relish *mostarda di Cremona*. Other fourteenth-century cookbooks speak of "Roman pastello," the torte from "Lavagna," and salt from Sardinia or from Chioggia.

We should not place too much faith in these denominations, for in many cases they may be occasional or celebratory names and not necessarily tied to local cooking traditions. To give an example, Giovanni Rebora maintains that the *torta lavagnese* is not a gastronomic preparation of Ligurian tradition but a dish intended to celebrate the ascension to the pontificate of Sinibaldo Fieschi of the family of the counts of Lavagna.[7] In other cases, the geographic designation seems more trustworthy on the level of gastronomy; however, it is not this that needs to be stressed but rather the fact that such denominations—leaving aside the real meaning of each one—indicate that people *believed* in the existence of local specialties. As Flandrin wrote, "Whatever may have been the true origin of national and regional cuisines, it is obvious that people of the time distinguished one from the other."[8]

That "local" culture was in some way shared and that this signified the factual existence of an "Italian cuisine"—understood as the common ground of exchange between diverse realities—are proved more by the recipes than by denominations, as well as by the effective circulation of those texts within the Italian territory, starting with two principal areas of diffusion that scholars have individuated as the Swabian-Angevine kingdom and the Tuscan commune.[9]

It was probably in the Angevine court of Naples in the early fourteenth century that the previously mentioned *Liber de coquina* was written, although based on her recent research, Anna Martellotti[10] holds that it was derived from a text of the previous century, compiled in Sicily at the Palermo court of Frederick II. The "southernness" of this cookbook was asserted by Marianne Mulon, the first to publish the text,[11] and her characterization was confirmed by the acute observations of Sada and Valente, based not only on formal aspects (many linguistic voices belonging to the "dialectal sources common to the Italian south," with particular emphasis, in the Angevine text, on "Neapolitan and Pugliese elements") but also on substantive ones (products and recipes traceable to the culture of southern Italy).[12] Thus, despite the objections raised by Bruno Laurioux,[13] the cookbook's "southernness" cannot be questioned. Its text is nonetheless an expression of a syncretic culture, international by nature, such as the one that was then in force in Europe and that was, in the case of southern Italy, particularly receptive to Arab influences.

From *Liber de coquina*, written in Latin, others were derived and translated into Italian vernacular, with various adjustments to local dialects such as the *Libro della cucina* (literally, the book of cooking) by an anonymous Tuscan at the end of the fourteenth century and the various texts of the following century—"variants" that Bruno Laurioux patiently examined in archives and libraries, arriving at the conclusion that "the *Liber de coquina* in its various incarnations was utilized until the end of the fifteenth century and was known all over Italy, and even beyond the peninsula, in France and Germany."[14] The book's European success can perhaps be explained by the fact that the fourteenth-century text was written in Latin, an "international" language. As for Italy, the geographic and chronological vastness of this circulation is the proof—and, in part, the instrument—of a gastronomic culture widely shared, though assuredly not homogeneous.

The same holds true for the second generation of cookbooks, whose earliest example was found in a manuscript from 1338–39, written in Tuscany, probably Siena. From there, it would seem to have radiated in all directions: manuscripts inspired by the Tuscan cookbook, with various adaptations of content and language, appeared between the fourteenth and fifteenth centuries in Bologna, Liguria, and the Veneto (in Venetian dialect) and in the south. If the family ties among these manuscripts are generally accepted, their relations are not assured, and among scholars, important differences of interpretation can be seen. Unlike the first group of cookbooks, these later ones never left Italy. On the other hand, they remained in circulation much longer—until the sixteenth century—traveling throughout the peninsula.[15]

The differing cultural and social orientations of the two groups of manuscripts (on the one side, the royal court of Palermo or Naples; on the other, a city of communal Italy) are reflected in the differing styles of the texts. Whereas those in the first group are directed toward a readership of gentry, explicitly stated in some of the recipes (for example, "Prepare the soup, add spices and serve to the lord along with the peacock"), those in the second refer to a group of friends: "twelve gluttons" (*XII gluttonous gentlemen, XII rich hedonists*) is repeated many times in the recipes with an insistence on the idea of "wealth," which does not evoke traditional nobility but rather the new aristocracy of money.[16] It is not the court but the house that is the point of reference in the second group of texts—not the nobility but the upper "bourgeoisie," a term, by the way, to be used with caution in a social context like that of medieval Italian cities, which viewed the families of traditional nobility and the new classes of merchants, artisans, and professionals as extremely mixed both in the exercise of power and in cultural models.

What appears to be very important is the specification—completely "bourgeois"—in the second group of texts, which provide the exact quantities of ingredients and look to costs and shopping. The *Liber de coquina* and the cookbooks stemming from it do not stoop to such details, limiting themselves to broader indications, on the assumption either that they are addressing cooks who are already well versed (and who must also have been the readers of the texts) or that their primary function was as a tribute to the lord, almost an object of display to celebrate the prestige of his table.

We can therefore imagine a bi-level reading of these texts: one "for show," intended for the buyers, the rich hedonists or the nobility; and the other more technical, intended for the cooks who served at their tables. To the latter are directed the warnings and the advice: on the subject of eel pie, "let it cool a bit or the rich people will burn their mouths"; when preparing ravioli, "make the dough extremely thin or it will not please the rich."[17] As for the cooks, however, there is an explicit recognition of their autonomy. It is almost taken for granted that they will freely vary the flavors and ingredients in the recipes according to market availability, their own ingenuity, and the tastes of the diner.[18] If one thinks of the typology of the buyers and readers for whom these cookbooks were intended, one cannot imagine a readership potentially more varied and extensive among urban dwellers. Apart from the rich bourgeois and the nobility, there was surely no dearth of ordinary inquisitive people, gluttons, and gastronomes, such those seen in literary sources as avid readers of culinary manuscripts. Gentile Sermini, a fourteenth-century writer, created the character of an epicurean monk, one Meoccio, who disguised his favorite cookbook as a breviary, which he read assiduously, pretending to be immersed in pious contemplation: the "breviary" was "entirely filled with recipes by cooks describing all the dishes and delicacies that could be made, how they should be cooked, with what herbs, and in what season; and it was all this and nothing else that filled his mind."[19]

There may also be a third type of manuscript—namely, *Fait de la cuisine*, a cookbook compiled by Maître Chiquart, cook at the court of Savoy in the fifteenth century.[20] But this is a work outside the circulation of recipe books within "Italy," more related to French customs even if it functioned as a bridge between the two cultural areas. Italy in the Middle Ages, and at least until the end of the sixteenth century, was an Italy without Piedmont.[21] The situation would slowly change, and, paradoxically, it would be Piedmont that constructed a political Italy.

After talking about manuscripts, indicating two principal families and a few avenues of diffusion of these two textual branches, we should now point out that these derivations are the subject of heated discussions among scholars. The fact is that derivations are never simple: they do not exclude—on the contrary, they regularly foresee—phenomena of selection and incorporation, cuts and additions, modifications and adaptations, all of which are inevitable in the case of texts for practical use such as recipe books. All this makes the work of philological reconstruction fascinating, but it would be hopeless to try to do this with criteria analogous to those used for literary texts. Scholars hypothesize the existence of lost codices from which others, apparently similar but in many ways divergent, might have been derived. They note the way entire parts were "forgotten" when a text passed from one region to another, as in the case of the Tuscan text, derived from the southern *Liber de coquina*, which omitted all recipes for saltwater fish for unfathomable reasons. In cases like these, the very notion of "variants" is inadequate. In short, the world of culinary manuscripts poses insoluble problems in view of the methodologies that have been honed and consolidated with regard to philology. Differences in dating related to physical aspects (typology of the writing materials, style of handwriting, etc.) are compounded by differences in evaluation of the contents: analysis of the recipes suggests a derivation of B from A in some instances and of A from B in others. The problems remain unresolved, and much of what has been written until now could be turned inside out like a glove tomorrow. But even this is the beauty of research.

In the second half of the fifteenth century, Maestro Martino de Rossi, the first important author in the history of Italian cooking, produced *Libro de arte coquinaria* (The book of culinary art). Despite its Latinate title, he wrote in the Italian vernacular, which marks a veritable leap in quality and content beyond the formal, compared with the earlier literature on this subject.[22] A native of the Ticino,* from the valley of Blenio, he is the exemplar of an interregional culture that traversed the entire peninsula. He worked in Milan at the ducal court of Francesco Sforza (presumably between 1461 and 1462) and then in Rome, at first in the service of Ludovico Trevisan, patriarch of Aquileia, and later at the papal court, where he held the delicate position of *cuoco secreto*, or private cook, to at least two popes, Paul II and Sixtus IV. During those decades, he became closer to the humanist Bartolomeo Sacchi, known as Il Platina, with whom he may have devised and executed the cookbook. After 1484, he was back in Milan, in the service of the great condottiere Gian Giacomo Trivulzio, at that time employed by the king of Naples. Precisely for this reason, we cannot exclude the possibility that Martino may have spent time in Naples, leaving behind a record of his work: an anonymous cookbook, written during those years in Naples and traditionally labeled *Cuoco napoletano* (Neapolitan cook) by scholars.[23] It is highly similar to Martino's cookbook. According to some, it is in Naples that Martino's[24]

*A canton of present-day Switzerland.—Trans.

professional formation would have matured, which would explain the frequent "southern" aspects of his cooking, particularly the Catalan influence (which others explain as merely the "culinary cosmopolitanism" of the papal court[25]). In any case, Maestro Martino's *Libro*, written in Rome in 1464–65 and then revised in successive versions, which fortunately have survived in manuscript, has a profoundly intercity and interregional tone, which contributed decisively to the definition of an "Italian" mode of cooking.

Martino was nonetheless quickly forgotten, at least as an author. Not so his cookbook, which continued to circulate and to enjoy extraordinary success, though attributed to others. A case of true plagiarism was that of Giovanni Rosselli, "the Frenchman" (identified by some as an authentic figure, by others as nothing more than an editorial phantom[26]), who presented Martino's text under the title *Opera nova chiamata Epulario* (New work titled Epulario) and achieved an amazing success. Another case was that of the so-called Maestro Giovanni, who in 1530 published his *Opera degnissima*, copied in its entirety from Martino.

But far more important was the European success Martino enjoyed, indirectly, thanks to his friend Platina's treatise "on guiltless pleasures and good health" (*De honesta voluptate et valetudine*), both in the original Latin and in the translations into Italian, French, and German. On a strictly gastronomic level, the derivation from Martino is direct and explicit: "What cook," wrote Platina, "can be compared with my Martino, from whom I have learned most of the things I am going to write about."[27] Platina's work, to be honest, has another cast, given that its recipes fall into a broader cultural and scientific context, stressing the role each ingredient plays in the culinary "system" from a dietary and convivial viewpoint. The pair of Martino and Platina set the tone of Italian cooking at the end of the Middle Ages, contributing decisively to making it an incontestable reference point of European culture.

Martino's importance in the history of Italian cooking lies not just in the contents of his book but also in the "rhetoric" with which the recipes are conceived and presented. With him begins a new style, marked by a search for clarity. The procedure is recounted in all its phases, taking nothing for granted and exhibiting a didactic sensibility that was lacking in earlier gastronomic literature. Until Maestro Martino, Italian cookbooks were rather approximative, the recipes looking more like notes for someone who already knows how to cook; the amounts are always missing, and the cooking times are never specified. The contents are not organized continuously, and the order of recipes does not follow defined criteria. Martino knows this tradition very well, so well that he includes in his text various recipes already present in previous manuscripts (those of the "southern family," as well as those of the "Tuscan family").[28] Martino's intention, however, is to innovate: among his recipes, three out of four are new. Moreover, he reelaborates, rewrites, lengthens, and abbreviates, all with the purpose of making the explanation clearer. He organizes the material in homogeneous chapters that correspond to a classification by products (meat, eggs, fish) or by dishes (soups, sauces, tortes, fritters; he presents, for the first time, pasta dishes as a "gender" in itself). He introduces new terms, like *polpetta* (meatballs) and *frittelle* (fritters), destined for long life in the gastronomic lexicon of Italy. He introduces products formerly ignored, such as eggplant. In this way, Martino places himself at a watershed: on one side, he marks the fulfillment of medieval tradition, and on the other, he founds modern tradition.

Platina is fully aware of this and declares the superiority of "his" Martino compared with the cooks of antiquity, such as Apicius and all the others: "There is no reason," he writes, "for us to place the tastes of our ancestors above those of today, for if they surpassed us in most fields, when it comes to taste we are unsurpassable."[29]

CHAPTER III

The Grammar of Food

AN ONION is an onion. But when Rabano Mauro explains to us, in one of those symbolic, allegorical, and figurative interpretations that weave through his book *De universo*, that onions and garlic "signify the corruption of the mind and the bitterness of sin" because "the more one eats them, the greater the torment," an onion has evidently become something other than an onion.[1]

Onions also became something else when Giovanni Italico, the biographer of Odo, abbot of Cluny, relates his encounter with an aged pilgrim during the return journey to Rome in the company of Odo. The old man had on his back a sack full of onions (along with garlic and leeks), and Giovanni, bothered by the stench, moved to the other side of the path. The intense odor of onions thus became the mark of peasant taste, which the fastidious monk found revolting.[2]

The onion (once again associated with garlic and leeks) also became something other than an onion when Liutprando, bishop of Cremona, was sent to the court of Constantinople as ambassador of Emperor Otto I of Saxony and viewed the custom of eating such foods as a sign of cultural inferiority. To indicate the nobility and prestige of *his* emperor, Liutprando pointedly rejected these odorous vegetables, unlike the "king of the Greeks," Niceforo Foca, who demonstrated his baseness by "eating garlic, onions and leeks."[3]

This intersection of symbolic implications—economic, social, political, and moral—gave rise to a tangle of meanings about our onion that went beyond the dimension of nutrition to that of *language*. The alimentary system in all societies works, in fact, like a veritable code of communication, regulated by conventions analogous to those that give connotation and stability to verbal languages. This ensemble of conventions that we call "grammar" replicates itself in alimentary systems; the result is not a simple compilation of products and foods or a more or less casual assemblage of elements but rather a structure inside of which every element acquires a meaning.[4]

Starting from this idea, it is possible to propose a few thoughts on European alimentary systems during the Middle Ages and on the modalities of their linguistic dimension, employing the double meaning of *internal* structure (the organization of an alimentary system within rules of usage analogous to those of verbal systems) and *external* projection (the use of the alimentary system as a means of social communication). I will concentrate on the first aspect by asking this question—particularly with regard to the centuries of the high Middle Ages: What was the grammar of food, and what were the vocabulary, the morphology, the syntax, and the rhetoric that constituted it?

The lexicon on which this language is based necessarily consists of the repertory of available products, plant and animal, like the morphemes (the basic units) that constitute the words and the entire dictionary. It is therefore a lexicon that defines itself in relation to local situations and is thus, by definition, variable—and all the more so during the high Middle Ages when the dynamic between the forest economy and the domestic economy, alternately integrated and complementary, anticipated broad discrepancies in both directions, for plants as well as animals. Animals that seem to us entirely domestic, such as oxen, also existed then in the wild; animals that seem to us wild, like deer, were then also domesticated, not to mention pigs and boars, hard to distinguish by their appearance and their behavior.[5]

This variable and, in a manner of speaking, experimental factor gave rise to subsequent social and cultural variants. The resources of the uneducated had a particular appeal to the aristocracy, which enjoyed the forest as the site of the hunt and of the confrontation with wild animals (in opposing[6] and also imitative terms). Even hermits appreciated the uneducated, seeing in them a simulacrum of edenic innocence and providential alimentation—in this case, vegetarian.[7] The monastic vocation, preferring the domestic to the wild (in agricultural as well as pastoral practices)[8] opted instead for peasant culture.[9]

In this variety of interests and outlooks, a few basic elements can be identified. The most important is the prevalence, primarily in the alimentary lexicon of the peasant population, of what in the documents is called *bestie minute* (small animals): pigs or sheep, raised for various alimentary uses. The pig is the ideal animal for meat and the ewe the animal for milk (or, more precisely, for cheese because that was the normal purpose of the milk). In only a few regions, determined by the environment (primarily in regions of forest or meadow) or by cultural traditions (largely in the Roman tradition), are sheep also important as a source of meat. The presence of cattle in the alimentary repertory remained minor, even if archeological data (rather than written sources) attribute greater importance to cattle raising during the Roman era.[10]

More common is the importance, during the high Middle Ages, of animals raised in conjunction with the development of forest-pastoral activities. Within the same context, fishing, practiced in the inland waters that are an essential part of the uncultivated landscape, was a positive contribution to the economy, whereas fishing for sea fish, which had been highly productive and commercial in Roman times, was a decidedly negative contribution in the Middle Ages and began to disappear from the alimentary horizon. Even in Ravenna, on the Adriatic seacoast, the regulations of the *schola piscatorum* (the corporation of fishermen) applied to the catching of river fish, totally ignoring sea fish.[11]

Among vegetable products, the primary role was held by grains, with a few significant innovations since ancient times. Early in the Middle Ages, two new plants, rye and oats, came under cultivation. Previously known only as invasive grasses, they slowly took over space given to such traditional plants as spelt and wheat by virtue of their high yield and singular resistance to adversities of climate. For the same reason, "small grains"—millet, panìco, and sorghum—acquired an important role in the economy of the high Middle Ages. However, the combination of barley and oats, documented in the early years of the tenth century on the lands of the monastery of Saint Julia in Brescia,[12] represents a juxtaposition of the old and the new: barley, a grain of very ancient Mediterranean tradition, and oats, a grain of recent success, known primarily in the northern regions of the European continent. To judge from local varieties, the grain lexicon of Europe in the high Middle Ages (and the alimentary lexicon in general) seems to be characterized by a common thread or, put differently, by a growing differentiation of resources so as to assure more protection in times of need.

Greater continuity, compared with the ancient alimentary tradition, can be seen in the cultivation of legumes, largely centered on broad beans, chickpeas, and beans (meaning the *dolico* or *fagiolo dall'occhio*, the only species indigenous to the Mediterranean region, all other beans having originated in the Americas), as well as a few species of lesser importance. In the high Middle Ages, the cultivation of green peas began to spread, enjoying enormous success during the centuries to follow. However, the sixth-century treatise by Antimo indicates no awareness of this, which may be significant in that one of the miracles attributed to Saint Colombano was that he made the *legumen Pis* spring from the rocks of the Emilian Appenines.[13]

There was also notable continuity in the repertory of vegetables, centered on cabbages, turnips, other root vegetables, and salad (as well as the onions, garlic, and leeks that were our starting point). We have to wait for the centuries of the full Middle Ages before coming into contact with the innovations brought by the Arabs to southern Italy and southern Spain, including such Near Eastern plants as spinach, eggplant, and artichokes.[14]

And, finally, with regard to fruits, we return to the theme of integration between cultivated and wild resources, typical of the high Middle Ages. The scarcity of documentation on domestic orchards[15] does not authorize us to deduce the absence of these products in the alimentary system; fruits were primarily obtained from a harvest economy, uncultivated to be precise, so their modes of exploitation are hard to discern in the written documents.[16]

This lexicon, as mentioned earlier, has multiple territorial and social variants: even if most of the morphemes are common, they take on a different meaning according to the context. Wheat, for example, is a luxury product almost everywhere, but there are regions, as in southern Italy, where the perpetuation of the Roman economy made the wider availability of this product not only normal but also popular.[17] The chestnut, which in the high Middle Ages became progressively widespread as an alternative to grains, became increasingly common in Mediterranean regions (in Italy, beginning in the Po Valley),[18] although in the north it remained an exotic product.[19]

The use of fats and beverages is also differentiated geographically,[20] but they, too, are part of that process of homologizing cultural models, that osmosis between the Roman tradition and the Germanic tradition, which, even in the domain of food, represents to my mind the most significant phenomenon in the history of the high Middle Ages in Europe. With regard to fats, the homology is articulated above all in liturgical rules that require all of Christendom, whatever the latitude, to alternate between animal and vegetable products according to the day of the week or the period of the year.[21] This is why olive oil, albeit more common in Mediterranean lands, was also exported to regions of northern Europe. In the *Colloquy* (a text written by Aelfric, an English abbot, for the purpose of teaching Latin), in which characters from different walks of life are introduced, the merchant declares himself an importer of oil.[22] Lard, on the other hand, is produced everywhere and represents one of the principal common denominators of the European model of consumption—and, let us add, the Christian model, making the pig an important mark of identity in the face of the Islamic world. The singular mode of transporting the remains of Saint Mark, filched in Egypt and hidden in a cargo of preserved pork, was not only a stratagem to foil the inspection of the Saracen guards but also a statement of cultural identity.[23]

As to beverages, wine had the most outstanding success by virtue of taste and prestige that went beyond its symbolism for Christians. Wine thus entered into competition with beer, which has different methods of production and different cultural traditions. Coexistence would seem impossible, given the almost perfect opposition of the two beverages in terms of use, whether nutritive or social, ceremonial or even religious. In this latter case, however, examples of their cohabitation are not lacking: "Should it happen that there is not enough wine," we read in the rule for canons written by Chrodegang, bishop of Metz, "we can console ourselves with beer."[24] Wine has always been recognized as having a higher value, so it was normal to find imported wines in the markets of northern Europe, whereas no one in southern Europe imported or produced beer. Aelfric's merchant imported wine as well as oil.

Beyond that, innumerable merchants from all European countries bought and sold spices, which, despite their exoticism, entered the alimentary language of the high Middle Ages in an organic way. Whereas the cuisine of ancient Rome used only pepper, during the Middle Ages spices multiplied and were differentiated as the repertory grew steadily richer.[25] In the case of spices, we are confronted with a special kind of lexicon that points to an exclusive group of consumers, delimited by those with access to markets of luxury goods. This may be the principal anomaly in a lexicon—viewed as a whole and, for the most part, shared on a social level—that defines differences in a primarily *quantitative* sense (during the high Middle Ages, to eat a lot projected an image of prestige and power)[26] and presupposes a common knowledge of alimentary resources, if not always of their uses. Within this unified culture, the qualitative differences—in particular, the absence of meat from the monastic diet[27]—would seem to be the result of cultural choices that, while rejecting certain common practices and values, nonetheless used the same lexicon.

If products constitute the basic alimentary lexicon, its morphology grows out of the ways in which these products are developed and adapted to the various needs of consumption: concrete gestures and procedures (modes of cooking and preparation) transform the important ingredients into words—that is, into dishes for various uses and functions. For example, with grains one can make polenta, bread, pies, and focaccia. The basic ingredients are the same; what is different is the gastronomic result, determined by the kind of procedure performed on them. It is always the gestures, the procedures (the recipes), that account for the relationship between the units of meaning. The linguistic phrase *tortelli di ricotta*, which uses the morpheme *di* (of) to designate the subordinate role of the second element in relation to the first, is expressed in culinary practice by the simple gesture of including ricotta in the tortelli. Every gesture has its meaning. The addition of a little honey, or raisins, or cooked must, or something more exotic such as dates is enough to go outside the nutritive and ordinary dimension of the dish and enter into that of delicacy, of festivity, of *dulcis in fondo* (which medieval taste also looks for, although unaware, at least in any rigid sense, of the distinction between sweet and salt more common in modern culture).[28]

Techniques of conservation also determine the morphology of products and confer a meaning. Conserved products (salami, cheese, meat, and dried fish) belong, by definition, to the alimentary "discourse" of the less advantaged, connoting the basic need to provide continuous provisions so as to avert the risk of an empty larder. The treatment of vegetables and fruits enters into this same logic, and the centrality of grains in the alimentary model of the peasantry is related to the particular preservability of these products, in addition to the many ways they can be used. On the other side, the pleasure of fresh products, whatever they may be, is a sign of social privilege and economic security—it being understood that even the larder of a well-endowed monastery, a powerful layperson, or the sovereign himself held a stock of conserved products (amply attested, for example, by the storehouses of royal courts, as we know from the chapter *de villis* by Charlemagne).[29]

The transformations resulting from culinary practices and cooking modes are filled with social and symbolic implications. A roast is typically seignorial, expressing—as Claude Lévi-Strauss has taught us[30]—the predilection for nature and wilderness (always ambiguous but a cultural choice[31] nonetheless) that we associate with medieval aristocracy. The comment made by Eginard on the culinary preferences of Charlemagne, who every day ordered his hunters to prepare spit-roasted game, "which he ate with more pleasure than any other food,"[32] not only suggests the emperor's personal taste but also involves more complex images that refer to an awareness of self and to class identity. Eginard further informs us that Charlemagne, though suffering from gout, quarreled with his doctors "because they urged him to give up roasts, to which he was accustomed [*assuetus*], and to eat boiled meat instead." That dish he found "particularly odious" and pushed it away with disgust.

Boiled dishes, in fact, primarily associated with the domestic dimension of food and with the use of cultural mediators such as pots and water for cooking, are typical of peasant food and express diametrically opposite values. On the material level, the prevalence of boiled dishes in the alimentary practices of peasant kitchens is confirmed by archeological data that provide evidence from medieval village sites of the precise correlation between the dimension of the pots and the size of the bones discovered in waste heaps.[33] The symbolic implications attributed to boiled meats began out of concern first for economy and then for the greater yield from this procedure: to cook in a pot rather than directly over fire prevented the loss of the nutritious meat juices, which were preserved and concentrated in the cooking water. The broth obtained this way could be used again for other preparations, adding other meats and vegetables. Furthermore, the use of water was indispensable when cooking salted meats, also typical of peasant food.

In the systems of cooking meat, there was also a motivation, explicit or implicit, of a dietary nature related to the canon of classification determined by ancient science and passed on by medieval medicine. That science, as is well known, based its observations on the notion of four fundamental "qualities" (hot and cold, dry and moist), which, when combined in various proportions and to variable degrees, defined the nature of everything edible.[34] And because the purpose of cooking, beyond those ranging from enhancing taste to promoting health, was to avoid all excess and to equilibrate the "humors" of the body (derived from the combination of the four "qualities"), boiled dishes, using water, were held to be ideal for meats of a "dry" nature as well as for those preserved with salt or from old animals (old age, according to the medical theory of the time, was presumed to contain an excess of dry and cold). The meat of young animals, being qualitatively moist, was treated instead with fire, meaning spit-roasted.

This kind of dietary culture—based not on abstract ideas but on perceptions that were instinctive for the most part—was shared by all social strata. Peasants were not ordinarily readers of dietetic texts, but their choice of boiling meat corresponded to their needs and to practices that integrated perfectly with the scientific canons. The meats they cooked, if not salted, were assuredly not from young animals. Only lords could allow themselves the luxury of regularly consuming the meat of young animals, prematurely taken from their other uses. The duality roasted/boiled therefore worked well from every point of view: the economic and symbolic values, the quest for gastronomic pleasure, and the observance of dietetic principles were rigorously maintained, each reinforcing and justifying the other in turn.

Syntax is the structure of a sentence that lends meaning to language and to its morphological variants. In the present instance, it is the meal that determines the order of dishes according to criteria of succession, accompaniment, and reciprocal relationship. As in the verbal sentence, one or more forceful nuclei (similar to the nucleus of subject/verb) stand at the center of the action. It can be a simple nucleus, as when one dish and a single course comprise the menu. Or it can be multiple nuclei (more foods, more courses) with increasing degrees of complexity depending on the ritual importance of the event and the social standing of the protagonists.

The model of the single dish, typical of the peasantry, is to be found in the meals distributed to the poor, according to available documents. Pope Adrian issued a decree, as recounted by Anastasii Bibliothecari, that one hundred indigents be fed every day in the Lateran basilica. This was accomplished by filling a huge cauldron with meat, grains, and vegetables, accompanied by bread and wine.[35] Into the *pulmentum* (porridge, or stew, or simply a "cooked dish") of this *caldaria* went pigs, wheat, and barley from a property on the outskirts of Rome: it is the exemplar of the "synthetic" organization of a meal in which all the ingredients are mixed together. Similarly, the priest Rissolfo ordered in 765 that the needy of Lucca receive a *pulmentarium* consisting of beans and *panìco* (foxtail millet), "thick and well seasoned."[36]

Pulmentum or *pulmentarium* is a term often seen in medieval documentation, designating fairly different preparations.[37] It does not indicate a specific composition; it can contain vegetables, grains, meat, or fish, according to the situation and the circumstances. Very simply, *pulmentarium* is the "dish," the "food." Generally, and precisely, it is the cooked dish as prescribed in the Benedictine Rule, two of which should be served to the monks at their daily dinner (*duo pulmentarium cocta*). This specification, emphasizing the monastic commitment to a communal and "domestic" life and dissociated from the solitary, wild, and "raw" model of the hermit's diet,[38] is characterized by the act of cooking—the morphology of the preparation—the action that allows the ingredients to acquire a meaning, to enter into an alimentary system that is shared by a society. But within this system, raw food also has its place: the third *pulmentarium* that may be offered to the monks is a dish of raw vegetables and fruits.[39]

Even richer and more complex models of menus are articulated around this basic structure through the elementary and extremely simple mechanism of multiplying dishes. The monastic regimen itself, proposing two or three dishes at each meal, follows this model and confirms it. One, two, or three *pulmentaria*[40] signify a greater importance given to food as an expression, for example, of joy: on feast days, the dishes will be more numerous. This is not about reorganizing the structure in a different way but merely about replicating and multiplying it. "During major holidays courses are added to lunch and dinner," states Cesario's *Regola per le vergini* (Rule for virgins).[41] And Valdeberto's Rule ordains that "on feast days, in honor of the holy solemnity, we will restore our body with a larger number of foods, that is, three or four dishes."[42]

The comprehensive nature of the expression *pulmentum* is defined by its components only in some cases. The statutes of the monastery of Corbie, in Picardy, specify that the *pulmentarium* of the monks is to be made of "greens of various kinds."[43] The first Camaldolese constitutions wanted it to consist of greens and vegetables but also of fish "and every kind of food that a monk may eat."[44] Elsewhere, outside of the monastic environment, one finds the component of meat—above all, where the territorial and cultural context assigned to meat a nutritional role of the first order. The *pulmentum* allotted to the canons by the Chrodegang Rule, in force in Metz during the middle of the eighth century, was organized into two separate elements: the "portion [*ministracio*] of meat" (one for two canons) and the more generic *cibaria*—with the proviso that "in case there are no other *cibaria*, they receive two portions of meat or lard." During Lent, meat was replaced by portions of cheese, to which was sometimes added a third *pulmentum* of fish or vegetables. With this Lenten food, they could find consolation (*consolacionem habeant*) during years when a scarcity of acorns and beechnuts prevented the raising of enough pigs to satisfy the usual "portion of meat."[45]

If *pulmentum* is a concrete unit, meaning the dish, its syntactic function (that is, its function in the context of dining) is expressed by the term *ferculum*, which indicates the *act* of the course rather than the *contents* of the dish.[46] The two do not generally coincide because each course contains multiple dishes. As we have already seen,[47] it was customary during the Middle Ages to serve a variety of dishes, all at the same time, among which the diners could choose. Such a system, in practice most commonly (though not exclusively) during opulent banquets, corresponded better to the culture of the time in its emphasis on the idea and the practice of sharing food. Around peasant tables as at lordly banquets, dishes were brought to the table on platters used by all the diners (or no fewer than two, as prescribed by ceremonial courtly rules of the early Middle Ages[48]).

This manner of serving food could give rise to embarrassing situations, as when a neighboring diner emptied the platter (or *tagliere* [cutting board] as it was sometimes called), taking advantage of his ability to swallow food that was still exceedingly hot. It was precisely for this reason that no one wanted to sit beside Noddo d'Andrea—the protagonist of an entertaining sixth-century novella by Franco Sacchetti[49]—who could gulp down "boiling maccheroni." Tragicomic instead is the account of the dinner—a genuine piece of theatre, written by Gregory of Tours in the sixth century[50]—that a married couple, she Catholic, he Arian,* decides to offer the priests of the two religions who are competing to

---

*Followers of Arianism did not believe that Jesus was of the same substance as God.—Trans.

be primate of the village. When the meal is ready, the host proposes to "his" priest that they play a joke on the "Roman" priest. He asks for the priest, as soon as the dishes are brought in, to "hurry and bless them with your sign so that he will not dare touch them and we, thanks to his sadness, will be cheered by eating." They agree. The first to arrive is a dish of greens. The "heretic" (so defined by the author) priest makes the sign ahead of the other priest. The wife, so as not to offend him, brings in another dish and offers it to the Catholic. But the heretic continues his blessings on the second and the third course (*in secundo et tertio ferculo*). At the fourth course, the drama begins. In the center of the platter is a handsome display of eggs scrambled with flour, decorated with dates and olives. Before the platter is even set down on the table, the "heretic" hastily raises his hand to bless the dish, immediately extends his spoon, takes up the food, and quickly gulps it down. Sadly for him, he is unaware that it is still burning hot. His chest flares up with intolerable pain, his belly erupts in a dreadful roar, and his breathing stops. The frittata has killed him. Unperturbed, the three survivors carry him out of the dining room, bury him, and go back to eating. Now that God has vindicated his servants, the "good" priest says to the master of the house, "Bring me something that I can eat."

In their relation to the principal subjects (the dishes) within the syntactical structure of the meal, the "complements" become defined in time as those things that precede, accompany, and follow: appetizers, intermediate dishes, side dishes, and "dessert" (as it is called today). Sauces can be seen as analogous to grammatical morphemes such as conjunctions or prepositions, bereft of autonomous meaning but essential for determining the nature and quality of the protagonists. Here, we must return to the relationship between alimentary practices and dietary science because sauces (almost inevitable in medieval cooking, as demonstrated by the space devoted to them in contemporary cookbooks) were selected and paired on the basis of the "humoral temperaments" borrowed from the medical tradition. For example, a meat that is cold and dry by nature—as determined by the characteristics of the animal but also by the way it is cooked—has to be accompanied by a sauce made of opposing products. From a rhetorical point of view, we could say that the prevalent figure of speech in medieval cooking is the oxymoron.

Condiments fall into the function of grammatical adjectives or adverbs. Their choice can be tied to reasons of economy (the availability of resources) or ritual (in Christian Europe the liturgical calendar with its "lean" [meatless] and "fat" requirements) that confer on foods a spatial/temporal connotation typical of adverbs. The alternation lard/oil, with the possible local variant of butter, signifies identity with a territory, a society, or a culture as well as with the day, the week, or the period of the year. The eighth-century document from Lucca, mentioned earlier, ordains that the dish intended for indigents should be dressed with "lard or oil" depending on circumstances.[51]

Bread plays a decisive role in this alimentary system, in a way both parallel and autonomous. Bread is the perfect "complement"; according to Isidore of Seville, "it goes with every food."[52] To turn this around, bread is the food that is accompanied by all other foods. This introduces into the alimentary discourse a kind of dualism: *pane e companatico* (bread and, literally, what goes with bread)—or, in the more typical terminology of the high Middle Ages, *panes vel pulmenta*[53]—means two entities that complement each other and are alternately integrated in inverse proportion. In some cases, the nucleus is bread: in the Benedictine Rule, bread is mentioned after and separately from *pulmentaria*, but the determined portion (a pound per day to each, every day of the year without distinction)[54] seems to guarantee on this nutritional scale the necessary minimum, integrated with other foods. When, instead, the nucleus is *pulmenta* (as in the diet of the Chrodegango canons of Metz), the attention is focused on meat, and the concern is to find "consolation" for the scarcities by turning to other *cibaria* such as cheese, fish, or vegetables. Bread, in this case, is limited to assuring that the canons eat *quod sufficiat* (as much as needed).[55] The contrast between the two models, at the same time territorial (southern and northern Europe) and cultural (monastic regimen, observing abstention from meat; canonical regimen, closer to the secular model), takes on social equivalence when compared with the aristocratic table, on which meat always holds a dominant place. In this case as well, bread *quod sufficiat* is never lacking, but it serves a supplementary function.

The case of bread can serve to illustrate the highly structured nature of the alimentary system and, within this system, the fact that everything has its place, the primary objective being to hold on to it. What comes to mind are the strategies used in the event of penury or scarcity, when the basic lexicon, the customary "repertory of products," is unexpectedly reduced. These strategies seem to reveal a general rule: despite the forced abandonment of usual practices, one must remain as close as possible to one's own culture, to the language one knows. The prevailing attitude is one of *substituting*, of locating something that can be used *in place of* something else. Medieval chronicles (and also those of later centuries) document all kinds of inventions for the purpose of adapting available products to familiar techniques and practices. If wheat was scarce, bread was made with inferior grains—a common practice among the lower classes even in normal times. Other times legumes were utilized (especially broad beans) or, in mountainous regions, chestnuts (not by chance is it called "tree bread") or acorns. Later it might have been roots and wild herbs. "That year," Gregory of Tours wrote, referring to events at the end of the sixth century, "Gaul was stricken with a terrible famine. Many people made bread out of grape seeds, or with the flowers of hazelnut trees, others used the roots of pressed ferns that were dried and reduced to a powder mixed with a bit of flour. Still others did the same thing with field greens."[56] In extreme cases, people had recourse to earth. In 843, according to the *Annals of Saint Bertin*, "in many places people were forced to eat earth mixed with a little flour shaped into the form of a loaf." Notice the expression of the chronicler: earth "shaped into the form of bread [*in panis speciem*]." The form, the morphology of the food, is what guarantees the continuity of the system.

"Bread of famine" recurs often in the sources. In 1032–33, Raoul Glaber related in a famous passage that "an experiment was attempted that has not been found to have been made ever before. Many people collected a white sand, similar to clay and, combining it with whatever flour and bran were available, produced a kind of roll in the hope of thereby alleviating hunger."[57] Unfortunately, they met with no success but did meet with painful consequences as regards digestion. This was nonetheless, as Pierre Bonnassie has rightly noted, the most "rational" response to famine[58] before falling into other kinds of behavior induced by panic and madness. Not only the consumption of certain products but also the renunciation of habitual practices of preparing and cooking food was seen as the abdication of one's identity, an indication of the descent into animalism: to eat grass "like beasts," without dressing it or cooking it—that was the decisive step. On the other hand, stealing acorns from pigs, grinding them with other chance ingredients, and trying to turn this into bread (as Geoffredo Malaterra informs us, referring to the dramatic famine of 1058 in southern Italy[59]) comprise a cultural gesture, born of an extremely refined and complex culture that, moreover, gave rise to survival techniques developed and transmitted by generations of starving people: "As is habitual among the poor [*sicut pauperibus mos est*], they mixed herbs with a bit of flour," records a chronicle about the 1099 famine in Swabia.[60]

What is striking about these dramatic events is the persistence of a direct reference to common alimentary practices. To recall the parallel between the alimentary system and language, this would be like modifying something in the lexicon without touching the morphological and syntactic structure of the discourse.

In only a few cases has there been a need for changes (generally temporary) by the substitution not of products, of ingredients that enter into the making of a given dish, but rather of the type of dish. For example, it might be necessary to replace dishes based on grain (soups, polenta, even bread) with meat or other animal products, which was possible only when the range of available resources was sufficiently broad. And this was the case during the high Middle Ages, when the models of consumption, based on an economy tied for the most part to the exploitation of forests and natural herding rather than agricultural practices, were fairly flexible, so that it was often possible to replace foods by turning to different sectors of production.[61]

The scarcity of bread has always caused serious alimentary problems, but in many cases, the agricultural crisis could be met with resources provided from the noncultivated economy.[62] The so-called Rule of the Father, composed in northern Europe, provided for a supplement of milk in the event that sterile lands made the supply of bread inadequate.[63] The *Life of Saint Benedict of Aniane* recounts that in 779 a multitude of starving people rushed to the gates of the monastery asking for bread; in the absence of anything else, they were fed every day "the meat of sheep and cows, and ewe's milk"[64] until the new harvest. More dramatic is the information given by Malaterra that during the famine of 1058, mentioned above, the consumption of "fresh meat without bread" was the cause of dysentery and death. This report may be less of a hygienic explanation than the reflection of a culture, such as the Mediterranean, viscerally associated with the idea of bread as crucial, even symbolically, to the alimentary system (not to mention the ulterior moral connotation because it was the season of Lent and meat should not have been eaten).

Reports of this kind seem to me typical of the high Middle Ages. The same consumption of meat during Lent, documented in various sources as a choice in cases of emergency,[65] seems related to an alimentary, economic, and cultural system in which a forest economy held great importance. Over time, the peasant diet became more uniform and monotonous, based more and more exclusively on grains. Starting in the Carolingian period, the extent of forested areas began to shrink and, most important, to be transformed into reserves for the pleasure of the powerful, accompanied by the double pressures of a growing population and the demands of the lords for larger agrarian yields.[66] From then on, meat increasingly became a mark of social privilege. If until then grains and meat were the equal subjects of a single alimentary discourse—differentiated on a social level but for the most part only quantitatively—from then on, there were two different discourses, one centered on meat and the other on grains.

The language of food, whose grammatical structure we have been examining, could not be fully expressive without the rhetoric that is the necessary complement of every language. Rhetoric means adapting the discourse to the argument, to the effects one wishes to produce. If the discourse is food, rhetoric is the way in which it is prepared, served, and consumed. To eat like "a famished lion who devours his prey"—as does Adelchi (the son of the defeated king of the Longobards) after intruding into the dining hall of Charlemagne to make known his presence and his avenging challenge[67]—signifies that voracity expresses strength, courage, and the sense of animal vigor that the aristocratic society of the high Middle Ages perceived as the fundamental value of its own identity. The huge pile of bones that Adelchi leaves under the table is a way of communicating all this; his adversary Charlemagne speaks the same language and understands it perfectly.[68] The monastic ritual of silence, requiring the monks to listen to sacred readings without speaking during meals, goes in an entirely different direction, expressing in the manner of consumption, beyond what is consumed, a control and a discipline of oneself imposed by the rule and the lifestyle chosen. About peasants we know little, but it takes no effort to imagine that they were as voracious as Adelchi, not for the purpose of adhering to aristocratic models of animal strength but to assuage their hunger.

What we see are collective gestures, a conviviality† that can represent the interests in force at the time precisely because of a common language

---

†In the etymological sense of living together.—Trans.

and the practice of sharing a meal that seems innate in humans, being the social animals that they are ("we do not invite one another so as to eat and drink," wrote Plutarch, "but to eat and drink together"[69]). This is the little secret that explains the extraordinary communicative efficacy of alimentation and its inherent ability to structure itself as a linguistic system. Every gesture made in the presence of others, along with others, acquires for that very reason a communicable meaning.

Here, as elsewhere, economic reasons bind with images and symbols. This may be what is most fascinating about the history of alimentation: to recognize the profound unity of body and mind, matter and spirit; to bridge the separation between levels of experience, that fictitious dualism that has for so long marked our culture. Historical analysis cannot account for this, and ideological interpretation is even less able to do so. Food in human societies takes on all kinds of values, but these do not supersede (nor can they supersede) concrete uses and modes of production, transformation, and consumption. The language of food is not discretional; rather, it is conditioned and, in some way, predetermined by the concrete, economic, and nutritional qualities of the lexicon utilized.

In the end, an onion is an onion.

CHAPTER IV

The Times of Food

BECAUSE THERE IS no life without food, the theme of cooking plays an obviously central, and even strategic, role in defining the relationship between "natural" time and "human" time—that is, between nature and culture. These terms are symbolically contrasting but, in fact, are interwoven in a multiplicity of complex and ambiguous relationships, held together by the particular position of humankind in the world, in its double identity of object and subject of the action. Humankind, too, is an element of the natural world, affected by nature's rhythms and laws, though to some degree the maker (or would-be maker) of its own destiny. In the physical space of the Mediterranean basin, humans at some point in time learned how to make bread, exploiting a "natural" element like grain but transforming it into something entirely artificial—bread does not exist in nature. Humankind is thus an eloquent symbol of the ambiguous attitudes that tend to govern the rhythms of nature by means of the rhythms of work, themselves partly based on natural rhythms but also partly destined to dominate them and modify them. That is why a food as seemingly "natural" as bread could become, in the ancient civilization of the Mediterranean, the symbol not only of the harmony of the natural world but also of humankind's ability to become emancipated from nature, acquiring a *civilized* and *human* identity for itself: "bread-eater" in Homer is the epithet for man.[1]

The time of food is therefore suspended between natural and human times—in other words, between times of culture and work. These two terms should be understood as twin meanings of the same word. The production of food presupposes the existence of a raw material, of a "natural" offering, so to speak—an offering that, from the day humans were cast out of paradise, was acquired with the sweat of their brow. Thus, this offering is not strictly speaking "natural," implying work, techniques, knowledge, and forms of intervention in the rhythms of nature. Humans had to start learning how to produce the plants and animals suited to their nutrition. Cast out of the unmoving time of an eternal edenic springtime, the terrestrial image of divine eternity, they had to adjust to the times of a difficult and capricious nature, always changing and deceitful. Hunters had to know the times when game could be found, gatherers the season when fruits would appear. Farmers had to adapt to the seasonality of the seeding, growth, and ripeness of plants to be harvested and reseeded. Shepherds had to adapt to the time for grass to grow and for trees to provide nuts for their animals. Dependence on natural rhythms determined the characteristics of every activity directed to providing food or, to be precise, the *time of work* in its essential function of assuring the daily survival of humans.

The hope that these rhythms would be regular, that the fertility of plants and animals would be guaranteed from year to year, became central to collective and individual concerns. "Oh, You who rule every single thing, why is it that the seasons are not always alike, distinguished only by four numbers?" This invocation by Merlin, appearing in a text by Geoffrey of Monmouth,[2] clearly expresses a common wish but one that is not exactly in harmony with a certain romantic image of the balance between humankind and nature that we often attribute to the medieval period and to the premodern era in general.

Medieval documents attest to the population's preoccupation with daily survival at every step. That there is a time for the harvest of wheat is obvious. That this time will be good (*bonum*) is a perpetually repeated, perpetually doubt-ridden wish seen, for example, in agrarian contracts where the amount of the share (of products owed by the tenant farmers to the owners) is subordinated to the size of the harvests, which are wholly dependent on the will of God: "*quod Dominus Deux dare dignaverit* [what the Lord will deign to give us]."[3] Or in the expressions of certain *polittici*, the inventories of goods and income of large properties: *per bono tempo* (in good times)—we read in the *políttico* of Migliarina, a property of the monks of Saint Julia of Brescia—1,500 *moggi* of wheat and 150 amphora of wine are produced.[4] In short, we are in the hands of God, or nature, which amounts to much the same thing. Alongside the *bonum tempus* wished for the grain harvest is the hope that the acorns will grow well on the oak trees to allow for a sizable herd of pigs: "when the acorn takes well [*quando glande bene prínde*] the tenth that we manage to collect amounts to 400 pigs"—we read again in the *políttico* of Migliarina.[5] No less important is the wish that the weather will allow for good fishing in the rivers (*quando ipsa pescaria bene podest pescare*), that cold or drought will not interfere.[6]

The succession of the seasons determines the supply of food and marks the time with a series of preoccupations, changing according to specific productive interests. A ninth-century Tuscan document divides seasonality into a "time of acorns" (*tempus de glande*) and a "time of lard" (*tempus de laríde*),[7] expressing rather clearly the attention given to the forest and to herding during the high Middle Ages and how much was derived for alimentary use. Later, this attention was concentrated in an increasingly linear way on the production of grain, and the cycle of wheat took on the leading role in the perception of "alimentary time."[8] Also noteworthy is that during the later Middle Ages the iconographic cycles depicting the work to be done in each month devoted much space to raising pigs under oak trees and to transforming them into food, operations of undeniable centrality in the fall and winter seasons, between November and January.[9] These representations are focused principally on three cycles of production—wheat, meat, and wine—with irregular digressions into fishing and the harvesting of fruit, and they offer incontrovertible testimony to the notion of seasonality, of a circular time to which the times of work and food are indissolubly connected.

I would like to return to the binomial *tempus de glande/tempus de laride*, which lends itself to a reflection on the relationship of nature/culture with regard to the food supply. *Tempus de glande* is clearly a "natural" time, measured by climatic and vegetative events. It is also a time that had become "cultural" insofar as humankind had learned to derive benefits from it by raising pigs under oak trees, a procedure that was not necessarily foreseen by nature. In any case, it is a time structurally bound to the natural growth rhythms of plants and fruits. *Tempus de laride*, on the other hand, is a wholly "artificial" time. Once we recognize what nature has (with our help) succeeded in doing, it tends to supersede nature, transforming seasonal resources—by definition, perishable and limited to a precise moment of the year—into conservable resources for the entire year and even (production allowing) beyond. *Laridum* is a term of multiple meanings, referring not strictly to lard but also to every part of the pig that can be stored. It is almost the definition of the human ability to make resources last beyond their "natural" limit through techniques of conservation that constitute the first and most important modification by humans of nature's schedule.

The fear of hunger was always on the rise. The "time of famine" (*tempus de caristia*) is recalled by annals and chronicles as a regular, recurring event, almost foreseen within an alimentary organization that was hardly stable.[10] Famine is "a structure of daily life," in the felicitous definition of Braudel.[11] The variability of harvests from year to year, the uncertainty of the future, and the ups and downs of a larder that was now full and now empty determined the perhaps dominant characteristic of a system, not only productive but also psychological, that profoundly affected medieval society. A "schizophrenia" between abundance and scarcity, a kind of collective psychosis in which "fear of famine" was more stressful than famine itself, has been admirably shown by Rouche.[12]

If the "time of famine" frequently affected whole populations, introducing a painful though not unanticipated variable in their perception of time, the principal means for defying it was having recourse to conserved foods. The techniques of conservation can therefore be seen as the prime agents in a strategy aimed at resisting the seasons and defeating the capriciousness of "natural" time.[13] In particular, it is obvious that peasant alimentation—the one most often jeopardized by seasonal variability—had always aimed at products and foods of long durability. For this reason, grains have always played the leading role in the historical development of civilization. As for perishable foods, much effort has been devoted to the development of the most diverse techniques for extending their season. As suggested by the sociologist Girolamo Suneri, "conservation is anxiety in its purest state." It is also a wager against the future. "Who would ever make jams without the hope of living at least long enough to eat them?"[14]

How do we preserve foods the way nature produced them (with human help)? In ancient times, it was thought best to keep them away from air: for example by wrapping apples in a layer of clay, as Aristotle

44

suggested.[15] The methods most commonly used were drying by the heat of the sun (in climates that permitted it) and smoking (in cold climates), but more generally, and in all climates, salt was the leading player in the history of food precisely because, aside from lending flavor to foods, salt has the ability to dry and thus preserve foods over time. Meat, fish, and vegetables under salt comprised the principal assurance of survival in a rural economy that could not rely on the daily market or the caprices of the seasons. During the Middle Ages, there were market centers in Italy—from Comacchio to Cervia, but mostly in Venice—that prospered primarily thanks to the commerce of sea salt.[16] In addition, every possible local resource was exploited, from saltwater wells and springs to rock salt mines. On the Apennines near Piacenza, the monastery of Bobbio extracted enough salt for the entire community.[17]

Other conservation procedures were based on vinegar, oil (the first much more accessible than the second), honey, and sugar. This last, introduced into Europe toward the end of the Middle Ages, long remained a privilege for the few. A contrast between the taste for sweet and the taste for salt came to be seen as an alimentary attribute of social differences.[18] In general, all of these substances (salt, sugar, honey, vinegar, and oil) made products preservable only at the price of *modifying*, more or less radically, their natural flavor. The same principle—of manipulating and modifying the natural qualities of foods—held for fermentation, another conservation technique in wide practice. Fermentation was decisive from a cultural standpoint (and even symbolic) in its expression of humankind's ability to turn a "natural" process, negative in itself, such as putrification, to its own advantage by controlling it.[19] From this ability came such extraordinary inventions as cheese, prosciutto, and other sausages that integrate fermentation with salting. The acidic fermentation of vegetables such as cabbage (kraut) was practiced in central and northern Europe and in other parts of the world.

The preservation of fresh produce was not the only way to alter the seasonality of foods. Another way was to affect production, diversifying the maturing times of plants: extending the times, making plants bear fruit as long as possible, going beyond the "natural" limitations of their growth and maturation. When Charlemagne recommends the cultivation in the imperial orchards of "different varieties of apples, different varieties of pears, different varieties of plums, different varieties of peaches, different varieties of cherries,"[20] he is thinking not only about the variety of flavors but also about the diversification of plantings that guarantee continuity in time. And all the better if some of the species cultivated are suitable for conservation: of the seven types of apples listed, the first six are "preservable" (*servatoria*); only the early ones (*primitive*) have to be eaten right away. Similarly, of the pears, four are "preservable." Peasants had all the more reason to follow this path: trees of many species, in orchards or in fields, made it possible to reposition the growing time of fruits. However, landowners also wanted to keep their larders full. Texts on agronomy from the late Middle Ages devote extraordinary attention to such matters, as they do in modern times. In this way, fruit was made available over a long span of many months, almost inconceivable compared to today.

To differentiate the available resources (along with techniques of conservation) was the surest strategy for preventing hunger. One need only think of the multiplicity of grains cultivated in the high Middle Ages to compensate for their meager yields.[21] The cultivation of rye, oats, millet, or spelt, in addition to wheat and barley, was a means of defense against the vagaries of weather. The varying times for growing and harvesting represented a measure of security against recurring climatic misfortunes.

Yet another strategy was recourse to the marketplace, it, too, capable, under certain conditions, of abrogating the narrow limitations of seasonality and diet. This, obviously, did not apply to local markets, which were the only ones available to the peasantry. Only distant markets that brought in products from far away made this further magic possible. It was the cities, above all, that managed to resolve a *carum tempus* (a time of scarcity) by flooding the markets with products from outside the region and by employing a shrewd municipal policy of rationing, even keeping prices artificially low.[22] Across commercial exchanges, there was space for infringing "natural" time—moreover, was the merchant not the very one who sold the time gained elsewhere?[23]

Questions perplexing medieval moralists arose from this substantial "denaturalizing" action on food (and much else), although these questions were not limited to mercantile activity. The major difference was in the elitist significance of the procedure in question. This struggle for control over space—an alternate or variant of the manipulation of time, this was an attempt to overcome the restrictions of the territory beyond the variability of the seasons—was reserved to the few and remained for a long time a social privilege and, even more, a mark of social privilege.

As Cassiodoro wrote in the sixth century, referring to King Teodorico: "Only the ordinary citizen makes do with what the territory produces. A royal table must offer everything and arouse astonishment merely to look on it."[24] In this way, it manifests and celebrates its difference.

Our consideration of the time of food has so far dwelled on the first phase of the alimentary itinerary, that of production and distribution. I would now like to enter into the phase of cooking—that is, the transformation of raw material into something edible. It is a preeminent cultural phase in which humans give form to their food, determining its use, its function, and its taste. I return to the example of bread. The agricultural act of cultivating wheat is in itself a cultural choice that, by adjusting itself to the rhythms of nature, "adopts" it so to speak, reworking it to suit human needs. The alimentary act (of transforming wheat into bread) adapts itself as well to the reality of nature because there would be no bread without the gluten of wheat. But that, too, presupposes active intervention, a combination of techniques and knowledge that are concentrated in the fabrication of bread, making it, even more than a food, a symbol of human ingenuity. This is what I mean by *cooking*—it is everything in the manipulation and combination of raw material that leads to the creation of what we will later eat.

On this matter of cooking, the first comment to be made is that the "time of cooking" during the Middle Ages was remarkably expanded compared with our idea of it today.[25] In general, cooking can be defined as techniques perfected for the preparation of food. But even in a simple definition like that, we can see that, depending on societies, times, and places, the whole of such techniques can be more or less inclusive, meaning that it can comprise a variable number of operations related to the specialization of the activities, their greater or lesser level of professionalism, and their eventual integration into the economy of commerce. For example, activities such as the milling or grinding of grains and the slaughtering and butchering of meat are excluded from the daily practice of cooking in contemporary Western societies, whereas they once were part of it (and still are in numerous traditional peasant societies). The complexity of culinary operations is not bound to the professional level of court cooks or urban upper bourgeoisie, to whom the cookbooks of the fourteenth and fifteenth centuries were addressed.[26] On the contrary, it was precisely for the preparation of the most ordinary subsistence foods that the most complex manual techniques were devised, those that demanded more time and ability. Once again, one need only think of the lengthy operations needed for the preparation of bread (or, on the other side of the Mediterranean, couscous, which at the end of the Middle Ages reached European cookbooks as well). Such operations demanded hours and hours of highly specialized work, handed down by means of experience and imitation. This was work accomplished daily by the women of the house (who make an occasional appearance between the lines of documents) in the city as in the country—the protagonists of kitchen work and the depositaries of the techniques that define it. This is not to overlook men in certain situations, such as monasteries, who took the place of women, developing their own skills and a specific culinary tradition that justified such stereotypes as the one, hard to dispute, about a monastic gastronomy, unquestionably competent and refined.[27]

To this broad and inclusive idea of culinary activity, requiring extensive work, can be added analogous cooking practices that are also of long duration. Meat was boiled for many hours in a cauldron suspended in the fireplace of every peasant house. This accounts for its characteristically tough consistency, either because the animals, free to move in open spaces for most of their lives, developed hard, compact muscles or because peasants commonly fed on old animals, previously used for field work—and, in either case, raised over a longer period to increase their weight. A shorter cooking time could be accomplished on the spit or the grill, more typical of upper-class cooking and normally reserved for younger animals.[28] In general, the few indications to be found in cookbooks imply not only prolonged but also multiple and repeated cooking procedures for meat: boiled before roasting, boiled before frying, roasted before braising, and so on.[29] This affected the consistency of the meat as well as its flavor.[30]

About the cooking of vegetables we know very little, but even in this case, we can easily imagine patient and prolonged cooking techniques, boiling and reboiling so as to make use of every leftover scrap. Practices like the one documented in the monastic rule known as *Maestro*, which instructs that every scrap be collected so as to be recomposed in a torte at the end of the week,[31] do not appear to be motivated by moral reasons alone; they were also prompted by reasons of economy, which every peasant family could hardly ignore. Thus, attention, respect, care of food, and *time*, much time, were dedicated to this essential protagonist in human life. In the *Consuetudines*, which he wrote for the Cluny monastery.[32] Ulrich describes all the phases in the preparation of broad beans, going into minute detail and defining the times of the operations with extreme precision. It is an extraordinary example of this attitude toward food and of the work required to prepare it. Of course, all the moralists teach that one should not live to eat, but eat to live. Quite so.

Long cooking times also applied to pasta dishes, which began to acquire a certain importance in the last centuries of the Middle Ages.[33] The cookbook by Maestro Martino, around the middle of the fourth century, prescribes cooking vermicelli "for a period of one hour."[34] When we think of pasta in the Middle Ages, the model is not the current Italian one of pasta al dente but the one still in practice in northern countries, particularly in the Germanic area, which, from this point of view, as in others, seems more generally conservative.

We have now arrived at the final phase of our itinerary: the consumption of food. About the times of day for meals we know little, except for the monastic communities, about which we know almost everything because every event of daily life was precisely determined by the rules. From those texts, we learn that the meals of the day were normally, as they are today, two (apart from periods of "fasting," when they were reduced to one) but at earlier hours than in most of Europe today. The first was in late morning and the second at dusk, with the circumstantial variations imposed by the length of the day depending on the season. The same mealtimes lasted virtually unchanged until recently in the peasant tradition, which reasonably goes back to medieval times. The timetable for meals evidently corresponds to the obligations of men, like peasants, who start working early in the morning, or of those, like monks, who are engaged in various activities, liturgical but also manual. The mark of social difference, in this case, lies in moving mealtimes ahead. The few studies made on this subject for the late Middle Ages and the modern era indicate that upper-class banquets started only in the afternoon and later in the evening, continuing deep into the night.[35] There are no accounts, however, about a breakfast meal, which only in the modern era took on it own structure and character. As far as we know, and that knowledge is minimal, in the Middle Ages what was eaten in the morning—if anything—only anticipated and replicated the same foods and models of consumption that followed throughout the day.[36]

As to the duration of meals, one need only observe the extreme variability of circumstances: from simple domestic conviviality to street food offered by rural and urban inns; from the quick meal of food brought from home and downed by the peasants in their fields to the *annona dom-nica* provided by the master on the days they worked in his fields;[37] from the Sunday banquet that ends the week, stressing the contrast between workdays and holidays,[38] to the political—even before gastronomic— event that accompanied aristocratic weddings and could last for days. If we are to believe the account of Donizone, the banquet organized by Marchese Bonifacio de Canossa for his marriage to Beatrice of Lorraine in 1037 went on for all of three months.[39]

So far this has been a rapid overview, but here I would like to linger on the criteria that regulate the choices of foods—for those who could do so—and in particular on the relationship, yet again ambiguous, between these criteria and respect for seasonality. With this, we return to the heart of the question, which is the dialectic between "natural" times and "cultural" times. On the scientific level, a general rule seems to be imposed by the advice contained in medical texts and manuals of applied dietetics: organize your own diet around seasonal foods, adapting your-self to the "natural" rhythms of the world around you. This completely coherent framework, based on the Hippocratic tradition reexamined and systematized by Galen and detailed by a long line of commentators throughout the Middle Ages, brought together microcosm and macro-cosm, human times and natural times, playing on the contacts among the four elements and the four humors, the four temperaments and the four ages of man, the four cardinal points and the four seasons. . . . What could be more evident, more "natural"? Except that, paradoxically, this same scientific tradition places food among the *res non naturales*, those items that belong not to the "natural" order of things but to the "non-natural" (meaning "cultural") order, determined by the will and action of humankind.[40]

The paradox is only in appearance because dietetic strategies have to take into consideration different and often contradictory variables that demand complex alchemies and a continual effort at adaptation, definable only as artificial. The fundamental correspondences are deter-mined by a logic of corrective compensation: cold, dry autumn required warm, moist foods; cold, damp winter required warm, dry foods; warm, dry spring wants cold, dry foods; and warm, dry summer wants cold, moist foods. Far from being perceived as a harmonious adaptation to natural rhythms, this series of rules is more like the exhausting chase after a goal never really reached. The adaptation looks more like stress because, as the texts of the Salerno school of medicine explain, *"reddit non paucis mutatio temporis aegros* [not a few maladies are caused by the change of seasons]."[41] This was the notion of ancient doctors when they recommended a change of diet to accompany the change of seasons.[42]

Moreover, seasonal variations were complicated by other factors, both objective and subjective: the particular climate of the location; the particular temperament of the individual; the person's state of health, age, sex; and so on. The interweaving of these factors generated situations that were hard to evaluate and to manage. For example, the requirements of seasonal adaptation (on the subject of *ex contrario* corrections) could conflict with the need to adapt the diet to the humoral nature of the individual—in this case, not in the sense of correction but in the sense of maintenance. The apparent simplicity of the basic rules left them open to every kind of discussion and alternative choice.

Monthly dietetic regimens, prescribed by the medical calendars of the high Middle Ages[43] and continued in the texts of the Salerno school of medicine, contain alimentary recommendations in a host of rules concerning bleeding, baths, physical exercise, sexual activity, and intellectual work. In February, one should eat (with certain precautions) chard, duck, and dill and banish from the menu legumes and water birds; in March, root vegetables are in order, along with roasts and boiled foods, seasoned with hot spices; in May, absinthe and foods cooked in goat's milk; in June, lettuce leaves and fresh vegetables; in July, sage and dill; in August, one should eat little and avoid wine and any warming food; in September, pears cooked in wine and apples cooked in goat's milk; October is the time for game, lamb, and poultry, to be eaten as much as desired without fear of stomach upset; in November, one drinks hydromel and wine laced with honey, ginger, and cinnamon; in December, cabbage is to be avoided and salad eliminated, but beans are encouraged, and drinks should be spiced with cinnamon. Rules like these, which I have selected only as examples from a monthly calendar of the Salerno school,[44] cannot easily be explained in the context of a "seasonal diet" as we understand it. The tie with seasonal food does appear in some instances, but the reference is mostly bookish, abstract, and often in conflict with the natural cycles of food production.

Scientific discussions—directed toward an elite audience but intended to reach across all of medieval society, in all of its cultural aspects[45]—were not the only point of friction between the "natural" and the "artificial" dimensions of the seasonality of foods. Other rules and other kinds of logic dictated another alimentary calendar, one that was also suspended between nature and artifice—the one imposed on Christians from the fourth century on by the ecclesiastic authorities, structured in tandem with liturgical times according to the two dietary models of fat and lean: when one could or could not eat meat or any animal products.[46] Alternating during the course of the year and the week, the two models eventually produced a kind of artificial seasonality during medieval Christianity that, by adding some priorities and superseding others, determined the priorities in the choice of foods. Before asking what there is in the larder or at the market, the cook will ask what day it is with regard to the liturgical calendar. In this way, even *Church time*—as Le Goff[47] came to call it—powerfully affected the definition of alimentary customs.

It is, above all, this idea of season that we find in medieval cookbooks. Let us look at a few examples from Maestro Martino. After having explained how to make *salsa agliata* (garlic sauce), he specifies that it can be "served and suited to all *fat and lean* seasons as you like."[48] Similarly, *l'agliata pavonaza* (garlic sauce tinted with black grapes) can be "served in *times of meat or fish,* however one wishes."[49] The same concept is inferred when, speaking of a turnip torte, Martino indicates that it can be varied "according to times and seasons."[50] Various recipes are specifically designed for the period of Lent[51] or else adapted to it: apple fritters, cooked "in good fat," meaning lard, "during Lent can be fried in oil."[52] The very structure of cookbooks was marked for centuries by this fundamental distinction: preparations for fat or lean, with or without animal products. Meat marks ordinary times and holiday celebrations; fish, eggs, and dairy products mark times of abstinence—although not necessarily of penance. I would add that it was precisely through its growth as a "lean" food that pasta slowly established itself in Italian alimentary practices, as of the late Middle Ages.[53]

It was the liturgical calendar once again that reinforced or, so to speak, absorbed and channeled the traditional custom of marking the principal recurring holidays with certain foods, often sweets. In medieval Italy, every holiday had its food, and a writer endowed with a sense of humor, Simone Prudenzani from Orvieto, could smile at the excessive piety of certain women who never missed a holiday: "If you knew the devotion / That she has to the lasagne of Christmas / And to the spelt cakes of Carnival / To cheese and eggs of Ascension / To the goose of All Souls Day and maccheroni of Fat Thursday / and also to the pig of Saint Anthony and the pascal lamb / No one could say in so brief a sermon / For all the gold under the stars / She would not let Ash Wednesday go by / Without eating a quart of fritters; / Sweet and ample wine is even more fitting / Nor would she add water for no reason / Because she says it cures every ill."[54]

Of course, it is possible, and even probable, that some of these products and foods became customary because they were associated with the "natural" calendar. The pascal lamb obviously evokes the Bible story, but it cannot be denied that is the "right" time to enjoy it. And to eat pork for the feast of Saint Anthony in January is "economically correct" because that is the season for slaughtering pigs. This also applies to other local specialties associated with particular holidays in the religious calendar. However, this is not true for many dishes (such as the *lasagne* and *maccheroni* of Prudenzani) and for many sweets (fritters, sweet breads) that, scattered throughout numerous holidays during the year, are not related to any seasonal production. It is then primarily the *forms* that signify the differences—in other words, human intervention in the natural product or, as in the case of sweets, in the filling. But even with sweets, ingredients such as raisins or candied fruit (typical enrichments of holiday pastries) do not seem to suggest a seasonal relationship; on the contrary, they seem to represent the optional use, on one occasion rather than another, of products "set aside" for long-term keeping.

Once again, the "time of food" reveals itself as a complex phenomenon. It lies at the point of intersection between cyclical time and linear time, between natural time and human time.

CHAPTER V

The Aroma of Civilization

Bread

IN THE LANGUAGE of Homer, "bread-eaters" (*sitòfagoi*) is synonymous with "men." Eating this food is essential and sufficient to being man—not men in general but the men of Homer: the Greeks, the bearers of civilization. Those who do not eat bread are for that very reason "barbarians."[1]

In point of fact, bread cannot be regarded as the "original" food of humanity. The ability to make it presupposes a series of complex techniques, not at all self-evident (growing grain, grinding it, turning it into dough, making it rise, baking it, and the like), that represent the fulfillment of a long history, a refined civilization. It was this that Homer had in mind, as did those who, along with him, were born and raised in the world that we are given to calling "classical," defined geographically by the shores of the Mediterranean. Even in the Sumerian *Epic of Gilgamesh*, the most ancient literary text known, the civilizing process of Enkidu, who lives as a "wild man" among the beasts of the forest, is accomplished when he learns to eat bread.[2]

From the time that agriculture was invented in the Stone Age, Mediterranean people based their alimentation largely on grains. People from others parts of the world did the same, given that grains provide incomparable advantages for survival. They are extremely adaptable with regard to gastronomy; they keep well and without much effort throughout the year. This is why in various parts of the world these "civilizing plants"—as Braudel felicitously termed them—took hold and became the center around which the whole human experience revolved: economy, society, politics, and culture.[3] Every aspect of civilized life was tied to grains, directly or indirectly. Intense efforts were directed toward producing these plants; control of their production (and the resulting commerce) defined the wealth or poverty of individuals; huge efforts on the part of public officials (the king or his delegates) were made to assure regular provisions to the people, to maintain order and stability (the very legitimacy of those officials depended on knowing how to solve the problem of daily hunger);[4] and, finally, it is around these products that cultural values, myths and legends, religious symbols, and every other form of intellectual creation evolved. This is what allows us to talk about "civilizing plants": for the populations of East Asia, rice; for the inhabitants of Central and South America, corn; for Africans, sorghum and later manioc; and for Mediterraneans, wheat. From wheat was created bread—a food to be mastered, invented day after day, and thereby handed down as a precious technological heritage.

The Romans, according to Pliny the Elder, did not have public ovens for baking bread before the second century B.C.[5] Earlier, they ate mostly soups, porridges, and flat bread. They then learned the art of leavening and bread making, which the Egyptians had apparently been the first to perfect, spreading it among the people of the eastern Mediterranean. The Hebrews certainly were familiar with it, although nevertheless maintaining an ambiguous attitude toward it. On the one hand, it was a fundamental resource of daily food. On the other, it was included among the products that did not enjoy elevated, sacred ideological stature,[6] insofar as it was a fermented food, making it "corrupted" compared with the original purity of the raw material. Christianity, instead, made bread—along with wine, another fermented product—sacred food, the instrument of eucharistic communion with the divine. It was a choice that knowingly signified the break with Hebraic tradition. Not by chance, one of the reasons for the conflict between the Roman and Greek churches, officially separated in the eleventh century, was the accusation made by the Orthodox against the Catholics that, with the introduction of the unleavened communion wafer, they had abandoned the "true" Christian tradition of fermented bread and gone back to the ancient Hebraic model.

The symbolic importance that Christian writers of the fourth and fifth centuries attribute to bread is remarkably intense. A sermon by Saint Augustine dwells with great precision on details of the metaphoric similarity between the making of bread and the making of a Christian:

> This bread tells our story. It arose as grain in the fields. The earth made it grow, the rain nourished it, and made it mature into a kernel. The handiwork of man brought it to the threshing floor, beat it, aired it, stored it in the granary, and brought it to the mill. He ground it, turned it into dough, and baked it in an oven. Remember that this is your story as well. You did not exist and were created,* you were brought to the threshing floor of the Lord, you were threshed by the work of the oxen, meaning the Evangelists. While waiting to become catechumens you were like grain stored in the granary. Then you lined up for baptism. You underwent the grindstone of fasting and exorcism. You came to the baptismal font. You were kneaded and turned into a unified dough. You were baked in the oven of the Holy Ghost and truly became the bread of God.[7]

But the ideal bread is Christ himself, "inseminated in the Virgin, fermented into flesh, kneaded in suffering, baked in the oven of the sepulcher, seasoned in the churches that every day distribute the heavenly food to believers," as we read in a sermon by Pietro Crisologo.[8]

The rise of bread as a sacred food undoubtedly aided the integration of the Christian faith into the value system of the Roman world. Or perhaps we should invert the argument and recognize in the ritual exaltation of that product the sign of a culture—the Roman, to be precise—that itself borrowed many aspects of nascent Christianity. Whether due to the prestige of Roman tradition or the galvanism of the new faith, the image of bread underwent an extraordinary elevation during the Middle Ages. Parallel to the affirmation of the Christian religion, bread became the preeminent food, not only for Mediterraneans but for all of Europe. Even those who were once called "barbarians," more closely tied to pastoral than agricultural traditions and to a primarily carnivorous alimentary model, yielded to the appeal of the new alimentary model

---

*Notice how Augustine insists on the idea of bread as an *invention*.

and contributed decisively to the propagation of the "culture of bread" throughout the continent.

And there is more to this. Beginning when Islam gained a hold on the southern shores of the Mediterranean, between the seventh and eighth centuries, that sea turned into a huge common lake, as it had been in Roman times, a sea of borders.[9] Here, two different worlds—two different civilizations, religions, and cultures—came face to face and perhaps even met, although from opposite shores. The world of the civilization of bread was obviously on the northern shore, or so it saw itself. There was great ideological tension among Christian writers who, during the period of the Crusades, regarded bread as the mark of their own identity and described Arab bread as "poorly cooked flat breads" that hardly deserve the name of bread. There is something more substantial here than gastronomic primacy. Bread by then had become an instrument of cultural conflict. And for that very reason, at the price of obvious force, bread became the symbol of Christian Europe. No force, however, was involved in the "Christianization" of wine, which, once banned from Muslim territories, was transformed from a Mediterranean beverage into the beverage of the European continent. It was like a comprehensive displacement to the north, the "continentalizing" of the Mediterranean alimentary model, corresponding to analogous political and institutional events. The bishops and abbots, described in hagiographic sources as intent on planting vineyards and using woodlands for agriculture, were in the forefront of the progressive change in alimentary habits.[10] The new "Roman empire" of the Middle Ages, that of Charlemagne, no longer had the Mediterranean as its axis; it had all of Europe.

In the north-central regions of the continent, the culture of bread took on new forms. Inserting itself into alimentary structures that had meat at their center rather than grains, bread changed its position from a basic food to an auxiliary food, though no less enjoyed and perfected. Quite the opposite, and not paradoxically, it was even more exalted in its specific gastronomic functions by being less basic. In northern Europe during the high Middle Ages, bread was considered a precious food, a rare food, and a fashionable food.

With time, bread became a common food and acquired central importance in the daily diet, not only for cultural reasons but also because of the modification of the economic and demographic situation. During the high Middle Ages, a largely woodland/pastoral economy guaranteed on every table the presence of meat, in perhaps small but nonetheless regular and continuous quantities. In those centuries, bread was not as irreplaceable in strategies for survival as it would become in the centuries after the year 1000. The growth of the population, the resulting expansion of agriculture, and the transformation of so many woods into private hunting grounds, taking them out of collective use, excluded the majority of the population from resources of meat, forcing it to depend almost exclusively on grains.[11]

From then on, the consumption of bread acquired a different social and cultural connotation. It began to characterize and to define the diet of the poor, to which peasants and lower classes in general were constrained. For all these people, the consumption of bread remained very high and decisive over centuries. In European countries, daily rations of bread from 700–800 grams up to a kilo and more have been documented as normal in the Middle Ages and beyond, at least up to the nineteenth century. Bread provided the most consistent portion of the daily caloric intake: 50 to 70 percent, according to calculations.[12] The expression *companatico*, which appeared in the Middle Ages to indicate everything that "accompanies" bread,[13] is the most convincing linguistic proof of an alimentation by then solidly based on that product.

In peasant houses, bread was eaten—God willing—every day. "As was the custom of rustics [*sicut mos rusticorum habet*]," a farmer, Gregory of Tours tells us, received bread from his wife, which he did not begin eating before having it blessed by a priest.[14] Let us not think that bread was freshly baked every day; obvious economic reasons demanded other choices. Until recent times, the large loaves of the peasant table were made to last for the better part of the week. Antimus, a sixth-century doctor, was therefore not referring to the majority in his treatise on diet when he recommended to the king of the Franks that bread, "well fermented and not unleavened," be baked every day, if logistically possible, because "such breads are more digestible."[15] This happened only in well-to-do houses or in monasteries. At Corbie, in northern France, the Statutes of Adalado direct that the 450 loaves necessary for the sustenance of the monks, their dependents, and their guests be baked daily. However, the "custodian of bread" (an office planned by the Benedictine Rule) had, in reality, to make certain that the quantity of loaves that came out of the ovens was commensurate with the number of persons actually present, so that if any loaves were left over, they would not be found later to "have become too hard." In such an event, "that bread will be put aside and another will be served in its place."[16]

Even aristocrats ate bread. At princely banquets, along with the many meats, bread was served de rigueur in "gilded baskets"—as Cherubino Ghirardacci mentions in his account of the elegant banquet held in Bologna in 1487 to celebrate the marriage of Annibale Bentivoglio to Lucrezia d'Este.[17] Except that this was a different kind of bread, which could be seen at first glance because of the color: the bread of the wealthy was white, made entirely of wheat; the bread of the poor was dark, made in whole or in part of inferior grains—rye, oats, spelt, millet, and foxtail millet—products that for centuries scanned the rhythm of peasant alimentation. In the cities, even the poor ate white bread so long as there was no shortage, but, in fact, bread became unavailable or scarce with despairing regularity. The great success that the scriptural "miracle of the seven loaves"[18] encountered in Christian Europe, where it was persistently referred to by a mass of aspiring saints, is also a sign of a demand too often thwarted and disregarded.

This same prevalence of inferior grains in the diet of the lower classes often made it impossible to produce bread: certain grains such as barley and oats are hard to make rise and are better adapted to boiling for soup or porridges (using farina) or simply to making it into a flat bread (such as focaccia or pita), to which we often see attributed, almost abusively, the name of "bread." A wishful bread, we might call it, just as the "breads of famine" are utopian and pathetic, the result of centuries of technical knowledge, handed down from generation to generation, on how to make bread in times of hardship when not only wheat but also other grains were lacking. That is when legumes and chestnuts came on the scene, or perhaps acorns, grasses, and roots were mixed in with a minute amount of flour—and on occasion a bit of earth.[19] Even cultivated men took pains to explain to the peasants—in texts on agronomy[20] or later in specific treatises—what they probably knew only too well: how to make bread out of field greens and wild plants.[21]

The use of fire required considerable experience and ability; it was hard to keep a steady temperature when baking loaves that were placed in different parts of the oven. Overbaking must have been a not infrequent occurrence if monks were authorized by the Rule to scrape up the burned crusts of bread; in the cities, there were special places for the sale of over- or underbaked bread.

During the Middle Ages, it was still common to find small ovens like those used in antiquity (and even today, by various peoples) in which the raw loaves were placed directly on the heated walls, to be detached once baked. This procedure, executed on overturned clay pots placed directly on the hearth, was better suited to unleavened dough, which would adhere better to the walls. Obtained this way was a bread called *clibanicus*,[22] similar to pancakes and flat breads that were cooked on a slab. With little yeast or completely unleavened was the bread cooked in embers: "the bread that is cooked by turning it in ashes," wrote Rabano Mauro in the ninth century, "is a focaccia."[23]

Bread made of wheat represented a luxury product throughout the Middle Ages, and it was precisely to reject this luxury that hermits chose to deprive themselves of it, replacing it with a barley bread having a clear penitential intent. This bread was little appreciated because of its sour taste and was considered barely digestible because of its reduced gluten, which did not allow for complete rising. If Roman soldiers could be given this as a punishment for having abandoned their posts,[24] no hermit would then deprive himself of it as a means of mortifying the body and the desires of the flesh, as did a philosopher in antiquity.[25] The complexity of such situations, including their symbolism, is witnessed by behavior such as that of Gregory, bishop of Langres, who did penance by eating barley bread. Because he did not wish to appear pretentious, he ate it secretly, holding it under the bread made of wheat that he offered to the others and pretended to eat with them.[26] Similarly, Radegonda "ate bread made of rye and barley in secret," so that no one would notice.[27] This penitential significance occasionally crossed the confines of the monastic or eremitic society. Gregory of Tours, in his *History of the Franks*, recalls that during the plague that hit Marseille in the sixth century, the king invited the people to do penance by nourishing themselves exclusively with barley bread, so as to obtain from God the end of that calamity.[28]

What is clear is that the criteria for the appraisal of bread varied from region to region: for example, whereas rye bread was considered *vilissima* (disgusting) in a French geographic and cultural environment,[29] in a German context it was seen as pulchrum (beautiful).[30] In the monastery at Corbie, in northern France, spelt bread was apparently much appreciated for it was distributed daily to everyone—monks, servants, vassals, and guests.[31] There are also cases of outstanding opulence, when precious wheat was used for every sort of preparation, even for polenta: "five bushels of the purest wheat [*ad polentam faciendam*]" were to be sent to the Parisian monastery of St. Denis under a decree from the emperor Charles the Bald in the ninth century.[32]

Widely used was a long-lasting bread that had been dried in the sun and subjected to double cooking (bis coctus). Roman soldiers[33] ate similar loaves, called buccellae; in the Middle Ages, for various reasons, it was mostly hermits and pilgrims who ate them. Hermits could assure their food supply with this twice-cooked bread, thereby freeing themselves from contact with society and the "world" from which they had fled.[34] Legend had it that certain hermits of the Thebaid had bread that lasted as long as six months. Pilgrims also needed an adequate food supply for the long journeys they undertook.[35] This bread was dry and had to be soaked in water (infundee) to make it edible.[36] At times, it was used as the basis for soups, being crushed and mixed with water, wine, or other liquids. Stale bread could be softened by a second cooking in water, with the eventual addition of other condiments. The raw dough itself was sometimes cooked in water to obtain a softer bread than the usual one, and the same result was achieved by the addition of milk or, in northern countries, the foam of beer.[37]

The high respect for bread went as far as the crumbs. In the sixth century, the Regula Magistri (Rule of the Master) ordained that the *micae panis* remaining on the table after each meal were to be collected very carefully and kept in a container. Each Saturday the monks were to put them in a pan with some eggs and flour and make a little pancake that they were to eat together, thanking God before the last hot drink that ended the day.[38] In less ritualized forms, but with the same concern not to waste any usable resource for daily survival, we can be sure that something of this kind took place in peasant houses as well.

CHAPTER VI

Hunger for Meat

IN THE MIDDLE AGES, meat became a primary food in terms of consumption—and even more so on a psychological level. The Roman era had not granted it similar importance with regard to choices of production or to dietary concerns and still less accorded it any ideological significance.

To make this clearer, Roman alimentary ideology was built around a triad of products: bread, wine, and oil. Following the Greek tradition, these products symbolized a certain idea of civilization bound, in both the Greek and the Roman worlds, to agriculture as a means of production, which characterizes humans. Separating themselves from the world of nature and animals, humans constructed their own artificial existence by inventing techniques for exploiting the natural environment, which they ultimately transformed. They designed a new landscape of fields and vineyards and planted trees from which humans, and only humans, succeeded in bringing forth the products—in turn transformed by techniques that are exclusively human—that provided food (bread), drink (wine), and fat (oil). None of these exists in nature, and for that reason, they symbolize the ability to create a civilized space in the midst of untamed nature (just as in the matter of habitation, humans became builders of cities, and in dress, they learned how to make clothes through a complex series of procedures).[1]

Herding and hunting also became activities of production, and meat appeared, plentifully, on Roman tables, not to mention cheese, eggs, and other animal products. However, meat was slow to acquire high, completely positive standing because it was associated with a way of exploiting the land that was seen as more "natural," less "civilized." It was primarily an ideological position, but ideology played an essential role in defining the behavior and attitudes of people. Meat was eaten, but Latin literature reflects images that assigned to vegetable products—the products produced by human labor—the task of identifying the true model of civilization. People who lived primarily on hunting and herding, making meat the core of their diet, were therefore represented as "uncivilized" or "barbarian"—judgments still found at the dawn of the Middle Ages when Procopius wrote that the Laplanders "extract no food from the earth . . . but devote themselves exclusively to hunting," and Jordanes speaks of Scandinavians who "live only on meat."[2]

During the Middle Ages, all of this suddenly changed because those "uncivilized" and "barbarian" peoples conquered the lands that had constituted the western part of the Roman empire and became the rulers of the new Europe. They thus imposed their culture, including their different ways of seeing the land and the modalities of its exploitation.[3] The economy of herding and hunting was of central importance because their diet gave pride of place to meat; it was, above all, their alimentary *ideology* that gave meat primary status. Whether in productive forms or in mental attitudes, meat became the star player, as did the forest, being the prime location for the production of meat. In the Middle Ages, that place was no longer *other*, disdained as being outside of "civilization," and became a *normal* place, central to daily life, and given full right to inclusion among productive spaces. Medieval documents regularly include hunting and herding along with fields and vineyards as relevant to every landed property. In inventories of the Carolingian period, it was common to measure land in pigs—the number being fattened determined the extent of the property. Analogously, fields were measured in bushels of wheat, vineyards in amphoras of wine, and meadows in wagons of hay.[4]

Why pigs? Because pork was, and long remained, the ideal meat. Pig raising took place mostly in forests, which in the Middle Ages were mostly oak—huge oak groves that extended largely in the plains, as well as at higher altitudes. The oak grove was the definition of a forest, the acorn its most prized fruit, and the pig the direct result on the economic and alimentary levels. This had its counterpart in the legends and myths of Germanic peoples. The Greek and Latin traditions had constructed images of fecundity around figures who symbolized the fertility of the fields and the rebirth of plants after their winter repose (just as Persephone—daughter of Demeter, goddess of the Earth, abducted by Hades, god of the underworld—was returned to her mother on the condition that she return to Hades for several months each year, like wheat seeded in the autumn that remains underground while awaiting spring's return). In contrast, the German epic told of game that, once eaten, was magically reborn from its own buried bones, or of a Great Pig that, in the beyond of the righteous, nourished vast squadrons of fallen soldiers, and each time it was consumed, it reproduced itself in the gigantic pot in which it had been cooked. In the meantime, from the udders of the Great Cow "flow four rivers of milk." Plants for Mediterranean populations, animals for populations of the continent—the wish for a table always laden, for a stomach always sated.[5]

Dietary thinking—related to social imagination, as well as to scientific considerations—underwent a similar change. Greek and Latin doctors had no doubt that bread was the most nutritive of foods because, by virtue of its being the most suitable food for humans, it provides proper sustenance for daily nutrition. "Bread contains more nutritive matter than any other food," Cornelio Celso wrote in the first century.[6] A few centuries later this would no longer be the case. The "new" culture of meat, introduced by the Germanic peoples and based on Roman tradition, as well as on preexisting cultural elements, slowly caused the modification of the earlier judgment. The Celtic pig is not an invention of the creators of Asterix and Obelix but rather an ancient symbol revived in the Middle Ages due to contact with Germanic culture and to its primordial value as food. Medieval doctors proposed not bread but meat as the prime food, the one best suited to humans. In the thirteenth century, Aldobrandino da Siena summed up this shift in attitude: "Among all the things that nourish man, meat is the one that nourishes him best, fattens him, and gives him strength."[7] This change did not annul the ancient prestige of bread, which, in the Middle Ages, was reinforced by Christian culture because bread, along with wine, became symbolic of the new faith that was slowly conquering all of Europe. But a kind of dyarchy was forming in which bread was expected to cohabit with the new protagonist in the alimentary model.

It was a difficult cohabitation at times because Christian culture—for obvious symbolic reasons, especially during the decline of monasticism, which had enjoyed such favor during the Middle Ages—not only continued to place bread on the pedestal of alimentary values but also, having inherited the ancient tradition albeit in a different context, challenged the culture of meat that had gained hold in the meantime. Among the norms of dietary regimen imposed by the rules of the monastic communities,[8] the renunciation of meat was always the first, with differences between one community and another. Some excluded it totally and at all times; others allowed it only for the sick; still others allowed poultry but not quadrupeds. Such norms, complex and diverse, implied significant diffidence toward the consumption of meat, a vegetarian vocation that was never explicitly declared but that can be easily surmised: the biblical image of an earthly paradise in which man, still immortal and happy, ate only fruits; the rejection of violence that inevitably conjoined with the killing of animals (even though the evangelical message excluded this kind of choice); options even subtler that refer to remote suggestions or to ancient religions and philosophies—all these reappear in the monastic attitude toward food and are part of an internal history of Christian thinking.[9]

Even the "climate" of the period, the changes of cultural coordinates that took place in the early centuries of the Middle Ages, must have counted heavily. When a monastic rule allows (or imposes) the use of meat to restore the strength of an ailing, physically weakened brother, the sharing of values with the culture of the time becomes obvious. Meat is the ideal food for nourishing the body, the one, going back to Aldobrandino, that "fattens him, and gives him strength" (to renounce it is precisely the paradoxical choice of one who rejects the needs of the body for those of the spirit; but at times, the first leaves no other choice). If a monastic rule had existed in Roman times, the renunciation of physical power would have manifested itself instead in the renunciation of bread (the principal food of Roman soldiers) and the recuperation of those powers in the resumption of eating it. If that position was now held by meat, it was also because the parameters of nutritional values had been overturned.

The subtle argument (at times even captious) that supports the renunciation of meat is typically medieval and operates on the level of dietetics and taste. If the classical vegetarianism of Pythagoras, Plutarch, and so many others, avoided meat as the source of wickedness—whether because it implied killing or because it represented the earthly corruptibility of human beings[10]—Christian vegetarianism rejected meat as an act of penitence: the renunciation of something good, not bad. Underlying this choice was the conviction, generally shared by medieval culture, that meat is the greatest gastronomic pleasure, the "pleasure of meat" par excellence. The image operates on a symbolic level (meat that nourishes flesh), but this presupposes that it operates on the level of dietetics and taste. Meat is the food best suited to human nutrition. Meat is the best and tastiest of foods. These views that monastic texts handed down to us, along with the stigmatization of meat eating, are the children of their time.

Lenten abstinence, as an act of penance imposed by the Church during the forty days preceding Easter (accompanied by analogous abstentions in other periods of the year or days of the week), fit perfectly into the framework outlined above. In some way, it represents the extension within the body of the faithful—even if limited in time—of the monastic alimentary model and once again confirms the exalted, powerful image projected by meat. If a denial has any merit, the thing denied must be an object of desire.[11] It is not by chance that abstinence from meat is on the same footing—in the Lenten practice as in the choice of the monastic vocation—as sexual abstinence. From this point of view, the "pleasures of the flesh"—or their rejection—follow one another in a play on words* that not only is linguistic but also reflects a very precise dietary culture that endows meat-as-food the function, among others, of stimulating the body-as-flesh, meaning sexuality.[12]

If one looks at ecclesiastic language and at common parlance as well, the Lenten diet is defined as "eating lean," whereas "eating fat" means eating meat. Medieval culture—which in this regard has endured until today—therefore identified meat with fat or at least placed them within the same frame of values, imbuing fat with the same positive image as meat.[13] This is confirmed on both the economic and the symbolic levels: if cuts of meat were all the more appreciated by being fat, the adjective *fat* denoted well-being and happiness. For Bologna, the epithet *grassa* (fat) was assuredly not coined out of derision,[14] and the Florentine upper class found no better expression than *popolo grasso* (a fat people)

---

*In Italian, *carne* is both meat and flesh, hence the double entendre.—Trans.

to define its own social stature at the height of its economic and political power.[15] Canons of values in those days were quite the opposite of today's; the request for "lean meat," so fashionable today, would have seemed highly bizarre to our forefathers.

In this complex matter of food (material and symbolic at the same time), the social image, and in a broad sense the political image, played an important role in medieval culture that was associated with the consumption of meat. If meat was the ideal strength-giving food, then it was the ideal food of power by virtue of an implicit exchange between the two (strength as a prime element of power), which medieval culture took for granted.[16] The powerful figure was the warrior, who could best fight enemies and was capable of defeating them. Strength is acquired, first of all, from meat. Meat is the food of the warrior, who builds up his strength, thereby justifying his right to command. In the ninth century, Emperor Lothair decreed that those tainted with a grievous insult to the sovereign were to abstain from meat, at the same time obliging them to lay down their arms.[17] For a nobleman who saw himself primarily as a warrior, to be disarmed meant the virtual annulment of his social status; denial of meat was its symbolic and functional equivalent.

This does not take away from the fact that in the Middle Ages meat, for many centuries, was a food for everyone, a daily presence on the table even of the most humble. It could not be otherwise in a period characterized by a hunting/pastoral economy that made of every peasant both a hunter and a shepherd. With the passage of time, however, this situation changed. The growth of the population, from the ninth century onward, forced many peasants to abandon the forest for cultivated spaces. A field of grain produces more food than an area of woodland. Even the nobility moved in this direction, encouraging peasants to extend the farmlands. The profits that resulted, from fees and tithes collected on the harvests, were higher and more spendable in food markets. In the end, noblemen reserved for themselves the right to hunt, which became essential to the definition and representation of the nobility.[18] Little by little the consumption of meat became socially diversified, above all, in terms of quantity. Peasants always ate less of it, and meat increasingly became a symbol of the lifestyle of nobility. This lasted for some time, almost turning into a social obligation, so that gout, related to the excessive consumption of meat, became the class hazard of European aristocracy.

The elitist character of meat consumption also came to be defined in qualitative terms: game was reserved, in a more or less stringent way depending on the region, for the tables of high society. Systematic practices of delimiting territory reduced access to forests to a very few and prohibited hunting in private preserves. Legendary figures such as Robin Hood, who rode through the forest in defiance of the restrictions imposed by the nobles, are also "the utopian image of a world in which one could freely hunt and eat meat," writes Hilton.[19] Similarly, meat—of every kind, ready to eat, cooked in so many different ways—is the most conspicuous food in the Land of Cockaigne, a land of plenty that was conceived by the popular imagination as provisioned with every delicacy, an alimentary utopia widely known as of the thirteenth century and continuing throughout the modern era, and that revealed its correlative: a quotidian land of hunger or at least a state of never being sated.[20]

Despite countless restrictions, the peasant still had the pig, thanks to the residual use of communal or seigniorial woods and to the new practice of raising pigs in stables, which in the last centuries of the Middle Ages gained increasing importance.[21] The peasant's meat was pork but mostly preserved. Salt was the leading player in peasant food, affording a little relief during the difficult months, a minimum of security against the caprices of the seasons. The upper classes, on the other hand, loved fresh meat, very fresh. Medieval usage occasionally allowed for the aging of meat—primarily the meat of wild animals, which is tougher—but often consumption took place immediately after slaughtering the animal.

Another significant locus of social difference was the city. Above all, in certain regions of Europe, like Flanders and central northern Italy, the city in the middle centuries of the Middle Ages affirmed its powerful cultural identity, defining itself in opposition to the country. To the opposition lord/peasant, inherited from the high Middle Ages, a new contrast arose between townspeople and peasants.[22] The difference resided principally in the influence of the market on determining their two alimentary styles. The style of peasants remained largely based on direct consumption—that is, on resources of their own production; as for meat, it was mostly pork, even though there is no dearth of evidence that, ever since the high Middle Ages, beef was eaten (the medieval forest also provided food for cattle) and, in regions of greater pastureland, lamb. There was also domestic poultry: chickens, geese, and ducks. The townspeople, on the other hand—the nobility and the middle class, of course, but to some degree even the lower classes—could count, under normal conditions, on a well-stocked and politically protected market. To guarantee food to a community is the first duty of every public administration, whether an aristocratic or a bourgeois government, a "republican" city or one ruled by a lord. The counters of shops or stands of a market were expected to fill every request, every wish, in keeping with a calendar determined by natural cycles and also by social and cultural obligations, such as Lenten abstinence. Once Carnival was over, no butcher could sell meat. In certain cities, the same corporations managed both the meat and the fish markets, until then coexistent but more often alternating during the course of the weeks and months.

What meat was sold in the city? A simple list would not tell us much about the changes that took place and the differences that arose. Now as before, in the city and in the country, the range of possible choices included pork, lamb, and beef. Municipal statutes and those of the guilds offer little more to the reader eager to understand. But contemporary archival sources, mixed with literary allusions, reveal that the urban public of the middle and late Middle Ages gave preference no longer to pork but rather to beef (and particularly to veal and to milk-fed veal) or even to mutton, ewe, or wether (a castrated sheep), which texts on nutrition consider the least healthful. A change of tastes? No doubt. But also one of image. Pork continued to be the strong point in the daily diet, but it had an inescapable rural, peasant, "traditional" flavor (or aftertaste). City people saw themselves as different, with food (as well as dress and manner of building) manifesting the difference between city and country, between inside and outside. In all of Europe, urban consumption seemed to disdain the formerly appreciated pork and to look elsewhere.[23]

The change was also a question of weight. To raise a pig, slaughter it, and prepare it properly, turning it into prosciutto, salami, and salted slices, is an activity perfectly congruous with the dimensions and needs of a peasant family. To raise and auction a steer is a market operation, where someone else butchers it and sells it to many. It is also a contrast between a subsistence economy and a market economy, which in turn is related to the important modifications in the landscape and the economy that took place in the last centuries of the Middle Ages. The Po Valley and other parts of Europe saw the spread of irrigated pastures and a mixed system of animal raising (free-ranging and stabled) that promoted the intensification of cattle raising. Sheep raising also intensified, whether because

the landscape changed (after the deforestation of the twelfth and thirteenth centuries, the demographic crisis in the mid-thirteenth century
favored the return of uncultivated land but in the degraded form of grazing land) or because the renewed needs of the wool industry encouraged
it. Superimposed on the diversification of city/country were the internal
differences between those who ate beef or mutton and those who ate
veal—respectively, the urban poor and the urban rich.

What the market lost, for the most part, was game. Though not
wholly absent (many municipal statutes from the late Middle Ages had
laws for regulating hunting), it was largely limited to personal consumption, be it ordinary citizens who enjoyed the right to hunt in communal
woods or the nobility who devoted symbolic time, energy, and attention
to hunting. Even the relation between hunting and power (like the parallel relation between meat and power) underwent significant changes in
the late Middle Ages.[24] During the Carolingian period, the aristocratic
imagination endowed hunting with the transmission of such values as
strength, courage, and military prowess. What hunting was supposed to
reveal was the ability of a nobleman to handle weapons, master a horse,
and fight, often physically, with a wild animal, which to a degree replicated combat with an enemy. In that cultural context, the ideal hunt was
for stag, boar, and bear. The meat of those animals—dense, bloody, and
highly nutritive—seemed the best suited to fortify the warrior and build
up his strength, symbolically as well as nutritionally.

A few centuries later the situation changed. In the fourteenth and
fifteenth centuries, no one seemed to doubt that the meat best suited to
the aristocratic diet was that of birds: partridge, pheasant, and quail—
still game but of a different type and related to different cultural images.
Birds fly and are therefore light, an observation as banal as it was crucial
in the scientific thinking, cultural perception, and social debate of the
period. Birds came to represent a different ideal of life, as symbolized
by images of birds in romances and poetry, and a different model of alimentation, as the nutritive values of birds were explained in treatises
on diet. Lightness meant refinement; it meant delicate meat suited to
an elite of courtiers (or urban upper bourgeoisie) who now manifest
their superiority in terms of intellectual capacity rather than muscular
strength. A ruler no longer had to demonstrate his strength now that
power was handed down to him through bloodline; he longer had to
conquer his land on the field of battle. Social domination was guaranteed

to him; now, he could play at politics, diplomacy, and, on occasion, cultural patronage.

The new image of power required new alimentary symbols, and this explains the new prestige of birds. Because they symbolized a "high" position in the natural world, they were perfectly suited to represent the "highness" of one who eats them. Many were the theories and systems built around this: in addition to birds, fruits (they, too, "high" in the natural world) were shown to be proper food for those who stood high in society.[25] This was a game played by many: agronomists and botanists, who demonstrated the greater purity of such meat and fruit; doctors, who maintained their greater healthfulness and lightness; authors, who illustrated their quality and virtue; and chefs, who cooked them in delicate dishes. Let us remember that a few centuries earlier birds were seen as properly suited to the monastic table precisely because of their lightness, which is congruous with a style of life that seeks to distance itself from the "heaviness" of the world.

The society of the thirteenth and fourteenth centuries thus developed new models of consumption, new alimentary images, and new symbols that were, in part, contradictory to the tradition inherited from the early centuries of the Middle Ages. One thing endured: the primacy of meat as an element of nutrition. Among many other things, the Middle Ages also bequeathed this to us.

CHAPTER VII

The Ambiguous Position of Fish

IN THE EUROPEAN gastronomic system, fish long held a highly ambiguous position—or "status," as Flandrin would have called it.[1]

What does this mean? It means that the experiences of our life are not merely what "is done" (or in this case, speaking of food, what "is eaten"); things have their own significance, a "meaning" within the system of values developed by each society. Foods, in short, have a *value*—and related to it a potential for communication. If I say "sardine," for example, I do not think only of a fish but also of a situation (in this specific case, food of the poor, a simple meal with simple people, certainly not an opulent banquet). If instead I say "sturgeon," I think, once again, not only of a fish but also of a costly delicacy that does not appear on the table of the poor or on the everyday table. The idea that comes to me in this case is one of wealth or festivity because sturgeon is expensive and is not often eaten. In this connotation, all our foods are weighted with expression, even emotion. And their "value" is not necessarily related to how good they are or whether I like them. Caviar might even be distasteful to me, but there is no question that it evokes an image of refined conviviality and sumptuous wealth. The "values" in question have a social dimension; they are collective images that cluster around foods. And that is their "status"—a status that changes with time and space, according to fashions and customs. The same food can be prized in one place and disdained in another; it can mean one thing in one period and something else in another.

The ambiguous status of fish in medieval culture (an ambiguity, moreover, that has lasted until today) is related to the fact that in the European tradition this kind of food has been accorded numerous statuses, almost all of them extreme. Fish is a mark of poverty, as well as prosperity; it is the humble bluefish that fishermen grill over a wood fire but also the costly whitefish that one eats at a seaside restaurant on a Sunday. What is generally missing is the normal dimension. Fish is not an ordinary food; it is not a "neutral" food. Why this contrast? Is it because the status of fish has so radically changed today in comparison with that of the past? There is no doubt that today fish is very much in fashion. And that is because it corresponds to contemporary dietary tendencies, to medical advice, and to the wishes of many consumers who prefer light foods that are easily digested. This is not as simple as it seems. On the contrary, fish reflects an inverse tendency with regard to a more than millenary cultural tradition. Fish has always been eaten, out of need or choice, but on the whole, the collective imagination has always regarded it with diffidence.

To understand the reasons for such diffidence, we must clarify an essential factor: for centuries, fish has been associated in Italian culture, and more generally in the culture of Europe, with the notion of sacrifice and penance. The Church, ever since the beginning of the Middle Ages, introduced the obligation to abstain from meat for a certain number of days during the week and the year.[2] Meat in that society was seen as the aliment of the highest value. The ruling classes consumed mostly game, which they procured by hunting; the peasantry raised many animals in woods and natural pastures, thereby integrating produce from the fields. Everybody ate other things as well, but the consumption of meat held first place in their desires.[3] Doctors considered it the most nutritive food, the one most capable of giving the organism strength and vigor, and this was most important in a world that attributed to food the primary function of "fattening"—that is, making one physically robust. In a period when there were no cars and no central heating, the calories expended were enormous, whether by the nobility who went hunting or made war or by the peasants who labored in the fields. For this, meat was the most important food in the daily diet. To give up meat, as the Church required, was a considerable sacrifice, a practice of humility that placed the needs of the spirit above those of the body, denying the body "its" specific nutrient for the purpose of loosening ties with the physical world.

This kind of alimentary sacrifice had important precedents in the Hebraic tradition and was also practiced by certain pagan philosophers.[4] Christianity spread it on a broader scale, turning it into a true mass phenomenon. In the fourth and fifth centuries, abstinence from meat was promoted as the model by hermits and monks, either as a personal choice or in observance of a monastic rule. Later the "model" spread to the whole of society through the prescriptions of ecclesiastic authorities, who imposed abstinence on all Christians on certain days of the week (Wednesday, Friday, and occasionally Saturday) and during certain periods of the year: the eve of important holidays; the *Quattro Tempora*, which marked the four seasons of the liturgical calendar, and evidently Lent, the forty days before Easter. All told, liturgical rules imposed the abstention from meat for more than one-third of the year, from 140 to 160 days.

It was therefore necessary to find alternative foods for those days and periods of the year. This explains the extraordinary success (both economic and cultural) during the Middle Ages of foods seen as substitutes for meat, such as vegetables, cheese, eggs, and fish. This last, in particular, was promoted to the rank of supreme substitute for meat, becoming the alimentary "sign" of the days and periods of "lean." It goes without saying that this development was not a straight line and did not go uncontested. In the first centuries of Christianity, there was a certain tendency to exclude fish as well from the Lenten diet because it is an animal product; this was followed by an attitude of tacit tolerance that did not prohibit it but did not prescribe it; and, finally, as of the ninth and tenth centuries, there was no question about the legitimacy of eating fish on days of abstinence.[5] Only "fat" fish were excluded from the Lenten diet, meaning large marine animals (whales, porpoises, and the like that are not really fish) whose flesh looks too much like that of terrestrial animals, perhaps because of the quantity of blood. Apart from such exceptions, fish (and whatever is born and lives in water) acquired as of then, and in an increasingly clear and unequivocal way, the cultural physiognomy of a "lean" food. It became symbolic of the monastic diet and of Lenten renunciation, and its difference from meat—initially vague, if not outrightly denied—became more and more established.[6]

74

The spread of Christianity thus played a notable role, perhaps a decisive one, in placing a "culture of fish" on a par with that of meat. The Venerable Bede observed that pagan Anglo-Saxons did not practice fishing, "even though their sea and rivers abound in fish." Among the first initiatives of Bishop Wilfred, who came to convert them, was to teach them "how to obtain food from fishing."[7] In other texts as well, one reads that the conversion to Christianity found its symbolic image in the acceptance of the Lenten diet. At the time of Charlemagne, Saxons who refused to abstain from meat during the periods imposed by the Church were punished with death.[8]

It took a few centuries before progress in methods of preservation could make fish a truly "common" food. Then the ambiguity mentioned earlier reappeared. If, on the one hand, fish became a symbol of humility, renunciation, and mortification, on the other, it remained a product not easily found and, above all, not easily transported or preserved in an era obviously lacking refrigeration. For this reason, fish came to be seen in the Middle Ages as a luxury product—which was something of a paradox, as the vast presence of water made fishing easily accessible (with unrestricted rivers, swamps, and lakes providing mostly freshwater fish).[9] Meat nonetheless remained a more "common" food, and for this reason, in contemporary documents, aside from praise for the monastic diet exempt from meat, we find attacks against the luxurious menus of monasteries and the delicacy of the fish eaten. In the twelfth century, for example, Peter Abelard warned his beloved Heloise against giving up meat to avoid having to rely on choice fish, which was rarer and more costly: fish, he wrote, is a delicacy for discerning palates and deep pockets—too expensive for poor people.[10]

During the Middle Ages, freshwater fish received uncommon attention in fishing and consumption. It became, so to speak, a "terrestrial" resource. This can be seen in every kind of document, from archival acts to literary sources, from dietary treatises to cookbooks. Praise of pike is sung in a poem by Sidonio Appolinare in the fifth century; Gregory of Tours, in the sixth, honors the trout of Geneva's Lake Léman. The epistle *De observantia ciborum* by Antimo, the Greek doctor who lived in Ravenna at the court of Theodoric, king of the Goths, begins his chapter on fish with a discussion of trout and perch and devotes most of his attention to pike and eel, mentioning only one saltwater fish, sole.[11] Trout and eel from Lake Garda, near Mantua, are listed in the ninth-century inventories of the monastery of Bobbio; particularly appreciated were sturgeon from the Po River, famous for their size. If the bishop of Ravenna could request that the fishermen of the Padoreno (a tributary of the Po that flowed near the city before emptying into the sea) bring him, before anyone else, sturgeon longer than six feet, it was because of the particular prestige of that fish. Throughout the Middle Ages, sturgeon indicated the table of the rich; in England, it was primarily reserved for the king's table. Preference for freshwater fish continued during the following centuries. The catalog made by Bonvesin de la Riva in the thirteenth century of the products that came to the market of Milan includes trout, dentex, carp, eel, lamprey, and river shrimp, this last heavily consumed in medieval cities. The statutes of Bologna, whenever there were problems concerning the sale of fish, never fail to add "and shrimp."

Saltwater fish had obviously not disappeared, but it is hard to estimate its volume during the high Middle Ages in the absence of specific documentation. Later, at the beginning of the fourteenth century, the *Liber de coquina*—the first cookbook to have survived from the Italian Middle Ages[12]—indicates a degree of interest in marine resources: not only the trout and lamprey already mentioned but also bream, anchovies, sardines, mullet, octopus, cuttlefish, shrimp, and lobster are the basis of various recipes.[13] Is this a rediscovery or a specifically Mediterranean phenomenon? The second hypothesis seems more likely because a few decades later a Tuscan translation of this cookbook eliminated recipes for saltwater fish and replaced them with recipes for fish from rivers or lakes.[14] This would suggest a diversity of alimentary usage between the Italian "continent" and the Mediterranean coast.

The central problem, and doubtless the greatest, was that of transportation, given the high perishability of fish. The good fortune of those who liked eel was that, according to medieval authorities, it could live for as long as six days without water, "particularly," Albertus Magnus advised, "if it is laid on grass in a cool, shaded place, and not prevented from moving."[15] It was mostly freshwater fish that ended up in the kitchen and on the table, being easier to catch and faster to transport. During a trip in Campania, Thomas Aquinas managed to eat fresh herring, which he liked, but only by miracle: a basket of sardines was brought to him, the story goes, that miraculously turned into herring. Fresh saltwater fish were indeed a rarity; only preserved fish reached the market. The practice of salting it (or drying it or smoking it or keeping it in oil) was ancient and allowed the mass of the population to observe as they could the obligation of abstaining from meat. At the beginning of the twelfth century, the perfection of preservation techniques, encouraged by the growing demand, in turn increased the demand for preserved fish, but fresh fish maintained its status as a luxury product.

It was precisely in the twelfth century that the large-scale commercialization of Baltic herring started. The following century Thomas de Cantimpré remarked that, kept this way, it lasted "longer than all other fish." Around the middle of the fourteenth century, the Dutchman Wilelm Beukelszoon devised a system for rapidly cleaning herring from the inside, placing them in salt, and stowing them in the same boat from which they had been fished.[16] This was how the fortune of the Hanseatic League (the association of German merchants in the Baltic) was built and, later, that of Dutch and Zeeland fishermen. But between the fourteenth and fifteenth centuries, herring fled the Baltic (it was a phenomenon of colossal proportions, the total migration of a species), so that Dutch and Zeeland merchant ships were forced to run after them off the shores of England and Scotland.

Even freshwater fish were processed this way. From the thirteenth century, documents from the lower Danube record large fish farms for the production of salted or dried carp, a species that appears to have been introduced by monks from southern Germany along with Christianity (here again, and not by chance, we find the Christianity-fish relationship). In time, carp became one of the principal items in the economy of the country. A few centuries later Venetian ambassador Giovanni Michiel remarked that Bohemia "has fish farms so filled with fish that they account in large part for the wealth of the realm."[17] In mountainous regions, carp farming gave way to that of pike and trout. Elsewhere salmon, lamprey, and sturgeon were fished, dried, and salted, a commerce largely conducted by Venetian and Genoese merchants.[18]

From the end of the fifteenth century, the commerce and consumption of fish saw the entry of a new competitor that slowly overtook herring, sturgeon, and other species: cod, fished for centuries in ocean waters but now discovered in inexhaustible supply off Newfoundland. An out-and-out war for the exploitation of those waters ensued, with the Basques, French, Dutch, and English battling in engagements decided by cannons. In the end, only the most powerful navies, those of England and France, retained access to those banks.[19] Dried and salted cod, known as stockfish and baccalà—the first sold by weight and the second by the piece—became a standard presence on the tables of the working classes, particularly in the cities.

Even then, the consumption of fish remained stigmatized by an ensemble of images that prevented it from acquiring unequivocally positive status and truly popular appeal. Preserved fish evoked poverty and lower-class social position. Fresh fish evoked images of wealth but a hardly enviable wealth because fish—people read and thought—*is not filling*. It is a "light" food, and for that reason "Lenten," and can be thoroughly enjoyed only by those who do not have to deal with daily hunger. In both connotations, fish labored to achieve a positive nutritional value. It was eaten, and even abundantly, but culturally it always remained a surrogate for meat. "Taste" and "need," Flandrin taught us, do not always go hand in hand.[20]

The revolution in fashion, which in the last century overturned this situation, bringing fish to the summit of positive values and spreading, by contrast, diffidence toward meat, signifies something very simple: we have evolved from a society of hunger into a society of plenty—from a society that lived in fear of an empty stomach (and for that reason sought, above all, filling and high-caloric foods) to a society that lives in fear of a full stomach (now oriented toward light and low-calorie foods). Lenten food has thus lost all meaning of renunciation, sacrifice, or penance. Fish has won the battle.

CHAPTER VIII

From Milk to Cheeses

THE IMAGE OF MILK is naturally associated with infancy. It is a positive thing, a source of life and health. Ancient and medieval doctors defined it as a kind of whitened, purified blood.[1] And blood is the very essence of life. It is therefore not surprising that milk also holds a place in religious symbolism as an image of life and inner salvation. In early Christianity, the holy meal of believers consisted of milk (along with bread or honey) and only later moved toward the ritual consumption of bread and wine.[2] At a certain point, wine replaces milk in the cultural and religious imagination, taking over its functions. This happens when milk loses its primary nutritional value, as in the passage from infancy to adulthood.

The profound connection between milk and infancy, which stands at the origin of the positive values symbolically attributed to milk, is also the limit of its role and its image, preventing it from assuming an entirely positive alimentary, and cultural, value. As a food for adults, milk (and here we are speaking of animal milk) is generally rejected. According to ancient medicine, milk is not a suitable food for adult humans. Hippocrates and Galen advise it only for medicinal purposes, emphasizing its many dangers from a nutritional standpoint.[3] These judgments were also made in the light of environmental issues: Greek and Roman culture developed in a geographic region, the Mediterranean, unsuited to the consumption of a delicate and perishable product such as milk. This was true in general but even more so in warmer climates, and it is not by chance that only certain populations to the north were described, not without amazement, as habitual milk drinkers. "Mare-milkers," Herodotus called the Scythians, who were great consumers of milk and milk products.[4] We see similar evaluations made by writers of late antiquity and the early Middle Ages. For example, Giordano, writing about the Goths, said that thanks to their contact with neighboring tribes, they discovered that marvelous drink of civilization, wine, but nonetheless remained faithful to milk, their traditional drink.[5]

The consumption of milk in adulthood thus became the alimentary characteristic of barbarianism—a notion analogous to infancy, transposed from the biological to the sociocultural: barbarians, who do not yet know "civilization," are to "civilized" man what the infant is to the adult. The paradox is that among the alimentary habits of mankind, the ability to drink milk in adulthood is one of the most heavily weighted with a cultural connotation, representing the outcome of a long and difficult adaptation that altered, more than other habits, the natural behavior of the species, yet today remains negligible throughout the world.[6] On a symbolic level, the image is reversed: milk drinkers are barbarian and primitive. This was the opinion of ancient and medieval writers who contrasted "evolved" agricultural societies with "primitive" pastoral societies and the foods developed and "invented" by humankind (such as bread and wine) with the foods spontaneously provided by nature (such as meat and milk).[7]

The milk in question is mostly ewe's milk. In fact, whereas today it is generally taken for granted that animal milk is chiefly from cows, in ancient and medieval times the preferred milk ideally came from ewes or goats. Until the Middle Ages, cattle raising was marginal compared with that of "small animals," as pigs and goats were called, because cattle were considered working animals rather than a source of food.[8] Isidore of Seville, in the seventh century, in the chapter on animals in his monumental etymological encyclopedia, saw a preliminary distinction between two categories of animals: "those that serve to lighten the labor of man, like oxen and horses, and those that serve to feed him, like sheep and pigs."[9] Oxen were used to pull carts and to plow, certainly not to produce milk or meat.

This classification corresponded to food habits and was reflected in categories of diet and taste: the milk of ewes and goats was regarded as the best on the dual grounds of taste and nutrition. Fifteenth-century humanist Bartolomeo Sacchi, known as Platina, in summarizing widely shared concepts and evaluations, wrote, "Milk has the same characteristics as the animal from which it was drawn: goat milk is reputed to be excellent because it aids the stomach, eliminates occlusions of the liver, lubricates the intestine; second is ewe milk, and third is cow."[10] It remains understood that "the excessive use of milk is not advisable"—a view shared by the physician Pantaleone da Confienza, author of the oldest known treatise on milk and milk products,[11] published in 1477. Milk, wrote Pantaleone,[12] is recommended exclusively for persons in perfect health, with many precautions: "it must come from healthy animals, be of high quality and freshly drawn; it should be drunk, in all cases, on an empty stomach, or no less than three hours after the last meal, and immediately after drinking vigorous exercise should be avoided." Furthermore, one must take care not to mix milk and wine in the stomach because the two are considered incompatible, based on the beliefs of traditional culture and for symbolic reasons as well.

It would nonetheless be a mistake to believe that milk had no place in the diet of medieval people. On the contrary, it played an important and at times decisive role in nutrition. Few drank milk, but the practice of turning it into cheese was fairly universal—and, moreover, an excellent means of assuring its long-term durability.

In truth, even with regard to cheese, medieval culture, like that of ancient times, remained very doubtful. The mysterious mechanisms of coagulation and fermentation were viewed with suspicion by medical science. Dietary treatises invariably expressed diffidence on the subject of cheese and warned against its consumption, placing many limitations on both quality and quantity. The greatest scientific authorities of the Greek and Roman world voiced these views, as did the Arab doctors who repeated them and transmitted them to western Europe. "*Caesus est sanus quem dat avara manus* [Cheese is healthful only when given by a miserly hand]," an aphorism attributed to the Salerno school of medicine, became a near commonplace in the literature on hygiene of the late Middle Ages.[13] Only when cheese is eaten in small quantities is it not harmful to the health.

Aged cheese was the primary object of such negative judgments. Platina, mentioned earlier, condemned it because "it is hard to digest, minimally nutritious, not good for the stomach or the intestines, generates bile, brings on gout, pain in the kidneys, sand and kidney stones." Fresh milk, on the other hand, "is very nourishing and in an efficacious way, it calms inflammation of the stomach, and is beneficial to people afflicted with tuberculosis."[14] Opinions like these recur insistently, almost as platitudes in medieval and modern treatises. They arise not only from theoretical prejudices (the processes of fermentation were often seen negatively in ancient cultures, and particularly biblical culture, because of their association with the corruption and putrefaction of organic matter) but also from practical considerations determined by the esthetic, gustatory, and olfactive characteristics of a product that not uncommonly—despite the massive amount of salt used to preserve it—looked rotten.

Medieval dietetics—based on the Hippocratic-Galenic theory of the four "qualities" (hot, cold, dry, and moist), according to which it is possible to classify foods in an infinite variety of combinations and "degrees"—set itself the task of arriving at a balanced diet that reconciled excesses by means of opposite excesses, taking into account not only the quality of the food but also the variables of the environment (location, climate) and the nature of the consumer (state of health, kind of life and work, sex, age, and so on). In conjunction with this kind of equilibrium, suggestions were made concerning combinations, type of cooking, and order of dishes. As for cheese, Platina maintained that it should be eaten at the end of the meal "because it seals the mouth of the stomach and eliminates the nausea caused by fat foods."[15] This "sealing" ability of cheese, proclaimed by the *Regimen sanitatis* of the Salerno school ("eaten after the other foods, cheese signals the end of the meal")[16] and repeated for centuries by dietitians, is the origin of customs still practiced today, not to mention proverbs, that do not consider a meal to be finished "until the mouth tastes of cheese."[17] It is interesting to note how proverbial traditions often take root in a premodern dietary culture in which the scientific particulars have disappeared but the practical precepts remain vigorously present.[18]

The recommendations of the doctors, in the case of cheese as of every other alimentary practice, found immediate and direct confirmation in the uses suggested by cookbooks of the time. Maestro Martino, the most important cook of the fifteenth century—whose close intellectual affinity with the Roman circles frequented by Platina[19] has recently come to light—makes a point of specifying that "cheese in little pans [*caso in patellecte*]," for which he provides the recipe, "should be eaten after the meal and very hot."[20]

All this, naturally, concerns only the small segment of society that has the luxury of choice. Every reservation falls by the wayside when it comes to need, when hunger imposes its own reasoning: "The poor, and how many are forced by necessity to eat cheese every day, are not obliged to observe the rules that we have set forth, being forced to eat cheese at the beginning, end and middle of every meal," wrote Pantaleone da Confienza without irony.[21]

Let us pause on this association of the poor with the consumption of cheese. It goes back to antiquity, as seen in the pages of authors and agronomists, from Cato to Varro, Columella, Pliny, and Virgil. In most of these texts, the social level that consumes dairy products seems decidedly "poor." Columella, however, points out a difference: cheese "serves to feed peasants" (in fact, it "fills them [*agrestis saturat*]"), but "it graces elegant tables."[22] On the tables of the poor, it is a main dish, a primary source of nourishment; on the tables of the rich, it appears only as an "embellishment" or an ingredient in more complex dishes.

This image carried over in part into the Middle Ages, framed however in a process of "ennobling" the product that led ultimately to a reversal—the definitive recognition of the economic, alimentary, and cultural value of cheese. A process of this kind, not without ambiguities, centered around the monastic alimentary model, hardly representative of the majority but nonetheless capable of imposing itself on the whole of society as an ideal reference point, being highly prestigious, and having great impact on the definition of collective behavior and attitudes. The essential element of the monastic model is the renunciation, partial or total, of meat. Prohibited to monks out of principle, albeit with many exceptions, meat was replaced by such substitute foods as fish, eggs, and cheese. Extending well beyond the monastic world, such renunciations (and such substitutions) came to be imposed by church regulations on the entire Christian society and ended up covering a good part of the year—as much as a third or more, as we have seen.[23] These choices and these requirements brought about important changes in the diet and in the "social status" of products. If, on the one hand, cheese was confirmed as a food of the poor and a substitute for a more prestigious and desirable food, on the other hand, it became "ennobled," reaching top billing in the diet, an object of the most concentrated attentions and, on occasion, of experimentation and innovative research. Almost paradoxically, the culture of renunciation was itself the origin of a new gastronomic culture, of an inquisitive and creative nature, from which many future acquisitions of taste arose. "Is it possible to single out any esteemed cheese that was not monastic in its distant past?" asked Moulin.[24] This is surely an exaggeration because those "origins" are often no more than mythic. But myths are themselves indications of a cultural climate, a common attitude that identified monastic centers—"the sites of renunciation"—as the sites where, paradoxically, gastronomic culture developed.

Moreover, when we speak of "monastic gastronomy," we must not forget the centrality of the peasant world in the evolution and diffusion of that culture. If monastic cheeses came to be produced and perhaps even "invented" within the monastery, this took place with the collaboration of the rustics who worked for the monks. In other cases, and perhaps in many, cheeses came from without, from farms that the monks owned but that others tended. The income in kind that the monasteries received from their tenants often included certain quantities of cheese. The monastery of Saint Julia of Brescia—as we know from the inventory of its holdings, drawn up in the ninth and tenth centuries—collected sizable rents in cheese from peasants living on monastic properties in Lombardy and Emilia. Requests were expressed in weight, with an indication of the corresponding pounds of *caseum,* or in the number of wheels.[25] Similar attention to cheese can be found in another ninth-century monastic inventory from the abbey of Saint Colombano in Bobbio, on the Emilian Appenines.[26] We have to imagine the fertile encounter of opposing parties: the long-established experience of peasant-shepherds confronted with the self-interested requests of the landowners to diversify and renew that experience.

In medieval gastronomic culture, cheese thus acquired—despite medical advice—a major renewal of image, a social boost that made it increasingly acceptable on elegant tables. In the fifteenth century, Pantaleone da Confienza could write in the *Summa lacticiniorum* that he knew "kings, dukes, counts, marquesses, barons, soldiers, nobles, merchants" who often and willingly ate cheese.[27] This direction will continue to affirm itself in the Renaissance and in modern centuries, when even literary and poetic works will sing the praises of cheese, such as the sixteenth-century triplets of Ferrara writer Ercole Bentivoglio.[28] The presence of cheese on noble tables is confirmed during those centuries by cookbooks, such as the one by Cristoforo Messisbugo, chef to the Este court in Ferrara, who lists "ricotta, cavi di latte, gioncata, cream, butter; hard cheese, fat cheese, tomini, pecorino [ewe's milk], sardesco [Sardinian cheese]; marzolini, provature and ravogliuoli [types of cheese]" among the indispensable provisions "to set a proper table for the arrival of any great prince . . . or for any other important event that might take place."[29] The vicissitudes of cheese demonstrate with singular clarity how values typical of popular culture can rise to the upper ranks of gastronomy[30]—an example of integration from bottom to top, not uncommonly paralleled by the reverse or, better still, by reciprocity and circularity.

Cheese was also widely used in cooking. As Platina tells us: "cooks used cheese in the preparation of many foods."[31] Its use is amply documented in the cookbooks of the time, between the thirteenth and fourteenth centuries, when they first appeared in Italy and other European countries.

Fresh cheese was mixed into eggs, meat, vegetables, and fragrant herbs to make all kinds of tortes and pasties—perhaps the dishes most characteristic of medieval gastronomy. The thirteenth-century cookbook preserved in a miscellaneous codex in the library of the University of Bologna, known as "Anonymous Tuscan"—cited here only as an example—proposes "fresh cheese [*cascio fresco*]" for the filling of "meat crepes or tortelli and ravioli," as well as for the stuffing of a lamb shoulder that must also include "fresh cheese, well blended with a fair amount of eggs." Along with "chopped meat," fresh cheese should go into *pastello romano*, whereas the *torta parmesana* should contain, in addition to fresh cheese, "an equal amount of grated cheese." This last ingredient also goes into "stuffed [deviled] eggs" and, of course, into lasagne.[32] In other cases, cheese is the principal ingredient of the dish and the qualifier of its name: a *casciata** is made of "fresh cheese washed and well drained, finely broken up with the hands in a bowl, then blended with eggs, herbs, lard, salt and pepper and baked in a crust." This is assuredly simple cooking, presumably of peasant origin but destined for the upper classes, as is made explicit in this cookbook, which, like all the others, was intended for the nobility or urban upper bourgeoisie. After the recipe for *cascio arrostito* (cheese roasted on a skewer over the open fire and served on a thin slice of bread or placed on a board of dried pasta), the writer of the text directs, "and bring it to the lord."[33]

---

*From *cascio*, the term more common in Tuscany than *formaggio*.—Trans.

Aged cheese also entered into cooking, as we have just seen in the recipes of the anonymous Tuscan. Although the fresh cheese was ground (with mortar and pestle), the aged one was grated, as the cookbook of Maestro Martino makes clear regarding a torte of spelt: "Take a pound of fresh cheese, and half a pound of good aged cheese, *grinding the first and grating the other*, as is customary."[34] In recipes for salty or sweet tortes, the two types of *cascio*, singly or mixed depending on the dish, are the principal ingredients.[35] They also make their appearance in fritters,[36] omelets,[37] and "deviled" eggs,[38] as well as in many other dishes.

Among the grating cheeses, parmesan, already in the Middle Ages, had acquired indisputable primacy (although at that time *piacentino* and *lodigiano* (similar cheeses from Piacenza and from Lodi) were equally famous.[39] The success of this kind of cheese, which was exported outside of Italy as early as the fourteenth century,[40] is also connected to the renown of a manufactured product that went particularly well with it: pasta. It is to parmesan, in all probability, that Salimbene da Parma is alluding in his thirteenth-century *Cronaca* when describing a monk, Giovanni da Ravenna, as a great lover of lasagne with cheese: "I never saw a man eat lasagne with cheese as eagerly as he."[41] And Boccaccio lavishly described as one of the major attractions of the utopian Land of Bengodi "the mountain made entirely of grated parmesan atop which people stood doing nothing but make macaroni and ravioli and cook them in capon broth."[42]

The practice of sprinkling parmesan on pasta, mixing in butter and sweet spices, is regularly documented from then on in treatises and literature, in chronicles of banquets, and in the recommendations of cookbook writers. Maestro Martino wants it on ravioli, Sicilian maccheroni, vermicelli, and lasagne and even on liquid first courses such as manfrigoli.[43] A novella by Celio Malespini, at the beginning of the sixteenth century, brings together a group of Venetian gentlemen who are delighting in macaroni from Messina seasoned with "more than twenty-five pounds of parmesan, and six or eight of caciocavallo [a type of provolone, the size of a fist, made in southern Italy], along with innumerable spices, sugar, cinnamon, and so much butter that they were drowning in it."[44] These are luxuries not available to the poor, who were limited to imagining them in their dream of Bengodi, that happy land of Boccaccian memory. Many people called it the Land of Cockaigne and perhaps believed it to be real. "They left with all their belongings and families," related a chronicler from Modena, Tommasino de' Bianchi, on the subject of certain peasants who fled beyond the Po in search of work, "and went to stay in Lombardy . . . because it is said that there they hand out gnocchi covered with cheese, spices and butter."[45]

Until the eighteenth century and its happy marriage with tomato sauce, pasta was customarily seasoned with butter, spices (chiefly cinnamon), sugar, and cheese. But not even tomatoes managed to replace cheese completely. The Neapolitan Ippolito Cavalcanti, who in the 1830s provided one of the first recipes for macaroni and tomato sauce, proposed that the macaroni, barely drained, should be well covered with cheese before adding the tomato sauce: "mix in aged cheese and provolone; and no matter how many other cheeses you may choose to add, they will only make it tastier."[46]

By the end of the Middle Ages, the traditional superiority of ewe's milk over cow's milk was no longer taken for granted. "At the present time," wrote Platina around the middle of the fifteenth century, "there are two varieties of cheese that are contesting primacy: marzolino, as the Tuscans call it, made in Tuscany during the month of March [*marzo*], and parmesan from the regions south of the Alps, that could also be called maggengo made in May [*maggio*]."[47] In fact, these differing times conceal a much deeper opposition, curiously not emphasized by the author: cheese made of ewe's milk versus cheese made of cow's milk. The growing success of parmesan was the proof of a culture that had begun to diversify and of a product that in some regions of Italy—"*cisalpine*," Platina calls them—had gained such strength that it could "contend the primacy" of the traditional cheese of ewe's milk. This became generalized in continental Europe during the late Middle Ages and early modern era. In Italy, beginning in the fifteenth century, the irrigated plains of the Po and the high pastures of Alpine valleys took on primary importance for raising dairy herds.[48]

In the meantime, regional specialties diversified and increased. In the sixteenth century, Ortensio Lando proposed a kind of "gastronomic itinerary" that stopped for the fresh *caciacavalucci* of Sorrento, the *ravigiuoli* of Siena, the *marzolini* of Florence, the ricottas of Pisa, and the *cacio piacentino*, which he remembers having eaten in Piacenza with apples and grapes and finding himself "consoled as though I had eaten a superb pheasant." Among the cheeses from the Po Valley, "the cheese of Malengo and from the Bitto valley" was also praised, and a final mention concerned *cavi di latte* (a cream-based dessert) from Venice.[49] Cow's milk cheeses held a position of great importance in the already mentioned *Summa lacticiniorum* by Pantaleone da Confienza, whose intention—called promotional in the language of today—was primarily to praise the gastronomy of the Po Valley and, in particular, that of Piedmont and Savoy. The cheeses of southern Italy and the islands, much appreciated and widely commercialized at that time,[50] are not even mentioned by him. That such a project was even conceivable marks a significant turning point that took place in the fifteenth century. Like Platina earlier, Pantaleone singles out as the best cheeses in Italy the *marcelinus,* or *marzolino,* also called *fiorentino,* produced in Tuscany and Romagna, and the *piacentino,* also called *parmigiano* (so identified by Platina) "because in Parma they make similar ones, not very different in quality." In the regions around Milan, Pavia, Novara, and Vercelli, they also began to produce some "a few years ago." The first is made of ewe's milk, "although some add cow's milk"; the second is of cow's milk.[51] It is, above all, this latter that in the centuries to come would cross the borders of Italy and become one of the signal traits of its gastronomic image.

CHAPTER IX

Condiment/Fundament

The Battle of Oil, Lard, and Butter

EMPEROR FREDERICK II liked to say that in his realm culture was the *condimentum* of power, represented by laws and weapons.[1] Scholars have pondered what meaning to attribute to this statement. Did Frederick see culture as a supplement, a kind of "feather in his cap," to make the structure of power more pleasing and acceptable, or on the contrary, did he see it as the foundation of power: *condimentum* as "condiment" in the first case (from *condire*) or as "fundament" in the second (from *condere*)? In the eyes of a historian of food, this is probably a nonproblem. It is obvious that the etymological proximity of the two terms (*condire* and *condere*) implies a substantive convergence: *condire* does indeed mean to add, to arrange, to season, but also to base, to give the style and meaning of what will be made on those bases. The "basics of cooking" are not called that by chance. Gastronomically and semantically, they are part of the same group as condiments, a group whose principal member is fat.

But there is more. Fats not only participate decisively in constructing an individual preparation or recipe but also represent one of the fundamental constructive elements of the alimentary "system" to which they belong: they define its character, specificity, and identity. Within the general tendency to repetition and self-reproduction, which distinguishes food habits and traditions, admittedly with many exceptions, condiments and basics were seen as strategic elements of continuity, to the point of having attracted the attention of ethnologists in addition to historians. Lucien Febvre, who in 1938 was studying (not accidentally within the context of the First International Congress on Folklore) the geographic distribution of culinary basics in France, remarked, "The preferential choice of this fat or another for home cooking or for cooking on grand occasions appears to be notably stable. Pretty much everywhere it has the solidity of habits that are not open to question."[2] Nonetheless, Febvre himself did not exclude the possibility of change over time: "The history of the substitution of certain fats for others would be fascinating."[3] The prevailing notion was that of permanence, of food customs (particularly with regard to fats) as an important cultural marker, traceable to a primarily geographic dimension. The cartography proposed by Hémardinquer in the 1960s grew out of this perspective: "a map of fats" based on surveys in the French provinces that afforded glimpses of a centuries-old stability in practices and habits, in spite of the radical changes taking place during the twentieth century.[4]

But the changes, others maintain, did not occur in the twentieth century alone. What might seem to be a period of extended duration, always faithful to itself, is only the flattening perspective of events that, on the contrary, are highly dynamic. Stouff, in particular, in his study of late medieval Provence, argued that only in recent times did olive oil become characteristic of Provençal cooking, whereas in the fourteenth and fifteenth centuries it was lard that served as the basic fat in daily cooking: "At that time, oil was used only for eggs and fish" and for a few other dishes; otherwise, "it was salt pork that provided the ideal fat"—above all, in the soups of legumes and vegetables that were the basic food of peasants and common folk.[5] With this, Stouff tried to restructure the presumed "regionalism" of alimentary traditions, placing in doubt the possibility of drawing a "map of fats" determined by geography. Carried to more extreme consequences by other scholars,[6] the negation of culinary regionalism and self-styled folklore of long standing—to be understood, in reality, as a very recent construction—was in turn contested by Flandrin, who, on the contrary, has supported the existence of highly precise regional and national distinctions in culinary practices ever since medieval times.[7]

In any case, the prevalent tendency today is to historicize as much as possible culinary habits and practices, extracting them from the generality of "tradition." And to historicize means to introduce into the research not only an incontrovertible chronologic dimension alongside the geographic but also the no less decisive variable of social nature. "In our maps," Hémardinquer admits, "we would have liked a special symbol to indicate particular socio-economic categories." A typical reply, recurring in the questionnaires used for the surveys, is "culinary basics vary with the social class."[8]

This is surely not an invention of the twentieth century. Pliny, in the twentieth-eighth book of his *Natural History*, wrote: "From milk one obtains butter, the most refined food of barbarian peoples, which distinguishes the rich from the poor."[9] Put together, these are two rather different notions: first, butter acts as a cultural signifier and, in a parallel meaning, as an ethnic signifier because butter is the fat of "barbarians" in contrast to the oil of the Romans, who are "civilized"; second, butter, as the fat of the elite, "distinguishes the rich from the poor." What seems to be missing, in any case, is a strict definition of "geographic." More important than places in defining the diversity of alimentary practices are the traditions of production and the ways of relating to the territory. The predilection for uncultivated spaces and herding over agriculture is in itself enough, in the eyes of Pliny, to qualify those populations as "barbaric." Moreover, when it comes to commercial exchanges, geography is superseded. Pliny himself informs us of the protective properties of butter, similar to those of oil, and of the custom of barbarians to spread it on the skin. "And we also do that with our babies," he adds, making us understand that even in Rome butter could be found and put to uses other than alimentary.[10] The same held for Greece, where (Hippocrates tells us) butter was imported from Asia to be used as an ointment.

In ancient times, the opposition oil/butter consistently represents the contrast between civilization and barbarity. "They use butter as oil," Strabo wrote, referring to the mountain dwellers of the Pyrenees.[11] But even in this case, the observation is more ethnic than geographic. On a social level, it would seem to go back to a context of poverty and marginality considerably different from the one to which Pliny alludes. Is it butter of the elite or butter of the poor? We cannot answer this question unequivocally because both situations can be present in differing environmental and social contexts. With regard to the Middle Ages, Flandrin believes that the social status of butter can be defined in terms of poverty, considering it a "popular" and "provincial" product that was not elevated to the status of an upper-class product until the beginning of the modern era.[12]

In ancient times, pork fat was also culturally demeaned as being "popular." Among Latin agronomists, only Cato—perhaps recalling traditional practices in the countryside—mentions a few recipes for cakes made with lard.[13] The refined cuisine of Apicius recognized only oil ("it is literally dripping with oil"),[14] and this alone would be enough to define its social position. Obviously, when Greek and Latin writers speak of olive oil as a mark of civilization,[15] it is to the civilization of the rich and powerful that they are referring for the most part.

It is nonetheless through these cultural prejudices that behavior and fashion took shape. Although the Romans did not disdain pork (the Po Valley, culturally modeled on the ancient Celtic occupation, was its greatest producer in Italy, even supplying the markets of Rome[16]), but it is also true that it was not until the third and fourth centuries that pork was among the meats generously distributed by the emperors to the people of Rome.[17]

Something had started to change—not only on the productive and environmental levels (with the decline of crops and farmlands) but also with regard to culture and attitudes. The influx of Germanic tribes, on the rise from then on, also led to an increase in the importance of a forest economy and its products, starting with pigs.[18] That was when lard attained full status among the top products of the alimentary system—so much so that the first medieval writer on dietetics, in spite of his cultural background (Greek by birth, he grew up at the court of Byzantium, winding up in Ravenna during the Gothic domination), was obliged to devote a disproportionate part of his treatise to the subject.[19] In his letters to Theodoric, king of the Franks, the sign of new times is unequivocal. "That lard is the delight of the Franks," wrote Antimo, our Byzantine doctor, "is almost superfluous to mention. I have also heard that they are accustomed to eating it raw, and I marvel that this represents for them so efficient a remedy that they require no other medication." As to the use of lard as a condiment, Antimo accepts that it can be used for vegetables and any other food "whenever oil is lacking." This is a qualification (*ubi oleum non fuerit*) that confirms the persistence, still in the sixth century, of the Roman cultural preference for oil. However, the overall context has changed in the interim: the political and social affirmation of the Germanic tribes has engineered a truly elevated image of animal fat and, more generally, of meat products— the alimentary result of an economy based in large measure on forest animals grazing in the wild. The forest, which in Roman times was alien to the dominant cultural and productive values, in the high Middle Ages was included among them to the point that it came to be "measured" in pigs, or in terms of production of pigs: the size of a forest was determined by the number of pigs it could fatten.[20]

The dominant classes in the new Europe, whether because they were the heralds of a new culture or because they were accustomed to the lifestyle and food models of the victors, were convinced consumers of lard, which never ran short in the storehouses of the great private and clerical estates so as to provide enough fat for the entire year.[21] Even monastic alimentation, normally so severe with regard to animal products and so ready to reject them, seems to have adjusted to common practice when it began to use lard for cooking vegetables and legumes.[22] The only exception was during periods of Lenten abstinence, when any animal product was prohibited.

With this, we have arrived at a decisive moment in the history of alimentary fats in medieval Europe. The requirements of the Church to abstain from animal foods for a certain number of days of the year (which we have estimated to be 100 to 150, according to place and period) were imposed on everyone, not just monks. During such days, it was inevitable that lard was replaced by vegetable oil. Because of this, an unusual situation of alternation between lard and oil entered into the alimentary culture of the time; they were no longer participants in different cultures and different ideological and social contexts, but rather they were integrated into the very system of consumption within the entire society.[23] This is to say that the encounter between Germanic and Roman cultures, with the determining intervention of Christianity, had produced a new system of values that in a way contained both of them. When in 765 a priest, Rissolfo, granted a free meal three times a week to the poor of Lucca, he did not fail to specify that the *pulmentario* of grains and legumes should be dressed *de uncto aut de oleo*[24]—presumably alternating between animal and vegetable fat according to the liturgical calendar.

The integration was nonetheless imperfect because it was only lard— along with all alimentary values associated with the consumption of meat—that had in effect entered into common use, encouraged not only by the social and cultural promotion already mentioned but also by the wide diffusion of specific productive choices. Olive oil, on the other hand, remained an elite product, not easily procured—without running into the expense of importation—outside of the restricted areas where the olive was cultivated. There is no documentation on the exportation of oil to northern Europe for the entire medieval period.

How, then, to resolve the problem of Lenten abstinence? One solution could be the invention of vegetable oils other than olive. As it happened, a veritable explosion of what could be called this "alternative" culture took place during the Middle Ages, after being virtually unknown in Roman times—or practiced in a highly limited fashion. Walnut oil began to be used first of all—the fruit and the tree enjoyed unimagined success in vast regions of Europe.[25] But it was lard itself, incredibly enough, that was transformed into a vegetable oil, cleansed of its animal properties by means of virtuosic lexical acrobatics. The Council of Aix in 816, not without obvious rhetorical exertions, granted the monks of Gaul the right to Lenten use of *oleum lardivum*, lard melted in the manner of oil, "in view of the fact that the Franks have no olive oil."[26] Later, a similar concession was granted to Charles V, king of France, in a bull of Gregory XI,[27] whereas the Spanish were authorized to use lard by the so-called *cruzada* bull.[28]

It was, above all, butter that was accepted as an alternative to oil for meatless days, first sporadically and then more generally. During the last centuries of the Middle Ages, this was conceded by Church authorities to various communities in northern Europe.[29] It should be pointed out that already in Charlemagne's *Capitulare de villis*, butter (*butirum*) was listed among the Lenten products (*quadragesimale*) made or stored on imperial estates.[30]

We would be mistaken to think that these various alternatives to olive oil (substitute oils, lard, and butter) were the result of simple economic considerations, dictated by the availability or cost of the products. In reality, the debate also arose out of questions of taste. Although the gastronomic and dietetic tradition of the Mediterranean basin unhesitatingly placed olive oil in first position for culinary uses due to its flavor and its infinite salutary virtues, this was heatedly contested in different cultures and societies. One need only look to Hildegard of Bingen, the famous German mystic and writer of the twelfth century, according to whom olive oil is good for a multitude of medical purposes but for the rest "is not worth much" (*non vale multum*) because "when eaten, it produces nausea and makes other foods distasteful."[31] This obviously personal view reveals the Germanic world's stubborn resistance to the culture of oil and its inability to appreciate olive oil's pungent flavor,[32] so unlike the sweetness of animal fats.

We do not know whether the campaign in favor of oil during the high Middle Ages succeeded in modifying this Germanic diffidence at least to some degree. What is significant is that Liutprando da Cremona, when visiting Constantinople, declared himself revolted by the foods dripping in oil served to him during a dinner that was "vile and obscene, saturated with oil as though they wanted to get drunk on it."[33] On the shores of the Mediterranean, as opposed to the continent, the flavor of oil was so enjoyed that giving it up could be a gesture of high penitential value. In some Spanish monastic rules of the high Middle Ages, the use of oil was prohibited during Lent,[34] which seems incomprehensible at first glance if we think of the Lenten purpose that oil represented in the eyes of the faithful. Obviously, oil for those monks constituted a special treat, and thus it was all the more meritorious to exclude it from the diet at certain times.[35]

Not paradoxically, the polemic between admirers and denigrators of olive oil became more bitter during the middle centuries of the Middle Ages, when intensified commercial traffic increased the possibilities of making it available in northern countries. At the beginning of the twelfth century, we see a huge increase in the records of merchants, mostly Venetian, who were selling oil coming from Adriatic ports, largely from Apulia[36] and the Marches but also from the Dalmatian and Istrian coasts, as well as Greece. Tyrrhenian oil (from Liguria, Tuscany, Lazio, and Campania) went instead to the Genoese market.[37] Most of this oil either did not leave Italy or was shipped to eastern markets,[38] but commercial documents from Bruges, Paris, and London attest to the arrival of oil from Italy—above all, from Campania and Apulia, which, along with Andalusia, were the major centers of exportation from the Mediterranean.[39] Catalan oil also reached Flemish and English markets.[40]

Aside from differences of taste and regional, social, and cultural contrasts, it is important to point out that all the factors already mentioned contributed to creating an integrated system within which each fat had its place: oil (or butter) in "lean" (meatless) cuisine, lard in "fat" cuisine. The battle between Lent and Carnival that appears in literature as of the thirteenth century and fills the cultural imagination of Europe for many centuries—with residual echoes still today[41]—was, in fact, a false battle because the territory had already been divided preventively (and peacefully) between the two contestants. If peas in lard are adversaries of peas in oil, if butter leads the armies of dairy products and "oil fights against lard"—as we read in the first medieval text from France whose topic is that so-called battle—in the end they "all agree to make peace."[42] Lent will go into exile but will return when the time is right, and Carnival will agree to reign for the rest of the year, it being understood that fish can also be eaten in "fat" times as well[43]—but, really, who would want to do that?

What holds on the level of religious rituals also holds on the economic level: the commerce and sale of fats, aside from local characteristics and differences, was often in the hands of a single enterprise. Oil entered into the inventory of *lardaroli* (lard merchants)[44] just as fish replaced meat on the stands of butchers.

One can see in all this a gastronomic logic. As Flandrin remarked, "fat fat," meaning lard, is admirably suited to the preparation of meats, primarily roasts, whereas "lean fat," meaning oil, is ideal for fish dishes (fried fish, in particular) and for salad.[45] The liturgical pairing thereby finds a confirmation in the gastronomic pairing. This became the rule in the cookbooks of the fourteenth century, which, expressing a culture oriented toward the international, reproduced the same alternation between oil and lard throughout Europe. Butter appeared only to a limited and marginal degree,[46] perhaps because its association with common people made it incompatible with the rules of written recipes, which were geared to the upper classes.

Slowly, however, things began to change. As soon as Church dispensations permitted, the upper classes of northern Europe introduced butter into cooking, elevating it socially and culturally despite its "popular" image. This was a choice primarily dictated by taste—or rather *distaste*, Flandrin maintains, referring to the pungent taste of oil, as unappetizing in the north as it was delectable in the south: "As soon as they had the legal permission, the elite ate meatless dishes prepared in butter. Is this not a proof that when there was no such possibility they ate food cooked in oil out of obligation and with some repugnance?"[47] This may be an embarrassing hypothesis for one who wishes to support the primacy of economics in history, "but these demographic, economic or technical transformations do not appear to explain this culinary revolution" that erupted in the late Middle Ages, becoming consolidated between the sixteenth and seventeenth centuries, expressing itself "not on the level of material conditioning but volition," and carrying in its wake important economic changes such as the development of animal husbandry and renewed attention to milk-producing animals.[48]

One thing is certain: butter gradually changed stature and, strengthened by its new image, made a breech in the alimentary customs even of regions traditionally devoted to olive oil. The decisive moment of this event seems to have occurred in the fifteenth century and included Italy. This almost amounted to "a second invasion"—again, the words of Flandrin—of Mediterranean gastronomic territories, other than northern cuisines, following the invasion in the high Middle Ages that spread Germanic customs and marked the adoption of lard into the culinary practices of all of Europe. The introduction of butter into the cuisines of the south marked a new turn in the struggle between the two alimentary models because Italy opened itself "to northern influences" at the very moment when French and English cuisines, having abandoned oil in favor of butter, "got rid of certain southern influences thereby enhancing their own originality."[49]

The two events, in truth, evolved in very different modes and tones. Whereas the "first invasion"—to continue the metaphor—involved a huge deployment of weapons and troops under the aegis of a culinary culture associated with images of power and social supremacy, the entrance of butter into southern kitchens came about almost surreptitiously. The fact is that it first appeared as a substitute for oil and was thus associated with the humble food of Lent (at least in the cultural imagination) and not yet elevated to the model of aristocratic cuisine, as would happen, above all, in France at the beginning of the seventeenth century. In this guise, it appeared, for example, in the *Register of Cooking* by Johannes Bockenheim, chef (and a German!) to Pope Martin V in the 1430s.[50] It is in the section devoted to Lent that we find, for bean soup, the direction to use "olive oil or else butter"; for braised carp, the direction to cook it with wine, parsley, and "oil or else butter";[51] and for herb pie (*herbulatum*), the suggestion to use spices "and fresh butter."[52] Finally, butter is recommended for fried eggs, a dish—our chef specifies—"suited to clerics and monks."[53] Meats, on the other hand, are always cooked in bacon fat or lard.

Butter also appears in Maestro Martino's most famous of cookbooks,[54] which, around 1450, proposed it to sauce pasta, combining it with the grated cheese that for centuries had been the most typical condiment. "Sicilian macaroni," Martino recommends, "should be cooked in water or in meat broth, and placed in plates with a generous amount of grated cheese, fresh butter and sweet spices."[55] This combination came to be confirmed and, in a sense, codified by fifteenth-century cooking, as we see in the cookbooks of Cristoforo Messisbugo (chef to the Este court of Ferrara)[56] and of Bartolomeo Scappi[57] (chef to the papal court of Pius V), as well as every other source, whether treatises or literature.[58] In the sixteenth century, the fanciful *Catalog of the things that are eaten and drunk,* by the Milanese Ortensio Lando, explains that Sicilian macaroni—in the Middle Ages, it was primarily Sicily, and later Genoa, that was the capital of the Italian culture of pasta[59]—"is commonly cooked with capon fat, and fresh cheeses oozing with butter and milk on all sides" and "liberally sprinkled" with sugar and cinnamon.[60] As for the poor, who were forced to do without these delicacies, they did not give up dreaming about them and on occasion chased after them: "They left with all their belongings and families," a chronicler from Modena, Tommasino de'Bianchi, relates, regarding certain peasants who emigrated north of the Po in search of work, "and settled in Lombardy . . . because it was said that there, people got gnocchi covered with cheese and spices and butter."[61]

It is understood that "butter is used for the most part by those who live in western and northern regions where oil is lacking," Bartolomeo Sacchi, known as Platina, reminds us in his manifesto of humanistic alimentary philosophy, *De honesta voluptate et valetudine* (Guiltless pleasure and well-being), written in the mid-fifteenth century in close harmony with the already quoted Maestro Martino.[62] Reviewing ancient and contemporary opinions on the subject of butter, Platina seems to have abandoned the old contempt for that "barbarian" fat, which can now be used "in place of lard or oil to cook any food whatever."

Others, however, like Michele Savonarola of Padua, writer of an important treatise on dietetics during that same century, unconditionally confirmed the condemnation of butter—a battle already fought and won—considering it unworthy of a noble table: "Many use it in place of oil," he writes, "but butter is bad for the stomach and the intestines, making them sluggish, and for those unaccustomed to it, it upsets the stomach."[63] There is less of a risk for those who use it regularly, but the fact remains that the "inflammatory" unctuousness of butter tends to corrupt the blood, generating "leprosy and similar ills." Savonarola goes so far as to insinuate "that it is perhaps one of the reasons why one finds so many scabby and leprous people in Germany." In short, butter "is not food for your Lordship." The "Lordship" in this instance is Borso d'Este, duke of Modena, Reggio, and Ferrara, to whom Savonarola's *Libretto* is dedicated. More generally, the book is intended for the upper class—the invariable referent of treatise writers—always very sensitive to the social status of foods, according to procedures and ideology extremely widespread throughout the late Middle Ages and early modern era. In that period, no food, no recipe, no food custom was unrelated to the "quality of the individual," meaning social position, not personal taste.[64] Food served to signal the differences among the classes, taking on symbolic meanings that teach us a great deal not only about collective imagination but also about actual practices and the economic value of products because there is no doubt that beyond its greater or lesser availability, the status of every product grows out of the prestige attached to it.

Savonarola is categoric about the exclusion of butter from the alimentary universe of the "Lordship," to whom—according to a model already described—olive oil and lard are better suited. When it comes to animal fats, it is better not to overeat them: one must not be excessive in the amount consumed, and, above all, they must not be eaten by themselves. "In the preparation of other foods," they are fine and therefore "can be used by your Lordship," albeit in "small quantity and only as a condiment," with preference given to pork fat (in keeping with Christian usage), leaving "goose fat" to Jews.[65] Among the many types of olive oil, first choice went to so-called raw oil, extracted from olives not yet ripe: "For health I say," Savonarola declares, "this is what your Lordship should use in his dishes."[66] What also emerges, and most curiously, is the habitual association of oil and the Lenten diet. Savonarola explains, in fact, that oil "fattens and greatly increases the size of the liver," which is why "monks who eat this way are fat" (adding, "I believe that eggs cooked in oil . . . are very fattening"). "Orientals" are also generally fat because they "prepare meat . . . entirely in oil."[67] In the eyes of this doctor from Padua, to use oil, even for cooking meat, is indicative of an alimentary culture that is fundamentally alien. However, the fact that oil "is more fattening"—for such seems to be his belief—is not necessarily a defect or a limitation seen from the optic of the time; if anything, it is a benefit, an ulterior motive for the appreciation of this product in a society given to *desiring* fat, to considering it a positive value, whether on the alimentary or dietary level or, in consequence, on the level of the imagination (and of esthetic preferences).[68]

An important result emerges from all this. Fats associated gastronomically and culturally with meatless cooking (oil and butter) long remained stigmatized as "weak," despite eventual evaluations, such as that of Savonarola, of oil's greater capacity to fatten. Aristocratic cuisine, the food of "lords," remained marked by the consumption of meat (and lard) as a symbol of power, whereas delicate foods (the fish and vegetables of Lent, along with oil or butter) were seen more readily within the framework of ecclesiastic gluttony. As for the popular imagination, it is hardly oil that flows in the Land of Cockaigne, where meat and animal fats reign, including prosciutto and sausages, chunks of lard, salted shoulders of pork, and fat geese.[69] In that land of plenty, it is always Carnival time, and Lent falls only once every twenty years. From that point of view, aristocratic culture and popular culture are absolutely harmonious and homogeneous.

Even in Alpine regions, which we might think were participants in a butter culture, it was not until the beginning of the fifteenth century that butter acquired acceptance by the ruling classes, having emerged from a marginal culture that until then had confined it to the impoverished valleys of the interior.[70] As late as the fourteenth century, the purchase of butter for the court of Savoy was extremely limited,[71] and Giovanni Albini, the prince's doctor, strongly advised against its use, claiming it to be better in medicine than in food.[72]

In the next century, the consumption of butter at the court increased, and the publication of Pantaleone da Confienza's *Summa lacticiniorum* in 1477 is certainly not without significance because this doctor was close to the court of Savoy. That was the first systematic work specifically devoted to products derived from milk. It is filled not only with topical references to scientific literature of classical derivation but also with original observations, fruit of the author's experience acquired during many professional travels in the countries of Europe, with interesting comments of gastronomic interest.[73] His focus, however, is almost exclusively on cheese,[74] and butter is obviously not on his cultural horizon. Pantaleone, in fact, is astonished that certain people have such a passion for butter that they "waste" their cheeses. After having described the abundance of pastures in Brittany, he says he ate only mediocre cheese, although the milk of those animals was "high in fat and unctuous." The reason for such a flagrant contradiction, in his opinion, is that Bretons extract from the milk the best part in order to make butter: "I think that if they devoted as much attention to cheese as they do to butter, their cheeses would be much better." Instead, they make so much butter that they export it to such distant places as Poitou, Anjou, and Touraine and even as far as Normandy. Much is consumed locally, however, given that "almost everything is eaten with butter, even fish, which the Italian doctor finds 'very unsuitable,' to the point of admitting that 'I have many times admonished them.' But to no avail: they so love butter as to justify the saying 'Butter is to the Breton as is the pear to the magpie.'"[75]

Similar opinions are found with regard to English alimentary usages: there, too, good pastureland abounds, but the cheeses "if made more buttery would be much better and not so crumbly, and thus so difficult to digest."[76] The same is true for German cheeses: "If they were aged," Pantaleone writes, "they would be too friable, and I believe that the reason for this is that extraction of butter," which the Germans love.[77] Also devoted to butter are the Flemish.[78] On the other hand, the mountain people of the Alpine valleys produce exquisite creamy cheeses to which, in large part, they owe their enviable state of alimentary health.[79] Coming from a Piedmontese like Pantaleone, this is a great compliment. Nevertheless, it reveals the considerable marginality of butter in Italian alimentary culture of the time.

It would be difficult to draw the geographic contours of butter-oriented Europe more precisely than did Pantaleone da Confienza: Brittany, Normandy, Touraine, Anjou, and Poitou in France, along with Angoumois and Auvergne;[80] England; the Low Countries with Brabant, Hainaut, and Artois;[81] and parts of Germany (of which Pantaleone knows only the southern part bordering on Switzerland). It would, however, be better to distinguish within the butter-based cuisines between "those among them who ate butter only in meatless periods, and those who ate it every day." Not for nothing—Flandrin remarks, quoting the fifteenth-century testimony of Bruyerin Champier—were the French mocked by the Flemish "butter-eaters," who "use it every day, at lunch and at dinner, and on holidays," even putting it ("God forgive them!") into beverages.[82]

Outside of the butter regions, the ideal "lean fat" was oil, though not necessarily from the olive. Olive oil was native to southern France (Languedoc and Provence) and later triumphed beyond the Pyrenees and the Alps, on the Iberian peninsula and in Italy (at least in Liguria, the center-south, and the lake region in the north, which from the high Middle Ages were producers of olive oil).[83] In Piedmont,[84] however, as in Burgundy, Lorraine, and the interior of Castille,[85] it was another oil, walnut oil, that replaced lard on meatless days.

The Romans found walnut oil disgusting. Pliny judged it to be "inert and heavy in flavor,"[86] good only—like all other oils that are not made from the olive such as myrtle and sesame—for medicinal use. During the Middle Ages, on the contrary, secondary oils enjoyed great success in the kitchen, a success largely obligatory due to the ecclesiastic interdiction of animal fats on meatless days; the prohibitive cost of olive oil for many; and the lack of appreciation for olive oil on the part of northern people because of its bitter taste, so enjoyed by Romans.[87] Those northerners, Flandrin writes, dreamed of a "colorless, odorless, tasteless" oil,[88] as far removed as possible from its original nature. Montaigne, who missed the strongly flavored oil of Italy[89] once he crossed the Alps on his return to France, represents the exception. More common were opinions such as that of Father Labat, who declared his repugnance for food cooked in oil (unhappily for him, his trip to Italy took place during Lent) but granted that he could eat it only if the oil looked in every way like water.[90] No differently, the Englishman John Evelyn, author of a treatise on salad written at the beginning of the seventeenth century, stipulated that salad should be dressed with an oil "lacking any perceptible flavor."[91]

This diffidence toward oil arose out of the variety of alimentary traditions but rested on the fact that Mediterranean merchants, perhaps counting on the consumer's inexperience, often exported products of inferior quality to the regions of northern Europe. Flandrin recalls the comment of Thomas Platter that the only oil to reach the northern countries from Provence in the sixteenth century was a second pressing: "And if one remembers the English saying of the fifteenth century 'brown as oil,' one may well ask oneself if the inhabitants of non-Mediterranean Europe could ever have known what good olive oil was."[92]

In Germany as well, what was wanted was the most delicate oil possible, and aside from the question of geographic contiguity and thus lower transportation costs, there was good reason that the oil from Garda, lighter in color and flavor than the oil of southern Italy, was long appreciated by those markets. When, in the early eighteenth century, representatives of Garda accused Venice of having monopolized the oil trade, sending to Germany oil from the south and thereby ruining the Garda market, one of the accusations was that Venetian merchants had "deluded the German taste" by mixing oil from Puglia with that from

Garda in diminishing quantities, so as to slowly modify the palate of the buyers. Thus, because of unscrupulous traffickers, oil from Garda, for a time "more desirable than what came from Venice, which, because of its natural odor, was inadmissible on civilized tables," was abandoned in favor of the Venetian import, which "presently almost everybody is eating." Only a few clients of high standing—the "great lords"—continued to prefer the more delicate but costlier oil "from the lake [Garda]."[93]

And here, again, is the social variable as the decisive element in food choices. Behind the cultural dynamics that set butter against oil and both of them against lard, it is not hard to find simpler and more concrete reasons in daily operation based on more prosaic reasons of economy— choices that give rise to substitutes and surrogates, oils of lesser prestige, butter of lower quality, fats from animals other than pigs. Already in the high Middle Ages, the *Capitulare de villis* mentions, along with lard, *soccia*, a fat extracted from "fat sheep and from pigs"; also a pair of fat oxen was destined *ad socciandum* (to become *soccia*) on every imperial farm.[94] Peasants were long forced to use this type of fat, but it was the urban poor—not often having a pig for family use like peasants—who had a harder time providing themselves with fats.

In an attempt to arrive at a conclusion regarding this question of when and where oil, lard, and butter were used, it is possible to draw various "maps of fats" in the history of European alimentary usages, which changed in time and space apart from social differences.

The first map is the ancient one, which opposed Mediterranean oil—the mark of a civilization founded on cultivating the land—to the "barbarians'" butter and lard, the alimentary symbol of a nomadic and pastoral civilization. Lard also appears within the Greek and Roman worlds but only among the poor and with a low cultural status.

The second map is the one that, in the early centuries of the Middle Ages, shows lard taking over as the fat of universal choice in European cooking. The outcome of new productive and cultural models, this increasing use of lard implies membership in a Christian community that in this way as well distinguishes itself from the Hebraic world (which used goose fat) and from the Islamic world (which used sheep fat or more commonly oil, bringing to the southern Mediterranean the most crucial tradition of Hellenistic and Roman cultures).

The third map, which can be superimposed on the second, shows oil also affirming itself as the universal fat, alternating with lard on meatless days. In a movement equal and contrary to the preceding one, it is the fat of the south, in this case, that conquers the north, enforced by ecclesiastic rule. Not always, however, is it olive oil: on this map, spreading like an oil stain, are many zones where independent productive choices prevail, where secondary oils, for the most part, were developed.

The fourth map slowly takes shape and becomes clear in the thirteenth and fourteenth centuries when the regions of butter retrieve an identity that had been obliterated by oil.

The fifth and final map, representing the fifteenth through the seventeenth centuries, shows an inversion of the two: now, it is butter that conquers the south, aligning itself beside oil and even replacing it—at first as a Lenten fat and then as an all-purpose fat—wherever climate, topography, and economic conditions permit. Within the same geographic and social boundaries, the image of lard fades, no longer capable of claiming the first place it once held in the alimentary culture of Europe. The growth of cattle raising, associated with the new business of agriculture, confined pig raising to more restricted areas, conferring on it a more typically peasant character. This is already evident in the late Middle Ages, when city dwellers, to affirm their own personal identity and different style of living, tended to reject the pig because it was a symbol of rural life, preferring other meats (beef and lamb) that were available at the markets.[95]

In later centuries, even figures viscerally bound to the culture of the pig—like Vincenzo Tanara, the Emilian author of a 1644 treatise on agronomy, in which he praises the excellence of pork and the "hundred and ten ways to prepare it"—do not fail to make us intuit the new social status of butter. No longer is it a "provincial" aliment, as it had been for centuries; now it is a fashionable product among its upper-class consumers. In reality, Tanara does not devote many words to butter, judging it not very practical in view of its high price: "In the eyes of our forefathers butter was the dividing line between noblemen and plebeians, between rich and poor." This is perhaps an echo of Pliny, according to whom butter, among barbarians, "distinguishes the rich from the plebes [*divites a plebe discernit*]."[96] Such a distinction, Tanara adds, mirrors the one between the prestigious substances in milk and the vile ones. This is a somewhat altered image taken from Saint Bernard, who "compares the life of the truly virtuous to butter . . . as the best part of milk," whereas cheese represents "the life of the wicked, whose heart is curdled like milk, and hardened."[97] Such literary quotations should not be disregarded as mere examples because Tanara could have chosen others: there are also deprecations of butter in treatises and literature. This declaration of the nobility of the product should be seen as related to the changing attitudes toward food evident in the seventeenth century, when the advances made by butter in elite cooking had become obvious in both French and Italian cookbooks.

By then, it should be mentioned, butter had even invaded the realm of meat, having definitively eradicated its Lenten imprint. That was when rich, butter-based sauces (or those alternatively made with oil) were invented, primarily to accompany meat dishes, replacing the thin, acidic, spicy sauces that were typical of medieval and Renaissance cooking.[98] The progressive rejection of those flavors—both acid and spicy—in favor of smoother, more delicate sauces based on fats is one of the key factors, according to Flandrin, in the "mutation of taste" that completely overturned the French gastronomic system.[99] The model soon became European as well, in the wake of a fashion related, as always, to the mechanics of power—in this case, the prestige of the French monarchy and its political centrality in the Europe of that time.

As for Italy, the change was already noticeable in that same seventeenth century. The cookbook by Bartolomeo Stefani, chef at the Gonzaga court in Mantua, printed in 1662, continued to propose acidic and spicy sauces such as those that had appeared a century earlier in the works of Messisbugo and Scappi and earlier still in the work of Maestro Martino and in the anonymous cookbooks of the fourteenth and fifteenth centuries. But along with them were sauces enriched with fats, such as the unequivocal "butter sauce" or "Angevine sauce," in which "a pound of vinegar, sugar and spices" are liquified in "good oil or butter over the fire."[100] Here and elsewhere, the old and the new were seen together: butter and oil appeared—rather timidly but perceptibly—in sauces constructed around ancient flavors, and not only sauces. Stefani's cookbook often and willingly considers the use of butter in a systematic way previously unknown.

Admittedly, Stefani is not the expression of all of Italian culture. Bolognese by birth, Mantuan by profession, he is the image of "Lombard" cuisine, or more broadly that of the Po Valley—which more precociously and with greater conviction adapted to the new European fashion of butter. Between the eighteenth and nineteenth centuries, the process continued, and in 1840, Carlotti, a native of Verona who grew olives in the Garda region, lamented that "for many culinary preparations butter is being substituted for oil, *qui divite a plebe discernit*"—once again, that old quote from Pliny carrying the idea of butter as an elite product,[101] only the reference is now to Italians and no longer to Pliny's barbarians.

At the end of the nineteenth century, Pellegrino Artusi could identify the Po Valley as a butter zone: "All people use for frying the fat that is best produced in their own region. In Tuscany preference is given to oil, in Lombardy to butter, and in Emilia to lard."[102] Sensitive as he is about placing diverse local traditions into a tendentiously "national" picture of Italian cuisine,[103] he is tolerant when suggesting which fat to use: make use "of the fat that you prefer"; fry "according to regional taste or your own"; dress with oil "where oil is good"; use lard or butter "where, for whatever local reason, greater preference is given to either of these condiments." In these and in similar recommendations,[104] we see his wish to respect tastes and traditions—specifically, in the case of fats. This is an almost ethnological approach to cooking—and we have come back to our point of departure—that we can accept only if we consider its historical stratifications, reading in "traditions" the meeting point of multiple factors of varying nature and meaning. Ancient oil, medieval lard, and modern butter come together in local Italian usages with a dynamic that is in no way fixed or immutable.

During the twentieth century, butter made new incursions, emerging at last from its elitist connotation and acquiring a vast public of consumers.[105] But the story is not over: ever since the beginning of the twenty-first century, olive oil has once again challenged animal fats, thanks to the discovery (or perhaps the invention) of the Mediterranean Diet by American doctors and journalists. The story, happily, goes on.

CHAPTER X

The Bread Tree

THE CHESTNUT, which grows spontaneously in a large area of the Mediterranean climate zone, remained outside the borders of commerce for a long time. At first, the Greeks did not even have a name to designate the chestnut, regarding it as a particular species of acorn or walnut.[1] Roman agronomists gave it little attention. Columella devotes a brief paragraph to the cultivation of the chestnut,[2] and Pliny the Elder makes note of "numerous varieties,"[3] but dietary science continued to refer to the wild species: "among all wild fruit," Galen wrote in the second century, "only chestnuts provide a significant amount of substances that are nutritional for the organism."[4]

This situation lasted throughout the high Middle Ages: when documents make mention of the chestnut, it is hard to determine whether they refer to wild or cultivated trees.[5] This holds true, for example, in the Longobardic law: "If someone cuts down a chestnut tree, a walnut tree, a pear tree or an apple tree, he must pay a fine of one *soldo*" (Edict of Rotari, A.D. 643).[6] It was only in the middle centuries that the chestnut was widely cultivated and became an important source of subsistence. The change occurred in the tenth and eleventh centuries in conjunction with an increase in population and a need for food. In regions of plains and hills, the expansion of cultivation increased at the loss of the woodland that had previously been the primary element of the landscape.

In mountainous zones, where grains are hard to grow, chestnut groves took their place. The two phenomena developed in a perfectly parallel way: fields of grain and plantations of chestnut trees grew at the same rate.[7]

Between the eleventh and thirteenth centuries, the spread of chestnut groves continued throughout the Appenine region of Italy, from Emilia to Tuscany, from Umbria to Lazio, and as far as Campania.[8] The same thing took place in south-central France, Spain, and Portugal and on the Balkan peninsula. Everywhere woods were transformed, becoming "domesticated." The forest-pastoral economy (i.e., herding and hunting), which in the early centuries of the Middle Ages had been the prevailing "natural" use of the forest, gave way to a new type of forest economy, more similar to agriculture in view of the constant care required to plant and maintain the chestnut groves. An Italian example: the forest of Santo Stefano, communal property of Mondovì in Piedmont, was leased in 1298 to fifteen individuals who, for an annual fee of fifty lire, contracted to make it *fertile and fruitful.* How? In part by tilling it and turning it to agriculture and in part by transforming it into chestnut groves: on that *sterile and infertile* terrain could be planted "*multa bona et domestica castagneta* [many good cultivated chestnut trees]."[9]

This "domestication" often took place at the price of oak trees. On the alimentary level, this produced a radical change in the popular diet, which increasingly turned from meat (pigs and game) to chestnuts, as that in the plains turned to grains. In both cases, a starch, a vegetable product, was chosen over meat because of its greater yield in weight and perhaps its greater adaptability in use. These were choices dictated by hunger, which followed side by side with the increase in population and expanding settlements. The chestnut became a "mountain bread" that replaced "genuine" bread where the latter could not be obtained: it was called "tree bread" in the region of the Mediterranean, and the chestnut tree came to be known as the "bread tree."[10]

This capacity to serve as a substitute is explicitly documented in many examples. In 1288, Bonvesin de la Riva, writing about the alimentary customs of Lombard peasants, said: "Often [chestnuts] are eaten without bread, or rather, in place of bread."[11] "Chestnuts are the bread of poor people" appears in a Tuscan statute of the fifteenth century.[12] Statements like these become more prevalent with the passage of time, as the alimentary conditions of the lower classes worsened. "In places where there is little grain, [chestnuts] are dried on grates over smoke and then ground to make flour, which is the substitute for making bread," explains Castor Durante in 1586.[13] Literary sources provide similar information: an anonymous poem from the end of the sixteenth century, describing the customs and hardships in the life of the inhabitants of the Tuscan Appenines, states that up there "bread is made of chestnuts."[14] In the seventeenth century, Giacomo Castelvetro, from Emilia, confirms this: "Thousands of our mountain dwellers eat this fruit in place of bread, which they never, or rarely ever see."[15]

Even with regard to nutritive value, one can see a certain resemblance between chestnuts and grains. Piero de'Crescenzi, the most famous Italian agronomist of the Middle Ages, returns to an opinion expressed in medical and dietetic treatises, quoting Galen, when he writes that the chestnut "is the most nutritious of all seeds insofar as it is the closest to the seed for bread."[16] The Spaniard D'Herrera confirms that chestnuts, "after wheat, give more sustenance to the body than any other bread."[17] Vincenzo Tanara as well, in the eighteenth century (invoking the authority of Galen), says that bread made with chestnut flour "aside from that made of wheat, is more nutritive than any other grain."[18]

In truth, as a substitute for bread, the chestnut is closer to the inferior grains than to wheat, whether because of the similarity of alimentary uses or because of its social destination—the lower classes, in particular. Bonvesin de la Riva, quoted previously, maintains that chestnuts, beans, and foxtail millet replace bread in the diet of many peasants. For the year 1285, the chronicle by Salimbene of Parma notes "the scarcity of small grains and chestnuts."[19] Indeed, the chestnut tree became a primary resource for many mountain communities, a genuine "plant of civilization"[20]—alongside and in place of wheat—around which local life and culture rotated.

Technical expertise for the planting and cultivation of chestnut trees was transmitted by example and by practice but also by written texts. Contracts with growers occasionally indicate with great precision the operations to follow. In 1286, two men from the mountain area near Bologna rented a property, contracting to prune the chestnut trees and cut old logs and to graft new suckers so as to increase production by using a specific variety of plants. The earth was to be plowed, tilled, and fertilized; for the first harvest, they would pay a reduced fee, barely equal to a fifth of the product. As production increased, they would pay half, according to the typical model of sharecropping contracts.[21]

Certain agronomists of the modern era recommended starting the trees from seed: "to have enough pairs [of chestnut trees] it is better to start them from seed than to plant them," performing the operation during the month of March and selecting a terrain "well spaded, well cleaned, and well mixed with manure" (so says Agostino Gallo from Brescia in the sixteenth century).[22] But a much older and more widespread practice is to plant seedlings, according to the classic dictum of Columella: "planting begins in the month of November."[23] Also widespread are the practices of grafting and suckering on old stumps, which we just saw in the document of 1286. Along with the labors of pruning and husking went the protection of the land against the outflow of water. As for manuring, Tanara in the seventeenth century recommends fertilizing the trees only with "their own shells."[24]

Particular attention is given to chestnut groves and to chestnuts in the statutes of rural communities, collectively involved in the protection and valorization of this precious resource. Special officials—in some cases paid in kind, meaning in measures of chestnuts—are charged with overseeing the forests and protecting them from damage caused by men or animals. Grazing under the trees is rigorously limited and at certain times of the year prohibited. The dates for harvesting, determined by the communal government, must be observed and apply to all. The conflict between the cultivation of chestnut trees and herding is particularly critical in communal regulations, which generally try to conciliate the two requirements in the hope of finding a balance that is difficult but not impossible. The statutes of Sambuca (in the Apennine region of Tuscany and Emilia) prohibit pig farmers from being found with their animals in the chestnut groves or in the nearby oak stands until the commune has officially proclaimed the end of the harvest (*abandonamentum*), after which grazing and digging—that is, gleaning under the trees—are permitted. Pig farmers could take their animals along the road going downstream only ten days after the chestnuts had fallen, keeping the herd close together and seeing to it that they did not go more than ten arm lengths beyond the path. In turn, the owners of the chestnut groves committed themselves to gathering the chestnuts before the passage of the pigs. The dates of access by the animals varied from place to place, depending on times of harvesting, which in some places continued through December.[25]

At times, instead of waiting for the chestnuts to fall spontaneously, the harvesting was anticipated by beating the trees with long poles. Both possibilities were foreseen by de'Crescenzi: "The chestnuts are gathered when their burrs fall to the ground, or else, when the burrs begin to appear the trees are beaten with poles."[26]

The importance of chestnuts in the diet of the poor was related to the fact that chestnuts could be stored for long periods. If the harvest was good, subsistence was assured for many months. "In our mountains," Gallo wrote, referring to the pre-Alpine region of Lombardy, "an infinite number of people live on nothing but this fruit."[27] In 1553, the captain of the mountains of Pistoia noted that the inhabitants of the village of Cutigliano "are so desperately poor that *seven-eighths* of the year they eat only *castagnacci*.*[28] This was also the case in many European countries: in certain regions of France, the daily consumption of chestnuts was estimated at two kilos (almost four and a half pounds) per capita for six to seven months a year.[29]

Clearly, this was possible because of perfected techniques of conservation but also because of the astute diversification of the various cultivars, which allowed for successive times of growth. For centuries, this was a fundamental strategy to protect the system of production, also entering into the choice of grains,[30] thereby better assuring that the needs of the peasants were met within the limits of an economy constantly suspended between the satisfaction of needs and the scarcity of resources. For chestnuts, like grains, growth times were varied so as to extend as long as possible the period of harvest. By this means, they managed to obtain harvests over a much longer period than is normal today.[31] The inhabitants of Mount Amiata, in southern Tuscany, were described in the medieval statutes of the region: "They only harvest chestnuts, and they are busy with that from September well into December so as to survive and sustain themselves throughout the year."[32]

As to techniques of preservation, which preoccupied agronomists beyond the daily practices of the peasants, there were principally two systems: keeping the chestnut fresh inside its burr and drying it in the sun or in the heat of the fire. The first system was described by de'Crescenzi, who recommended beating the chestnuts out of the tree when they are still green. Then they are gathered and "piled up inside a bush, to keep them from the pigs. And when they have been closed up this way for a few days inside their burr, they open up, and these are the best ways to keep

*A kind of flat bread made of chestnut flour.—Trans.

them fresh . . . inasmuch as they can be kept green all of March." Instead, if they are gathered on the ground already ripe, "they will keep barely two weeks."[33] Unripe chestnuts can also be kept "in sand," as de'Crescenzi[34] informs us, and in the sixteenth century, Gallo advises: "Whoever wants to preserve these fruits should gather them by a waning moon when they are half-ripe and completely dry, and place them in sand in a cool place, or, still in a cool place, in some kind of crock that is so tightly closed it does not allow any air to enter, otherwise in a short time they will rot."[35] Considerably later came the method of "curing," which involves immersing the chestnuts in water for a few days, causing a light fermentation. No agronomist makes mention of this until the eighteenth century.[36]

When drying was used, it took place in the open in special buildings situated within the chestnut grove. The chestnuts "no sooner gathered are placed on a grate under which smoke is made and a fire is kept going for many days until they are completely dry, as dry as stones," Tanara explains.[37] Castelvetro explains that when dried by smoke on grates and then peeled, "they can keep for two years and more."[38] Sixteenth-century texts replicate medieval practices. The fruits, kept semifresh, were eaten whole: "Our women," Castelvetro explained, "keep the chestnuts in baskets or in boxes with rose leaves, where they become tender and very fragrant." Those that were dried were successively ground to make flour. In certain mountainous regions, mills ground chestnuts exclusively, and in payment, the millers received a portion of the ground chestnuts.

The chestnut was first and foremost a product of subsistence intended to fight hunger among the poor in mountainous areas. Its presence was less prevalent in the plains, and, more generally, in the cities chestnuts were consumed more as a delicacy than a necessity. Even in this instance, the product's importance was related to its particular aptitude for conservation, which made possible its prolonged presence on the market. Documentation from the mid-fourteenth century indicates that even in the month of May "fresh chestnuts, candied chestnuts, dried chestnuts" could be found for the prestigious table of the priors of Florence.[39] A few centuries later, Tanara observed that chestnuts could be served even in the summer "out of eccentricity."[40] The two aspects (need and whim, hunger and "eccentricity") are not mutually exclusive; rather, they reinforce the story, which can be seen in the sixteenth-century statutes of the town of Popiglio, in the Tuscan Apennines: the inhabitants extracted from "the chestnut groves and the forests" both "the daily requirement for their food" and "the necessary money to face their every debt, whether public or private."[41] This means that they *sold* the chestnuts.

The preservable qualities of chestnuts were obviously most appreciated on the commercial level, and during the Middle Ages, these qualities were singled out in different varieties.[42] In the thirteenth and fourteenth centuries, chestnuts from Lombardy were on the markets of Paris, and those from Campania went as far as Egypt and Constantinople.[43] Foreign export was controlled by the merchants of major cities, who got their supplies from local marketplaces. For example, the chestnuts from the Apennines of Romagna ended up for the most part in Venice and from there went to the markets of the Levant.

The urban merchants sorted the local production, selecting a part of it for foreign export and a part for local consumption. At times, the commerce was in the hands of specialists, as in Treviso, where the produce vendor Diana, in the middle of the fourteenth century, contracted with the peasants of the region to secure for herself in advance the harvest of their chestnut groves; she sold a portion of the chestnuts in the city and sent the rest off to Venice.[44] The trade went on for some time, at least four or five months, until well into the winter.

The needs of hunger and those of the market occasionally came into conflict—or at least into competition. This is why in periods of famine the exportation of chestnuts could be prohibited. A ban in Bologna in 1593, which attested to a good harvest "of marrons and chestnuts . . . allowing for the hope that the poor will have an abundant supply," prohibited the product from being appropriated by merchants and leaving the territory; if by chance the harvest exceeded the need, it could be sold only "in the markets of the province of Bologna or in the marketplace of that city."[45]

Roasted, boiled, or fried, chestnuts of regular dimensions were consumed fresh or semifresh, preserved within their burr or in sand. These latter were tenderized, Tanara explains, "by soaking in rose water," and even better, "if they are interspersed between these same roses in May" they taste like fresh ones and are "eaten with delight."[46]

The way to prepare chestnuts is well described by Castelvetro in his little opus on all the fruits and vegetables of Italy (composed in England in 1614). In his native country, he explains, "most people when cooking them roast them in a pan with holes on the flame of the fire or under hot ashes, and eat them with salt and pepper." He further adds that in

Italy they are flavored with "orange juice" but not with sugar "as they do here [in England]." Boiled chestnuts, he considers more plebeian: "they are eaten more readily by children and the lower classes than by civil and mature people." He also mentions the custom of stuffing poultry with chestnuts: "Having left them to soak in fairly hot water, the second shell is removed and then various dishes are made, by cooking them in cream; and they are very tasty; and they are used to stuff the capons, geese, and turkeys that they wish to roast, with dried plums, raisins, and bread crumbs."[47] These are customs that the Europeans successfully passed on to the American continent.

The practice of steeping chestnuts in orange juice was already documented a century earlier by the physician Durante: "Lightly cooked in embers and peeled, they are then cooked in a pan with oil, pepper, salt and orange juice" (with the enigmatic specification that in this way "can serve as truffles").[48] But even the use of sugar—contrary to what Castelvetro seems to imply—was common in seventeenth-century Italy: for the month of November, Tanara proposes a recipe for "marrons cooked in embers, served with salt, sugar, and pepper on top."[49]

These choices of flavorings are strictly related (as are so many others) to dietetic ideas. Tanara himself informs us that the roasted chestnuts "served with salt and pepper, are also served with sugar, whose presence makes them healthful."[50] The idea also appears in medical texts that justify this scientifically. According to Durante, "chestnuts roasted under embers and eaten with pepper and with salt, or with sugar, are less hard to digest."[51] Mattioli broadens this by explaining that roasted chestnuts "eaten with pepper and salt, or with sugar" lose all their noxious properties.[52]

Tanara lists many other ways of preparing chestnuts. For example, "placed in sweet wine they are delicious, and if the wine is new, all the better, but one has to have a strong stomach." Or chestnuts, once cooked, "can be cooked again with pork, and are tasty when mixed into a soup made with vegetables, in particular with the white beans with which ravioli are made. . . . Chestnuts are also good with cheese and with milk," and can be cooked in wine and dried in embers. A particular preparation from Piedmont is to cook them in wine with fennel, cinnamon, nutmeg, and other spices, "but first the outer shell must be removed," and served hot.[53]

Dried chestnuts, on the other hand, are used after they have been ground into flour, with recipes of every kind that faithfully follow the various preparations of cereal flours. We have some from as early as the fifteenth century when Bartolomeo Platina—in his book on guiltless pleasure and good health, drawing for the gastronomic part on the most famous cookbook of the time by Maestro Martino—included a recipe for a chestnut pie (*Torta ex castaneis*): "Boil the chestnuts and grind them in a mortar, pass them through a strainer with a small amount of milk and than add the ingredients for a spelt tart.[†] If you want to give it some color, add some saffron."[54] Bartolomeo Scappi, the chef of Pope Pius V and author of the most important work on Italian cuisine of the Renaissance (published in 1570), included among the elegant recipes in his book two recipes that use chestnuts and chestnut flour: one is "a pie of fresh and dried chestnuts" for which he advises chestnuts not yet ripe, gathered in the month of August; the other is a "soup of chestnut flour."[55] These are recipes that seem to go back to peasant cooking, reinterpreted with more complex procedures and expensive ingredients: the addition of generous amounts of butter, sugar, and Oriental spices (cinnamon and pepper) suffice to make these preparations worthy of an opulent table. Nonetheless, their "peasant" nature is not entirely eradicated, testifying perhaps to an unexpected proximity between peasant cooking and upper-class cooking, despite the prejudicial ideological opposition between the two worlds, evolved from aristocratic culture dating primarily from the fourteenth to the sixteenth century.[56]

Regarding this proximity, the presence of chestnuts in elite cookbooks is one of the most obvious clues. They are found everywhere, from Italy to France to Spain. For example, a recipe for *castanas piladas*, enriched with costly spices (cinnamon, cloves, ginger, and saffron, mixed, however, with oil and onion), appears in the *Libro del arte de cocina* by Domingo Hernandez de Maceras, published in 1607 in Salamanca.[57] Even books on pastry make use of the chestnut, or rather the marron: *Le confiturier françois* (published many times in the second half of the seventeenth century) lists a delicate *compote de marrons*, made of "marrons cooked in embers, apricot syrup, and Spanish wine."[58]

Interesting recipes for desserts are provided in the seventeenth century by Tanara. It is delicious to mix into chestnut flour, dissolved in rose water, parmesan or some other tender fat cheese and "then make

---

[†]Fresh and aged cheese, pancetta or cow's udder cooked and ground, spices and sugar, and eggs.—Trans.

castagnazzi in the shape of fritters, fried in a pan with butter" (a variant adds honey to the flour, "for flavor, and health").[59]

Dietetic science not only contributed to the definition of certain types of condiments for chestnuts aimed at minimizing their presumed ill effects but also provided the guidelines for the proper place of these products within a meal. Because astringent properties were attributed to chestnuts (Mattioli: "they constipate the body"; Durante: "they constipate"[60]), it was concluded that the right time to consume them was at the end of the meal to "seal" the stomach, which had previously been "opened" by such acidic fruits as citrus fruits. "Chestnuts are astringent . . . if eaten after a meal": this incontestable declaration by Tanara[61] brings together observation and practice consolidated over centuries. At the end of the thirteenth century, after having provided detailed directions for the gastronomic use of chestnuts in the region of Lombardy, Bonvesin de la Riva points out that "they are generally eaten after other foods."[62] In the same period, in 1266, a curious agrarian contract drawn up in the region of Asti by one *dominus Pacia* stipulated that the tenants were responsible for two annual dinners, which were to begin with a lemon, followed by various meats accompanied by appropriate sauces and a dish of vegetables, and to end with a "paradise fruit" and six chestnuts.[63]

CHAPTER XI

The Flavor of Water

WATER HAS NO flavor, but it is the element that carries all flavors, allowing them to exist. This notion, formulated by naturalists and philosophers in ancient Greece and taken as the basis of medieval scientific thought, contains in essence all the ambiguity of any discussion of water focused on the theme of flavor—or taste, which perceives and distinguishes flavors. If water has no flavor, then the two terms have no reason for standing together, and our discussion would end here. But flavors arise out of moisture, meaning water, and there is no discussion of taste that is not, by definition, a discussion of water. As Guillaume de Saint-Thierry explained in the twelfth century, each sense is bound to one of the four elements in the universe: sight to fire, touch to earth, hearing to air, and smell to air as well (or rather to smoke, which is a kind of variant); in short, taste is "of an aqueous nature."[1] The relationship of water to taste is therefore an essential one.

But before we investigate the taste of water, we must first go over a few preliminaries. Water must *exist* materially because without water there is no life. This primary, essential value, stunningly simple, is what the documentation makes clear first of all. "How can we live here, without water?" the monks ask Abbot Brendano when they land on an island in the middle of the sea.[2] The same monks, during their peregrinations, meet an old hermit who lived only on water: "He lived for sixty years without any food other than this source."[3]

To live solely on water is an extraordinary feat, but to live without water is impossible, which is why the people of the high Middle Ages, "a time of scarce water,"[4] were constantly in search of springs, wells, rivers, and lakes for drinking water. During the Roman era, such sophisticated public works as aqueducts[5] could transport water across great distances, but in the Middle Ages, what mattered was the *local* availability of water, a criterion for distinguishing between one village and another, one territory and another. Rural and urban settlements, noble fortresses, hermetic solitudes, and monastic centers literally laid siege to springs and water courses. The *luogo ameno*,* in which fresh water flows abundantly, was a literary cliché that corresponded to a genuine need in daily life.

Innumerable proofs of saintliness mentioned in hagiographic literature relate to this need: the miraculous production of water that flows out of rock or arid land is a recurrent theme in Christian texts as of late antiquity.[6] The illustrious precedent of Moses, who succeeded in quenching the thirst of his people in the rocky desert,[7] is the explicit reference,[8] so that the prayer for invoking water can be made "according to the Mosaic ritual [*Moysaico ritu*]."[9] But textual references are not all there is to it.[10] The miracles attributed to the saints are not pure and simple replicas of models to imitate but replies to a request, a need, a genuine thirst that has to be appeased. A miracle is always a response to a specific request.

The typology of miracles is extremely varied.[11] It can concern provisions for monasteries, as in the episode narrated by Gregory the Great in the *Dialogues*, whose protagonist, Benedict of Norcia, constructed three monastic houses among the cliffs of the Apennines. For the brothers, it was tiring and dangerous "always to have to go down to the lake to draw water." For this reason, they went to him and suggested moving to another site. That night Benedict climbed to the summit along with a boy named Placido; he stopped to pray, and with a simple and solemn gesture, he placed three stones to mark the right place. He returned to the monks and exhorted them to go up to the summit and, "where you will find three stones one on top of the other, dig a bit. God will make water flow from now on to spare you the fatigue." They went and found that the rock was already oozing,

---

*An expression, used earlier by Virgil and later famously by Ariosto, which came to mean an ideal place, from monastic texts of the high Middle Ages, indicating a good place for building a monastery.—Trans.

and they prepared around it a cavity into which the water could flow, and from the top of the mountain, the water was directed below.[12]

Elsewhere, the miracle concerns solitary hermits. Again in the *Dialogues*, Gregory writes about the hermit Martino, who lived in a cave in the mountains of Marsica, in Abruzzo. His first miracle, when he had barely settled into that place, was that "from that very same concave rock in which he had arranged a little grotto for himself, a drop of water emerged," no more or less than he needed every day to survive.[13] Even more astonishing was the intervention of Colombano when he lived in a grotto near Annegray. A young man, Domaolo, responsible for bringing him water, complained about the hardship of not having water available in the immediate surroundings and the fatigue of having to carry it up amid the sharp rocks of the mountainside. Colombano, reminding the young man of the miracle of Moses in the desert, commanded him to strike the rock so as to replicate the miracle of the water. Suddenly, "a spring began to flow from it, which is still flowing to this day."[14]

The allusion to the perpetuity of the spring generated by the saint, which remained available to the inhabitants of the locality, is a common narrative device used to attribute greater credibility to the episode or to associate it with the genuine needs of the population. In a similar way, the *Life of Gualtiero* tells of the saint and some of his companions, who were traveling to Jerusalem across arid lands lacking all water and were suffering terrible thirst. Gualtiero stopped to pray, he then struck the earth with his walking stick, and out came clear salubrious waters that not only served to slake the thirst of the pilgrims but also, from that day on, produced a perpetual spring.[15]

In some cases, the collective or *social* needs are not fulfilled as a secondary happy outcome but rather are the original motive of the miraculous gesture. Leufredo, traveling to Tours to visit the church of Saint Martin, passed through the territory of Vendôme and in the evening arrived at a village where he asked for water. The host replied: "Alas, holy man, our town is suffering from a terrible shortage of water: we do not have a well or a spring." The holy man turned to his brothers, saying that they should get to work and ask God's help to make water come out of the earth. As soon as he finished the prayer, he struck the earth with his stick a good ten times, and out came a spring "that endures to this day."[16]

The frequency of such miraculous interventions—oriented toward the resolution not only of contingent situations, such as those of the

hermit on the mountaintop, but also of those of a structural and endur-
ing nature, such as the siege by the monks and peasant villages—mirrors
a particularly urgent and disregarded request. To produce water, as do
the saints, also serves to astound and convert unbelievers.[17] Similarly,
they dominate natural forces by invoking or stopping rain, modifying the
direction of the flow of water,[18] or preventing water from flooding the
land. In some cases, intelligence rather than faith is the subject, as when
a pious figure found in thick vegetation springs that were unknown to
the local inhabitants.[19] In others, the protagonist becomes the labor, the
effort of man who, tools in hand, finds the means to overcome the environmental hardships in order to make the area livable. This is the direction toward which a passage in the *Life of Senzio* moves: when he saw the
inhabitants of the Tuscan coast afflicted with insufficient water, he took
the initiative and provided the example himself by taking up a shovel and
starting to dig in the earth. Suddenly, out came "extremely cold water
[*aqua frigidissima*]" that still now, the biographer guarantees, exists on that
spot.[20] This kind of "work miracle" reminds me of a splendid expression of Cassiodorus, minister of King Theodoric of Ravenna in the sixth
century, who, in a letter, compares the public administrators responsible
for constructing aqueducts to Moses (him again), who made water flow
out of rock: Cassiodorus remarks, "What Moses did with a miracle, others can achieve with work [*Hoc labore tuo praestas populis, quod ille miraculis*]."[21]

In contexts like these, the image of water defines itself in terms of pure
necessity. The same idea is implied in penitential books: by indicating a
diet of bread and water as the model for mortification of the flesh,[22] they
presuppose that one can do without all the rest but not without bread and
water. The contrast is between necessity and pleasure. To satisfy the first
is legitimate and, in fact, obligatory; to renounce the second is possible,
even meritorious. The problem is that the line of demarcation between
necessity and pleasure is very fine and often imperceptible; when one eats
or drinks, the two go together, inextricably bound. It is precisely from this
observation that a culture of deep suspicion developed in the Christian
tradition toward the daily gestures of eating and drinking, so innocuous
at first glance. Augustine explains this very well: any discussion of the sin
of gluttony is complicated by the difficulty of understanding, in any particular case, whether it is necessity that legitimizes the resulting pleasure
or whether it is pleasure that surreptitiously disguises itself as necessity.
On this, Augustine confesses that he has not yet arrived at a clear idea:

"consilium mihi de hac re nondum stat."[23] The temptation of pleasure is always lying in wait, and medieval texts abound with admonitions intended to separate necessity from pleasure, which is to separate the inseparable, to decipher the indecipherable. And because by nature this is impossible, the fear of pleasure (bitter enemy of holiness) ends up creating diffidence even toward the most necessary necessities, such as water.

If even water can be pleasurable, one has to approach it with caution. Monastic rules advise against excessive consumption of water[24] because even water can "inebriate the senses" (we read in the *Regula Magistri*). It can affect sexual desire, encouraging the production of semen, quite simply because it can give pleasure. In the hagiographic writings, we find a certain Livinio of Ghent who practices mortification of the flesh by mixing his bread with ashes "and with an extremely sparing taste of water [*parcissimo aquae gustu*]."[25] The practice of penitence can lead to total renunciation. Abbot Lupicino, according to his biographer, did not drink water for eight years, not even during the height of summer heat, when his stomach and his legs pulsated from his dreadful thirst and unbearable dryness. His only concession was to moisten bits of bread in cold water and eat them with a spoon.[26] The pleasure of water must have obsessed Lupicino in particular, as another story of his life (related by Gregory of Tours) attributed to him a most original technique for hydrating his parched body. The abbot had a bucket of water brought to him, and he immersed his hands in it. Amazingly, his flesh managed to absorb it as though it had passed through him by mouth. With this kind of natural drip, Lupicino satisfied his thirst, while preventing the satisfaction of his taste buds.[27] Another excessive saint, Emano, ingested salt in place of water, mocking his own body and parched mouth: "Take this, insatiable mouth, and let it replace the sweetness of water [*hoc sit tibi pro dulcedine aquae*]."[28]

Also, bad water could be a means of penitence. According to the *Storia Lausiaca*, the Egyptian hermit Pior, "having dug in the place where he lived, found bitter water and until he died he remained in that place, accustoming himself to the bitter taste of that water to prove his steadfastness. After his death many monks competed to stay in his cell but did not have the strength to hold out for an entire year."[29]

More moderate was the spirit of penitence in those who used water to diminish the flavor of foods. Beverages, explains Guillaume de Saint-Thierry, in certain cases increase the tastiness of the foods that accompany them; in others, they decrease it, "attenuating the flavor."[30] Francis

of Assisi also availed himself of this quality of water to mortify the pleasure of the palate: he added ashes to his food or diluted it with cold water
to make it less appetizing.[31]

In contrast to these uses of water, which we can define as "antigas-
tronomic," are more normal strategies of consumption, directed toward
the choice of good water, simultaneously good-tasting and healthful
(two concepts closely related in the Middle Ages).[32] The water most recommended by dietary manuals was rainwater, uncontaminated by the
impurities of the soil: "*est pluvialis aqua super omnes sana*," the doctors of the
Salerno school assured.[33] This was an ancient idea; "for drinking, water
from the sky must be preferred to any other," we read in the treatise on
agronomy by Palladio written in the fourth century,[34] but we can go back
even further to Pliny and other ancient authors. In fact, there was no lack
of organization in the Middle Ages for collecting and keeping rainwater in appropriate cisterns.[35] Nonetheless, the water most often discussed
is from wells, springs, rivers, and even lakes—water drunk with caution
out of fear of contamination. "Do not drink stagnant water or water that
does not flow freely" is one of the few recommendations that a knight
makes to his son before dying.[36] The custom of flavoring water with acidic
fruit juice (raspberries, blackberries, blueberries) also helped produce a
light fermentation, which disinfected it.[37] Similar results were obtained
by boiling: "use cooked water [*aquam coctam usitare*]" is a recurrent recommendation in dietary calendars, which also suggest cutting it with wine or
enriching it with herbs and spices.[38] In addition, it was common to add
vinegar to water. Medieval documents attest to the persistent use of *posca*,
the traditional drink of Roman soldiers[39] (which they gave Jesus on the
cross out of compassion, not contempt: here, the historian of food can
trust only the gospels of Matthew and John rather than that of Luke).[40]

The practice of drinking water with wine, normal in the Middle Ages,
goes back to Roman times, not only for gastronomic reasons but also, in
some measure, for hygiene because the alcohol content of wine helps to
counteract the bacteria in water. To drink only water, as did certain monks
to signify the mortification of the body, could produce undesirable effects
on the health.[41] Moreover, mixing water with wine corresponded to the
rules of dietary science, which, in keeping with the Hippocratic-Galenic
tradition, classified substances into four principles or qualities: hot, cold,
moist, and dry. Water, cold and moist,[42] could reequilibrate the humors
during the summer, but in general, it was not advised to drink it at the end

of the digestive process, which was understood then as a true "cooking" of the food in the stomach.[43] This "cooking" required heat, and water, with its coldness, interfered: "cold, in point of fact," we read in a translation from late antiquity of a text in the Hippocratic tradition, "constipates the humors of the body and numbs it."[44] In short, water cools the stomach and prevents it from digesting food, leaving it "raw," as we read in the *Flos medicinae* of the Salerno School: "Drinking water is very bad when one eats, because it cools the stomach and leaves the food raw."[45]

Wine, on the contrary, with its heat helps the digestion: "To digest, drink good wine."[46] Therefore, if one really wants to ingest water, it would be wise to drink some wine on top of it: "Wine drunk after water serves as a remedy," recommends Adamo of Cremona.[47] But even better would be to mix the two liquids before drinking, so as to equilibrate their contrary qualities. Wine tempers the cold nature of water (an effect obviously intensified if the mixture is made with heated water),[48] and water in turn modifies the hot nature of wine. Both beverages benefit from this mixture.[49]

By insisting on the hygienic and dietary aspects of the problem, I do not mean to discount the social and symbolic aspects: hygienic preoccupations (which seem to me undebatable) are superimposed on cultural prejudices that aim at combatting the "banality" of water by altering it with additives of various kinds and playing with the temperature when served—modifying in essence the "natural" state of the product. From an overall view, I would say that the dietary concern was precisely what constituted the meeting point between hygienic preoccupations and sociocultural attentions.

Consideration of alimentary, dietary, and, generally speaking, gastronomic uses of water has slowly brought us closer to the question of taste and flavor, a question (as already noted) that is contradictory by its very nature. The idea that the Middle Ages inherited from ancient science is that water in itself has no taste but potentially contains them all—in the same way that although it is formless, it is virtually the matrix all forms.[50]

That all flavors are present in water had been maintained, with various nuances, by Empedocles, Democritus, and Anaxagoras. Their theories were conflated in Aristotle, who defined flavor as the result of a modification produced in the aqueous humidity of the earth's dryness by the action of heat.[51] Thomas Aquinas, commentating on Aristotle, confirms that water in itself would have a natural tendency to be insipid but is nonetheless the root and principle of every flavor. He adds that if water itself has a flavor, that is because some element of the earth has been mixed into it.[52] For that reason, Guillaume de Conches explains, water can assume any flavor, depending on the substances that have been dissolved into it: "If it flows out of sandy and stony soil, it will take on a sweet taste [*dulcis*]; if it crosses a salty stretch, it carries away a salty taste [*salus*]; if the soil is muddy, its taste will be flat [*vapidus*]; if it runs over sulfurous or calcareous rocks, it becomes bitter [*amaro*]."[53]

Another way of classifying the flavors of water—more theoretical and more abstract, in a manner of speaking—is to evaluate the orientation of the spring. Cassiodorus explains in a letter that the waters going east and south are generally sweet and clear (*dulces et perspicuas*), light and healthful; those instead that go to the north and west emerge too cold (*nimmis frigidas*) and are excessively heavy and dense (*crassitudine suae gracitatis incommodas*).[54] We find considerations like these in scientific texts of late antiquity, by Oribasius, up until those of the early Middle Ages[55] and on into the modern era,[56] and all tend to isolate specific flavors of water (*sapores aquarum*), variably pleasing to the taste, variably good for the health of the body. No less than wine and any other beverage or food, water is evaluated, judged, and selected. It is perceived not at all as an indistinct reality but as a differentiated universe rich in nuances.

Among the positive attributes that describe the taste of water, the most common is assuredly that of sweetness. Good water is sweet; bad water is salty or bitter. "No one can enjoy sea water," Augustine writes.[57] And it is truly a miracle that the Lord performs every day, making the salted waters of the sea evaporate in the air, "cooking" them in the heat of the sun, and transforming them into the sweet water of rain.[58]

Even temperature is an important factor. If tepid water is nauseating,[59] cool water restores and quenches—to confirm this, it is useful to go back to the biblical metaphor: "like cold water for him who is thirsty."[60] Satisfaction of the palate guarantees beneficent effects on the body's health: an idea consolidated in the scientific literature is that the pleasure of food and drink certifies their conformity with physiological needs.[61] In this sense, aside from being pleasurable (*in that* it is a pleasure), "cool water is salutary," as we read in one of the many pseudo-Hippocratic texts that have been transmitted since the Middle Ages, so long as it is not "too cold," in which case it becomes "inimical and hostile." Hot water, on the other hand, "weakens everything."[62]

The discussion can also become overtly gastronomic. Water, Cassiodorus writes, "gives flavor to foods." On the subject of the works ordered by Theodoric to restore the aqueduct of Ravenna, Cassiodorus comments that no food is pleasing if not accompanied by the sweetness of water: *"nullus cibus gratis efficitur, ubi aquarum dulcium perspicuitas non habetur."*[63]

The flavor of water appears to be understood not only qualitatively but also quantitatively: excellence is intimately associated with abundance. Water that miraculously flows from the rocks to provide for the needs of a monastic siege is defined as plentiful, beautiful, limpid, and flavorful. The onlookers ask themselves where it came from, how it could have "such and so much flavor [*talis et tantis saporis*]."[64]

All this does not alter the fact that in general water considered the best is tasteless and odorless, without any suspended substances. "What is the best water?" asks the twelfth-century *Liber de digestionibus* of Sorano; the reply is "clean, transparent, without any smell or taste, light in weight and, after resting for some time, does not release any impurities."[65] Pliny had already written that "salubrious waters should have no taste or smell."[66]

From this point of view, the identity of water is defined negatively, in the sense of *absence*: its true nature is to be *without* smell, taste, or color. The meeting between this basic idea and the multiple evaluations of the flavor of water ends by producing a kind of conceptual oxymoron that conveys two contradictory notions: perfection and incompletion. Water is perfect in its natural state, meaning odorless, tasteless, and colorless—when it corresponds to the basic requisite of absolute simplicity (*liquor simplicissimus*).[67] Similar values expressing notions of purity, lightness, and noncontamination, are implicit or explicit in every description of water fit to drink. Water, Cassiodorus writes, is a gift all the more precious when "it retains its natural purity."[68] On the other hand, completely tasteless water would be incapable of quenching thirst (as anyone knows who tries to drink water in the mountains where it is still low in mineral salts). Let us consider this metaphor of Massimo of Turin: the catechumen, not yet a true Christian, is "like water without taste or smell, that has no value, no usefulness, nor does it please him who drinks it, or allow itself to be preserved."[69] This is to say that only water with taste and smell can be considered precious because it is pleasant to the palate and more readily suited to storing.

A few centuries later, in a text by Galbert of Bruges, we read that the assassins of the Count of Flanders were subjected to this singular punishment by God: wine began smelling acidic, fetid, and tasteless to them, bread putrid, and water insipid—and in this way disgusted, they were forced to suffer hunger and thirst.[70] The expression used—"*aqua insipida eis nihil prodesset*"—presupposes that only water that is *not* insipid can quench thirst.

If the perfection of water is ultimately perfectible, then it is not perfect. The simplicity of water is also its limitation. This connotation, in particular, is expressed in the metaphors in medieval literature that juxtapose water and wine, almost as though the latter represented the complement, the perfection of the "unfinished" nature of water. Ambrose, commenting on the Gospel passage of the marriage at Cana, writes, "as the steward pours the water, its smell becomes inebriating, its color changes and it takes on a new form, and thus does faith increase with the new flavor."[71] Changing smell, color, and flavor, water miraculously acquires a new and more complex identity, losing its "inferiority": "from that inferior water," writes Maximus of Turin, "he wants the guests to enjoy the flavor of an excellent wine."[72]

The addition of flavor ennobles the watery substance, and the transformation of water into wine assumes the metaphoric value of adding meaning. "We were water and have become wine," writes Augustine— which is to say that we were insipid and God gave us flavor, making us wise.[73] According to Baldwin of Ford, "fear without love does not yet have the flavor of wine, but is like insipid water."[74] And according to Geoffrey of Monmouth, the conversion of water into wine is the image of an "insipid and watery" heart that "acquires the flavor of wine" by means of the sweetness of contemplating God.[75]

The paradigm of the event remains that of Cana: by converting water into wine, writes the Venerable Bede, Jesus "saturates their insipid mind with the flavor of celestial knowledge."[76] The same words reappear in Alcuino,[77] whereas Maximus of Turin explains that the apostles, admiring the transformation of water into wine, are transformed themselves and change nature, "and just as water turned into wine is seasoned with flavor, color and warmth, so their insipid knowledge acquires flavor, their pallid grace acquires color, their frigidity is warmed by the heat of immortality."[78] To the already noted qualifications of tasteless, odorless, and colorless, the notion of cold is added here, an implicit echo of medico-dietary science that has already been discussed. Only a portent can give water more flavor than wine, which is what happened to the virgin

Lidewig, who, through the exceptional grace of God, while drinking the water of the Moselle, found it so tasty "as to surpass the flavor of wine."[79]

The question of flavor deserves additional reflection. In medieval culture, flavor was regarded not as a simple attribute (Aristotle would have said "accident") but rather as a "substance" of things and, even more, as the means by which things can palpably manifest their individual nature.[80] Flavor thus assumes a formidable cognitive ability, which justifies (in an ontological sense, so to speak) the etymological relationship of *sapore* and *sapere* (flavor and knowing): by virtue of flavor (or taste), I am capable of recognizing the essence of a thing. The insistence on the theme of flavor that recurs in evangelical commentary is therefore not strange: in Cana, water acquired the flavor of wine, which means its nature changed. "*Aquam in vini saporem naturamque convertit.*"[81] There is no dearth of differing opinions, but even those who argue that Jesus succeeded in changing the flavor of water without modifying its nature[82] only confirm—in fact, reinforce—the prodigious, *unnatural* character of the episode.

The transformation of water into wine is a proof of holiness that was particularly dear to medieval culture, not only because it replicates the miracle at Cana but also because it corresponds to the widespread diffidence toward water, various examples of which have been provided. On the other hand, in at least one case, it would seem that an inverse miracle occurred when wine was amazingly transformed into water. The episode is related in the *Chronicle of the Monastery of San Michele della Chiusa*. Giovanni, the protagonist, was a hermit who had withdrawn to live in solitude on Mount Pirchiriano. Fascinated by his fame, Count Ugo d'Alvernia came to see him with many followers. After a difficult climb, the visitors were tired and thirsty, but there was no water to drink. There was only a little wine in the cruet that the hermit kept by his side, barely enough to celebrate mass. The saint invoked the power of the archangel Michael, and a miracle took place: "the cruet began to erupt like a spring that gushes from the depths, and everybody who had come drank to their satisfaction."[83] That wine was turned into water in this instance is not all that explicit and can be doubted.[84] Not for nothing, in a later version of this episode, in which the visitors are not Count Ugo's gentlemen but ordinary pilgrims, is the "remedy for quenching their thirst" found in *merum*, the crude wine in the cruet that multiplied with stupefying abundance, so that they all left "restored."[85] But this "normalizing" of the miracle, brought back to a more consolidated typology, does not make the first hypothesis[86] less fascinating, justified in the *Chronicle* by words and expressions intimately related to the world of water: after prayer by the saintly hermit, the cruet literally floods those present "like the stream of a spring that gushes from the depths [*quasi ab imo scaturiente vena fontis*]."[87] This is the typical vocabulary that in hagiographic texts signals the miraculous finding of water sources: "*ab imo terrae venam fontis scatutire.*"[88]

Thirst can also be quenched with wine—even better than with water, Baldwin of Ford seems to think.[89] However, the image of liquid bursting from the vein of a spring cannot but evoke the idea of water—at times, more desired than wine: "such is the absence of water to which we are subjected," we read in the *Lives* of the Egyptian anchorites, "that we use it with parsimony such as no one uses with the most precious of wines."[90]

I return to the "impossible question" from which I started: Is there a "flavor of water"? Or must we simply admit, along with Aristotle and Thomas, that water makes it possible for other flavors to exist but has none of its own? To this impossible question, medieval naturalists had an incredibly ingenious reply: add insipid to the other flavors.

The "system of flavors" in practice during the Middle Ages derived directly from Aristotle, who, examining the sense of taste, identified eight fundamental flavors: sweet, fat, sour, pungent, tart, acidic, salty, and bitter (then to make them fit into a septenary canon, symbolically preferable, he eliminated fat, including it in sweet as though it were a subspecies).[91] This classification was modified in various ways by medieval authors. For example, they separated tart into two flavors of differing intensity (*stipticus* and *ponticus*), or they stressed spicy (*acutus*),[92] which had achieved a new gastronomic centrality with the growing use of spices in cooking.[93] And then the great invention: even *insipidus* was admitted to the paradigm of flavors, which rose from eight to nine, and at times to ten, depending on the text.

The first writer to speak of this is Guillaume de Conches in his *Dragmaticon*, a dialogue on physical substances written around 1125: "Among the nine flavors, one is insipid, which is that of water [*unus est insipidus, qui est aquae proprius*]."[94] By the next century, the "promotion" was consolidated: whether the "Regimen sanitatis" of the Salerno school, or Bartolomeo Angelico (*De proproetatibut rerum*), or works devoted to the subject such as the anonymous *Summa de saporibus*, all include insipid among the fundamental flavors.[95] The Salerno "Regimen" explains that insipid "is called that because it does not affect the tongue very much, which does not, however, indicate that insipid is without flavor [*sic nominatur, / quod lingua per eum parum immutatur; / nec tamen insipidus sapore privatur*]." The fact that this flavor does not produce any "reaction" in the body, rendering it inefficacious both for medicine and for food,[96] does not prevent it from having, like all other flavors, specific humoral qualities— obviously, those of water were cold and moist.[97] In the overall picture, it is classifiable, along with sweet and fat, among the so-called temperate flavors, which, because of a particularly balanced nature, have less need for corrective interventions intended to modify their characteristics.

In the face of such conceptual acrobatics, one can only remain impressed. But it is these same medieval texts that, on occasion, de-dramatize the subject. The last word comes from the *Chronicle* of Salimbene of Parma: "*Et quid est aqua nisi aqua?* [And what is water if not water?]"[98]

CHAPTER XII

The Civilization of Wine

"THE GRAPE HANGS from the vine like the olive from the tree . . . but the grape does not become wine, nor does the olive become oil before being pressed."[1] Turning the image of the press into a metaphor that signifies the tribulations and spiritual perfection of man, Augustine also proposes the idea of *work*, which transforms and gives meaning to nature. Without the operation of the press, the grape would remain a grape and the olive an olive. This alone would not be insignificant, given that it was man himself who planted that vine and that olive tree. To make wine and oil is the ultimate goal, in which toil and ingenuity, labor and culture come together.

For precisely this reason, wine, along with oil and bread, were taken by the Roman world—and even earlier by that of the Greeks—to represent its own identity. Those products not only were the focus of production, circuits of trade, and eating customs but also became the vehicle of an ideology that understood civilization as the ability to invent one's own life and to shape nature—wine, oil, and bread do not exist in nature.[2] It is in this dual view, mental and material, that wine takes on the role of indicator, the marker (in the language of sociology) of Roman-ness.

At first, this identity seems to follow a logic that could be called "national"; Rome was as proud of its own culture as it was protective of its own economy. "We," Cicero declared, "do not allow people from the other side of the Alps to plant olive trees and grape vines that exceed our own in number."[3] And if the Gauls—according to a motive already widely diffused among Latin writers and revived in the Middle Ages by Paolo Diacono—descended into Italy[4] galvanized by their desire for wine (*aviditas vini*), Caesar bears witness to a similar pride in their own culture among the "barbarian" populations of northern Gaul and Swabia, who long prevented the importation of wine into their territories, fearing that the effeminate drink of the Romans would lead to a moral decline.[5] Vineyards expanded along with the expanding Roman empire, but the idea of wine as a "national" drink is still perceptible in the edict of Domitian of the year 92, which, beyond prohibiting the planting of new vines in Italy, ordered that they be uprooted in at least half of the province.[6] This order (never carried out, however) was aimed at protecting the production of grain for rationing supplies. Nonetheless, the difference in the treatment of Italy and "the provinces" is noteworthy.

In the third century, Emperor Marcus Aurelius* authorized the planting of vineyards throughout Gaul, Pannonia, and Britain,[7] also for practical reasons (in this case, more political than economic, as the intent was to assure the fealty of the populations allied against the threat of the "barbarians").[8] Evidently, the mental attitude had changed, which leaves no doubt about the now imperial, and no longer national, character of the production and sale of wine. For some time by then, the itineraries of exchanges had ceased to be unidirectional, from south to north; they now crossed in all directions.[9]

In the passage from antiquity to the Middle Ages, the cultural prestige of wine remained intact, thanks to the interest of the new "barbarian" rulers in the Roman legacy and later, to what I call the "image promotion"[10] of these products as they were incorporated into the new Christian religion. As of the third century, it had entwined its own interests with those of the Roman world, assimilating values to which new meanings were given and "transporting" them into the medieval world.

"Wine, oil and bread are the most reliable aliments in life," wrote Massimo of Turin.[11] But the metaphoric values with which these products were now imbued are not only those developed by Roman ideology (the ability of man to transform nature). They also contain the idea of spiritual perfection: the "nature" that is transformed is human nature itself, which grows and surpasses itself by listening to the voice of God.

---

*Marcus Aurelius Probus Augustus, referred to as Probus in Italian.—Trans.

Ambrose, as Augustine relates, recalling their meeting in Milan, "distributed to your people the flower of your wheat, the joy of your oil, the sober inebriation of your wine."[12] Christianity later amplified the image of wine (and bread and oil) as the mark of "civilization," by then extended to the confines of the empire, but then went beyond even those confines by proposing that these products are universal necessities. A message that claims to be universal has to be founded on universal symbols.

Symbols, indeed—but first of all, *instruments,* real, concrete substances, have to be produced or in some way procured. Wine, oil, and bread are the instruments of a liturgy that seems to be based on the Mediterranean alimentary triad, as well as on ritual traditions borrowed from the Judaic religion and from Greco-Roman rites. The Eucharist requires bread and wine (all believers, until the thirteenth century, took communion with both),[13] and oil is needed for the sacred ointments and votive lamps.[14]

Here we see once again, within the limits of possibility, the cultivation of more vineyards. The bishops and abbots, protagonists of so many hagiographic tales and legends, are now engaged in viticulture. On the subject of this "episcopal and monastic wine-growing," a decisive element for the conservation and propagation of the culture of wine during the centuries of the high Middle Ages, the pages of *L'Histoire de la vigne et du vin* [The history of the vineyard and of wine] by Dion are unsurpassed. Despite a half century since its appearance, it continues to be an indispensable historiographic reference,[15] but in these same pages, there is a possible overvaluation of the phenomenon because, as various scholars have remarked, the nature of the sources available to us, primarily ecclesiastic and monastic, are for that very reason only a partial view of reality. According to Unwin, it was not Christians who "saved" the culture of wine, which the "barbarians" had not at all forgotten and even less destroyed; churches and monasteries assuredly contributed to the transmission of techniques of cultivation and vinification, passing them down over time, thanks also to their continuous ownership of lands. But these properties, along with the vineyards contained within them, in many cases fell to religious institutions as a result of donations made by lay noblemen, so that, Unwin concludes, "this should rather confirm the theory that after the fall of the Western empire, it was the lay nobility who saved winemaking."[16]

Matheus also tends to re-dimension the wine-making crisis that followed the fall of the Western empire, seeing it as a quantitative rather than a qualitative phenomenon. Offering as evidence that in the regions west of the Rhine "a population of Gallo-Romance speakers . . . taught the art of producing wine even to the people who in subsequent periods migrated to and settled in those regions," he insists on the involvement in that activity of lay proprietors alongside church landowners, the latter being better documented by virtue of archival transmission. As for regions east of the Rhine, "wine growing did not see its dawn with the Christianization of those territories, but . . . was present long before the border was set."[17] Even the expansion of vineyards beyond the English Channel, between the tenth and eleventh centuries, later spurred by the Norman invasion, seems to have taken place principally on lay properties both large and small.[18] This argument was made earlier by William Younger to reject a platitude that had been considered undebatable: in a brusquely polemical manner, Younger stated, "The Church had little or nothing to do with the transmission of wine making from the ancient to the Christian world."[19] Stated so categorically, this affirmation would seem hardly acceptable; however, we must also admit that too much verbiage went into praising the Church and the monasteries.

Ecclesiastic and monastic institutions were only one factor that guaranteed not the survival but the vigor of wine making during the high Middle Ages. They contributed, in this as in every other sector of the economy, rational elements and good management related (not incidentally) to religious and cultural choices. Today, however, we can no longer think that they were "the principal agent of the transmission of ancient techniques and cultivation"[20] in the field of wine making, an area of experimentation and innovation whose true entity remains to be proven. "It is certain," writes Archetti, "that [the monks] instructed their farmers, when they themselves were not doing the work, both on how to plow the land and on various crops."[21] In monastic libraries amid liturgical and moral works, it was rare not to find a text on agronomy. Personally, I would like to think of peasant know-how being passed on orally, perhaps by someone working for the monks. As Fumagalli wrote, "[Medieval] agriculture was left almost entirely, with regard to plantings, techniques and the use of implements, to the inventiveness—or rather to the hard labor—of country folk"[22] (it should nonetheless be noted, as did Fumagalli himself, that there was a partial but significant exception to this abdication in the case of viticulture).[23]

During the centuries of the high Middle Ages, the culture of wine continued to expand north, leading a process already begun in Roman times to extreme consequences; a second decisive phenomenon, which became apparent beginning with the seventh century, was the Europeanization of that culture, parallel to the establishment of Islam on the southern coasts of the Mediterranean (and the south of the Iberian peninsula). The Muslim prohibition against wine, albeit subject to numerous distinctions and heated discussions,[24] created an unprecedented boundary between Christian Europe and Islamic Africa. And because identities are also founded in differences, Christian Europe had all the more reason to characterize itself as wine-drinking Europe. From then on, wine lost its original identity as "Mediterranean" and took on a new one that can be called Roman-barbarian (or indeed European).

A few episodes from the hagiographic literature clearly indicate the convergence, with regard to wine, of the Roman-Christian world, which had reinterpreted the ancient world, with the "barbarian" world, which had adopted its interests. The *Life of Remigio*, by Incmaro of Rheims, relates how King Clovis, defender of the "true faith" and founder (with papal support) of the Frankish kingdom, while he was repelling the decisive attack by the Aryan Alaric, king of the Visigoths, received from Bishop Remigio (who had converted and baptized him) a flask of wine that had been blessed, from which (so long as it lasted) the king drew the strength and fervor to fight. Thus, "the king drank, and the royal family as well, and crowds of people, and they sated themselves abundantly; but the flask did not empty itself and continued to replenish itself as though it were a fountain." Naturally, this led to victory.[25] The strength attributed to the wine is evidently a moral strength that translates Christian faith into muscle. But even in the Roman tradition, wine was understood—on a strictly alimentary level—to be comforting and restorative to soldiers in war. The troops of Gaius Pescennio, defeated by the Arabs in 194, vindicated themselves and their leader by arguing that in those regions they had been unable to drink their usual ration of wine.[26]

The lack of wine is lamented even during the Middle Ages in regions of northern Europe, despite the extraordinary expansion of vineyards mentioned above. The monk Alcuin, writing from York in 790 to an Irish student living in Tours, complains with multiple biblical citations that he has no wine and is obliged to drink "bitter beer," adding "drink to our health, and give my greetings to our brothers in Bacchus."[27]

As Gautier[28] has remarked, what Alcuin is saying is technically wrong. In York at the close of the eighth century, there was an important Frisian community that specialized in the sale of wine.[29] The complaint is more like a cliché, going back to the widespread commonplace about drunken Englishmen and beer drinkers (whereas the Franks were known as wine drinkers; a poem by this same Alcuin celebrates the Carolingian court "where wine flows abundantly"[30]).

Is this an antinational issue? Certainly not. Alcuin is proud of being English and speaks of himself as a gluttonous eater of porridge (*pultes*).[31] But he does not want to be confused with beer drinkers, a stereotype even his friend Theodulf of Orleans tries to pin on him, describing him in one of his poems as a drinker for whom wine or beer go down equally well.[32] Instead, Alcuin—I am following Gautier in his subtle textual exegesis—wants to show that albeit English, he is part of a diverse community that places itself among the devotees of Bacchus. He expresses his participation by declaring his membership in the "Palatine school," the circle of intellectuals who gathered around Charlemagne. The argument of wine over beer provides Alcuin with an identity that is cultural and religious, political and social. In this way, too, he wants to separate himself from an Anglo-Saxon milieu that he considers corrupt and confused, neither Roman enough nor Christian enough. Beer, often presented in archival sources as a pagan drink,[33] became the mark of a society that was non-Roman, non-Christian, non-international, and uncultivated; an ecclesiastic community, "vernacular, pagan, and popular," that in its way of eating, drinking, and dressing; in its physical appearance; and in its poetic and literary tastes did not adequately demonstrate its distance from pagans.[34] The pagans in question are, of course, Anglo-Saxons, not those of ancient Rome who no longer pose a threat, having been completely transformed in their new Roman-Christian identity. The serene, sunny reference to "brothers in Bacchus [*fratres nostros in Baccho*]" is a palpable proof thereof. Bacchus often appears in monastic literature, always in a key position: in fact, the *Consuetudines* of the abbey of Fleury informs us that the monk assigned to the vines "was called by metonymy brother Bacchus [*vocatur metonimice frater Bachus*]."[35]

Although an identifying mark of a Roman-Christian identity, wine for Alcuin was also a mark of social prestige—for the most part, a variant of a new meaning because in Roman society wine could be an element of alimentary luxury, but on an ideological level, it was seen as a common good, shared by the entire society. In the Middle Ages, things changed. As Dion pointed out, wine became "an accessory that was necessary for the existence of high rank," regarded as "one of the palpable expressions of every social dignity."[36] For this reason, "in the aristocratic society of the high Middle Ages . . . not to serve wine generously to a guest shows a lack of respect."[37] Devroey, referring to the concept of "distinction" developed by sociologist Pierre Bourdieu (and applicable to alimentary styles as well), also sees wine as "a key element in medieval *distinction*."[38] And yet the phenomenon cannot be generalized: its place is more precisely in the realm of culture and geography. Devroey, restructuring Dion's thesis,[39] designates two different situations related to traditions of production in individual regions and to the different roles played by wine in alimentary systems. In the regions of northern Europe, where wine was produced with great effort and acquired at high cost, it automatically became a prestigious drink, whereas beer was seen as a drink of ordinary people (this is why Alcuin's argument is valid). In regions of traditional wine making, on the other hand, wine remained, as in Roman times, a product held in "common." In these cases, Devroey writes, behind images of aristocratic wine, a mark of distinction for lay and ecclesiastic elites, we can discern a whole world of producers and drinkers, "a little population of wine makers, tavern keepers and straight-out imbibers";[40] behind the cult and the pomp was "all the freshness of a conviviality founded on the sharing of wine."[41]

Social distinction was nonetheless possible: all wines are not equal. King Childebert, who rejected the "bad wine of the peasants [*rusticitatis musto*]" offered to him by the pious Carileff,[42] demonstrates that he aspires to a very different kind of liquor. But within wine regions, these differences do not exclude a common culture—in fact, they presuppose one. In 806, when Charlemagne condemned the "shameful profit" of speculators who bought up grain or wine merely to resell it at high prices,[43] it was of the wine *for everybody* that he thought, the wine that, like grain, was part of the daily needs for survival. Food distributed to the poor normally included wine,[44] considered an integral part of the daily diet (Augustine called it *victus quotidianus*[45]).

In France and Germany, in Spain and Italy, wine for the gentry came for the most part from the lands of peasants, in keeping with land fees that required the consignment not of grapes but indeed of wine, which is to say the product already made, a share of which was due the landowner (in varying proportions according to the zone), whereas a share remained to the peasant. This indicates that it was the peasants themselves who possessed the implements and techniques for making wine.[46] The lord, or rather his lackey, came on the scene when it was all finished, when it was time to divide the product—not only the wine of first extraction but also in certain cases that of the second or third, the wine produced by the press, when water was added to the marc.[47] These same peasants, within the manorial system, worked on the vineyards of the domain on days of statute labor and, along with the domestic servants, participated in the various phases of wine making on the property of the lord of the manor.

The variations of the "social status"[48] of wine, according to geographic and cultural regions, is mirrored in the typology of the miracles that place it at the center of hagiographic texts. A multitude of saints undertake to replicate famous evangelical precedents, multiplying wine or producing it out of water or, more simply, assuring that it will appear.[49] The query behind these prodigies is obvious: Wine is often lacking, but to whom?

In the regions of northern Europe—once again, it is Dion who comments on this—"these miracles ordinarily occur for the benefit of high personages":[50] bishops and kings, counts and abbots, with pious figures in the role of host or guest who in some way are the providers in difficult situations. It can be a holy abbot welcomed at the residence of a lord momentarily short of wine;[51] it can be a king received by a bishop.[52] In any case, the story ends happily, with the prodigious retrieval of the desired drink.

It is not true, however, that in the high Middle Ages "miracles related to grape vines and wine were accomplished solely for the benefit of nobles and churchmen," as Pini wrote, generalizing Dion's intuition.[53] On the contrary, Dion's argument must again be corrected, primarily because the protagonists of these episodes, although wearing clerical garb, are not always definable as "high personages." In so many cases, entire communities are involved, and they have need of wine for daily use, not just for particular events.[54] Among the many possible examples, I propose one concerning a community of women, which shows that the consumption of wine in the Middle Ages had no gender boundaries. The *Life of Odile, Abbess of Hohenburg*, in Alsace, relates that one day a nun in charge of wine was distressed because there was no more wine left in the cellar "to serve our sisters," except for the one "ration of that day." Odile reassures her: "He who sated a multitude with five loaves and two fishes will also think of us." When the moment arrived "to pour wine for the sisters as was usual," the *vas vinarium* (wine barrel) was found to be full.[55]

In certain cases, the request to which the miracle responded was strictly "popular." The *Life of Crotilde*, at the close of the eleventh century, describes a group of workers who, in the employ of the queen, are building a new monastery in Normandy, at Les Andelys. The region does not produce wine, "but the workers ask for it." The queen is tormented by her inability to accommodate them. Suddenly, a lovely pure spring appears in the precincts of the monastery. A dream tells her to draw water from that spring when the workers ask again for wine. The following day, under the blistering summer sun, "the workers grumble and ask for wine." The queen did as was told to her and miraculously "the water changed into wine and the workers said they had never drunk a better one." Notice that from this appreciation we can deduce that they were accustomed to drinking wine. They thanked Crotilde, repeating that "they had never tasted so good a drink."[56]

In the Mediterranean region, we find "popular" miracles even in earlier texts. Gregory the Great, in the sixth century, relates in the *Dialogues* the miracle performed by Boniface, bishop of Ferentino, who, from a few clusters of grapes remaining on a vine destroyed by hail, barely managed to obtain a little wine and, after blessing it, poured it into the bottom of the barrels that he had normally been able to fill. He then had the poor people called in to distribute it as charity, and the wine "began to increase, filling all the receptacles that the poor had brought with them." Once the needs of the poor had been met, Boniface also thought of the needs of the Church. After locking the cellar, he returned three days later, reopened it, and found the barrels filled to overflowing.[57]

Wine in the medieval imagination thus constitutes a decisive reference point with regard to identity. Its prestige gives it a paradigmatic value, according to which *other* realities are defined in opposite terms, which is to say negative. This is, above all, relevant to geography and territory: a region can be defined as *not* producing wine, which frequently serves to justify the need for miraculous interventions such as those mentioned above.[58] A miracle is decidedly an easy way to remedy situations of penury, but the complicity of an available saint is not an everyday affair. Other solutions are more normal—in particular, two: recourse to the market and the geographic relocation of properties.

During the early centuries of the Middle Ages, which saw a decrease in trade around the Mediterranean, the commerce of wine did not cover great distances,[59] but it did seem to develop in peripheral areas of viticulture such as northern Europe. Surprising, in a passage by Gregory of Tours, is the superposition of the two possibilities, miraculous intervention and recourse to the market, when he relates the embarrassment of the priest Edazio, who, for the anniversary of Saint Vitalina, arranged a dinner for widows and poor people but was lacking *vinum bonum*. The saint appeared to him in a dream, pointing to a tree under which he would find the money necessary to acquire wine worthy of the occasion; "having bought the wine, he was able to give refreshment to the poor."[60] The story takes place in Arthona in Avernia and, with its insistence on the quality of the wine (*bonum, dignum*), seems to suggest the need to turn to the market for a product of quality. In this connection, I notice that the alternation between production/exchange, and auto-consumption/market might be a new way of analyzing the typology of alimentary miracles in the lives of saints.

The interregional articulation of great estates was another strategy for acquiring wine in places that did not produce it. In that case, the internal exchange replaced recourse to the market—or was close to it. Devroey[61] cites a fine example concerning the abbey of Mouzon, founded in 971 on the shores of the Mosa. Because grapes did not grow there, the archbishop of Rheims thought it wise to give the monks other lands in the diocese "so that the absence of good wine not aggrieve you."[62] From this same perspective, Matheus demonstrated the interest of Bavarian monasteries in acquiring property in the South Tyrol and in Austrian viticulture zones.[63] This process did not involve only churches and monasteries. In 842, the division of the Carolingian empire among the sons of Louis the Pious gave Louis the German the eastern parts—"that is, all of Germany up to the banks of the Rhine"—but to that were added various cities with adjacent lands on the left bank of the river "because of the abundance of wine."[64]

Finally, the shortage of wine was compensated by alternate products— seen, however, as substitutes for something to which a higher value was attributed with regard to image if not always taste. The case of beer is an example. In various countries—above all, in the north—a proud tradition spread its use as an everyday drink with a powerful sense of identity. It defined "national" areas of consumption, marked by very specific peoples and regions. Giona, author of the *Life of Colombano*, incorporated both ethnic and geographic coordinates to delimit the world of beer drinkers: "it is used by the people who live around the Ocean, that is, Wales, Brittany, Ireland, Germany," and also certain Balkan peoples.[65] In each instance, *boundaries* are marked indicating where beer is a "provincial" product. This is not the case for wine, except in the negative sense: a region that does *not* produce wine. We have already seen that during the Middle Ages wine tended to lose its "national" or "territorial" connotations, turning into a potentially universal product. Beer, on the contrary, retained and even accentuated its "local" character. From this point of view, Alcuin's perception, discussed above, is exemplary.

The inequality of values between the two drinks is clear. In a text from the tenth century, the main character is the Count of Rennes, Juhel Berenger, who is dining with the nobles of Brittany. The larder is well stocked with beer and hydromel, and no one seems dissatisfied. Suddenly, guests of the Count of Anjou arrive, and they want wine, but there is none. A peasant finds on the port of a nearby island a barrel that came from no one knows where.[66]

Cohabitation between beer and wine was possible (as proved by the episode of Juhel Berenger), but the hierarchy between the two products is indisputable, as even beer drinkers concurred. The rule for canons by Crodegango of Metz, around the middle of the eighth century, is quite explicit: "should it happen that there is not enough wine for their needs . . . a measure of beer will be added to console them."[67] Also addressed to the canons are the dispositions of the synod of Aix in 816, careful to distinguish among the different local institutions and to establish precise relations between the daily measure of wine and beer, determined by a single basic principle: the lack of wine is to be compensated by a greater quantity of beer. The instances foreseen are three, depending on whether the community is large, middling, or small; the daily measure of wine is fixed, respectively, at 5, 4, and 2 *libbre* (pounds) per capita. But this applies only "if the region produces enough wine." If not, the 5 *libbre* go down to 3 (plus another 3 of beer), and 4 *libbre* go down to 2 (plus 3 of other drinks "made with various products") or even to only 1 *libbra* (compensated by 4 *libbre* of various drinks); the 2 *libbre* of wine granted to the canons of poorer churches, "in the event that the region is lacking in grapes," will be replaced by 3 *libbre* of beer along with 1 *libbra* of wine "if resources make it possible to procure it." In these "tables of correspondences," the attention to wine is uppermost and almost obsessive, as confirmed by the final considerations of a general nature. Because "in numerous provinces there is not an ample supply of wine," it is opportune to have it come "from bordering wine-making provinces," compensating for the lack with the integration of interregional resources and relying on the managerial abilities of the bishops.[68] Judging from data of production in local areas, one can imagine fruitful exchanges among the ecclesiastic provinces.

Similarly, in Benedictine communities the custom of compensation with a double ration of beer appears to have been practiced at Fulda and Corbie and has been documented in cases of an insufficiency of wine: "where there is no wine, the measure of *cervisia* [beer] is doubled."[69]

At this point, it is time to speak of wine. With all these considerations of the "expressive" function of alimentary products, of their ability to serve as *indicators* of an economic model or of a cultural and religious affiliation, what has been lost from view is *their* identity, their material essence before they became symbolic. That wine served to define an identity (or many identities intermeshed in different ways) is clear by now. Now let us turn the discussion around and ask, What would be the purpose of defining the identity of wine?

I start with the assumption that if something stands at the top of a hierarchy of symbols, it must have its own positive value. An analogous reflection, which I find particularly apposite, was made by Flandrin with regard to bread. Its very special role in the Christian tradition— which had the power to encompass, by metonymy, the complexity of man's alimentary needs ("give us this day our daily bread") and whose values were far-reaching and exalted—would not have been possible, Flandrin believes, without an equally lofty intrinsic value. Documents provide clear evidence: the smell, the taste, and the quality of bread were regarded very highly, endowing it with an alimentary, gastronomic, and dietary "status" that justified the exalted nature of its symbolic values.[70] In the same way, wine could not signify "the mystery of human nature, the ardor of the Holy Ghost, the knowledge of the Law, the word of the Gospels, spiritual understanding, the blood of Christ, conscience, contemplation, love"[71] if it were not itself a product of excellence. Rabano Mauro expressed it perfectly: wine was chosen, along with bread, to concretize the Eucharistic miracle because these products surpass in dignity and preciousness all other fruits of the earth (and human labor).[72]

Wine is (and must be) *good*. Pleasure is its original attribute. It was given to man "for his pleasure [*causa delectationis*]," Ambrose explained, commenting on the biblical story of Noah.[73] "We were water and we became wine," writes Augustine. In other words, we were insipid, and God gave us flavor, making us wise.[74] The ambivalence of the terms[†] is much more than word play: in medieval culture, it led to a profound reflection on flavors, not only as a metaphor but also as the instrument of knowledge, because it is flavor that reveals the nature and quality of things.[75]

"To question allegory," wrote Tombeur, "is to ask oneself how reality was perceived."[76] A mental image filled with metaphors, drawn from multiple fields of experience, from the physical to the moral, from music to the sciences, has always accompanied wine in an attempt to describe its nature.[77] In the Middle Ages, the first attribute of good wine is *sweetness*. This is the taste most sought after, but at the same time, it is extremely rare. Many medieval wines seem to have been low in alcohol and quickly became acidic. Sweetness is hard to achieve. According to a striking image from Honoré of Autun, the six stages of the world (represented by the six stone containers in which the water they held was transformed into wine) correspond to six different wines whose sweetness continues to increase as the project of salvation continues to improve.[78]

The preference for sweet wine, which is long lasting,[79] explains the prestige of Mediterranean wines, denser and higher in alcohol, which even in the Middle Ages we see appearing in the markets and on the tables of Europe, as confirmed by numerous documents. Venanzio Fortunato remembers Falerno (perhaps the most renowned wine of antiquity) along with the wines of Gaza, Crete, Samos, Cyprus, and Colophon.[80] Aside from Falerno, Sidonio Apollinare cites the wines of Gaza, Chios, and Serapte.[81] Those of Laodicea and Gaza are praised by Gregory of Tours as "the strongest of wines."[82] According to Paolo Tomea, it would be a mistake to reduce these examples to mere rhetorical or literary models—perhaps valid for such wines as Falerno from Campania or Chios from the Greek island of the same name, famous in ancient sources—but certainly not to the wines of Palestine that began to be documented "just around the fifth and sixth centuries."[83] As to Falerno, very often mentioned in texts of the high Middle Ages,[84]

[†]Only in Italian: *sapore/sapere* (flavor/knowledge), *sapidità/sapienza* (tastiness/wisdom).—Trans.

Émile Brouette maintains that from the time of Gregory of Tours, the denomination had lost its ancient indication of origin and had ended up, sliding semantically toward the generic, simply designating any wine of high quality.[85] However, Tomea observes, Gregory's enological indications seem too precise—to the point of constituting "one of the emblems of his social culture, the senatorial class to which he belonged[86]—to be considered generic or inaccurate. Perhaps "the root stock of Falerno was in fact transplanted to certain zones of Roman Gaul."

In our sources, there seems to be a perfect awareness of the territorial diversities of wines, whether the place of origin or the characteristics of environment, soil, or exposition—what today we call *terroir*. It would nonetheless be anachronistic to place the medieval culture of wine in "territorial" categories that did not acquire an important significance— in production, marketing, or consumer choices—until the beginning of the modern era. In the Middle Ages, the *typology* of the product, largely related to its sensory characteristics, was much more important than provenance for distinguishing one wine from another. The *Secretum secretorum*, a text dating perhaps from the seventh or eighth century, of which a fourteenth-century French translation (*Segré de segrez*) has survived, classifies wines according to age, color, flavor, nose, substance, and potency (but also according to the soils and region in which the vines grow).[87] We see the same thing in lexical inventories: Papias, in the eleventh century, classifies wines on the basis of color, clarity, flavor, consistency, alcohol content, method of vinification, and purpose.[88] These criteria remained valid for centuries. "Wine," wrote Aldobrandino of Siena in the middle of the thirteenth century, "varies in color, substance, flavor, perfume, age, and because of its diversity affects the human body differently."[89]

Even questions of health played an important role in defining the uses of wine. It not only entered into the fabrication of many medicines but also was itself held to be a medicine, perhaps the best of medicines, to which infinite benefits were attributed: it could prevent and cure illnesses, preserve the health of the body, aid digestion, purify the organism, and eliminate bad humors—and better still, it could cheer the spirit, an indispensable condition for living well. The exoticism of certain prescriptions, such as the use of aged wine as an antidote to poison,[90] is only one point on a vast therapeutic spectrum that held wine to be a "universal remedy" for every kind of ailment. This conviction had its roots in the medical culture of antiquity, but the Christian tradition also took many important references as models. Throughout the Middle Ages, a passage in the first epistle of Paul to Timothy was frequently cited—and even abused[91]—in which wine is recommended to relieve the sufferings of the body: "Do not drink only water," the apostle writes to his friend, "but also take a little wine for the sake of your stomach and your frequent indispositions."[92]

Diffidence toward water—held to be unreliable with regard to hygiene and to be "cold," and thus damaging to the digestion—was shared by the entire medical literature.[93] That is why it was normally mixed with wine, which, in fact, was the only trustworthy drink, and why abstinence from wine, dictated by penitential choices and the terror of inebriation, was intermittent and contradictory. Those monks who, upholding a utopia of absolute renunciation of earthly pleasures, tried to give up wine completely were later forced to go back on their decision because of the unpleasant consequences that ensued. This happened, for example, at Fonte Avellana, where, as recalled by Pier Damiani, only water was drunk for some time, reserving wine for the celebration of the mass. But at a certain point, the monks became weak and fell sick, and no one entered the monastery because of that excessively rigorous practice. For that reason, "we decided to indulge the weakness of the brothers, or more accurately the weakness of everyone, and conceded that wine be served while maintaining sobriety and moderation." The inevitable end of the story is, needless to say, the allusion to Paul's epistle to Timothy.[94]

Along with these collective experiences—a few centuries later the same thing happened to the monks of Monte Oliveto[95]—there are individual ones. The biographer of Atanasio, bishop of Naples, relates that "at first he wanted to abstain from drinking wine, but because of physical problems was unable to do so."[96]

The therapeutic benefit of wine, attributed to the very nature of the product, was at times confused with a miracle. The vineyard planted by Saint Orso produced a wine to which divine grace granted such benefits "that if someone afflicted with any infirmity drank that wine he immediately recovered."[97] The same held true when the wine was blessed[98] or when it was used to dissolve miraculous powders that were scraped from the tombs of saints.[99]

The use of wine for protecting or recovering health was such an indisputable axiom, and so evident to all, that there was no need to refer to it. In 853, Pardulfo, the bishop of Laon, wrote to Incmaro, the archbishop of Rheims, having heard that he had just been ill. Pardulfo gave him various suggestions about food—among them, that he select "a wine that is neither too strong nor too light, but of medium strength. Rather than the wine produced high in the mountains or down in the valleys, select a wine made of grapes from the hillsides."[100] That wine is good for the health is taken for granted.[101]

The choice of a wine of "intermediate" quality was also normally advised by the *Regimen sanitatis* of the high and early Middle Ages. Arnaud de Villeneuve advises "a wine of medium age, between young and aged, pale but moving toward red, of good nose and good flavor, that is neither sour nor sharp, sweet nor smokey, heavy nor too delicate, and of *media vertù*, that did not grow in a dark mountainous area, nor in flat fields suitable for cultivation, but in hilly land facing south, and unshaded, in a region neither too hot nor too cold." This would be the "wine of choice, the best for a regimen of health."[102]

The classification of wine in the Middle Ages (as shown by Grieco) operated on a binary system, contrasting wines that were "sweet and strong" with those that were "sour or bitter, and thus weak," along with an unlimited series of intermediate flavors. The more a wine was deeply colored, sweet, and aged, the more it was considered "hot" by nature. Inversely, wines held to be less "hot" were young wines that tended toward white and were acidic.[103] In this system, the choice of the "right" wine never had an absolute value but had to take into account (as a compensatory function) the humoral constitution of the individual (determined by age, gender, and health), in addition to spatial-temporal variations (the time of the year, the geographic location) and the foods that the wine was to accompany. Within these cultural coordinates was the idea that wine is better suited to older people than to the young because, as Clemente Alessandrino observed, to give wine to the young, given their hot nature—boiling hot, to be exact—is like "adding fire to fire," whereas when age cools the body, wine is not harmful but on the contrary becomes a remedy that reconstitutes natural heat.[104] For this same reason, young white wines were advised for young people and aged red wines for older people.[105]

This rule makes us want to reexamine the idea that medieval wines did not keep from one year to the next.[106] The widespread opinion that "after the fall of the Roman empire the predilection for aged wine disappeared for a millennium"[107] should, in fact, be corrected because wines generally held up for three to four years.[108] The already mentioned *Secretum secretorum* defines wines as "young" when they are only a year old, "medium" when they do not exceed three years, and "aged" when they have gone beyond four years, up to seven.[109]

On the other hand, wines were not considered to be and, aside from rare cases, were not used as a "finished product"; rather, they were a primary matter to be blended with herbs, roots, flowers, fruits, spices, honey, and all kinds of aromas. Gregory of Tours would have one believe that only young light wines were treated this way. When Claudio, emissary of King Gontrano, tries (with nefarious intentions) to convince Eberulfo to let him enter his house, he says he is curious to know "whether your wines are treated with aromas (*odoramenti inmixta*) or whether your power requires that you drink strong wines (*potentiores*)."[110] From this, one would deduce that the wines intended to be flavored with *odoramenti* would be the lighter ones, not the *potentiores*. Even in later centuries, monastic documents from central Europe associated the idea of spiced wine (*pigmentatum*) with the younger, lighter *clarum* or *claretum*.[111] Because of these additions, the taste of wine at the very moment of drinking it was determined as much by who consumed it as by who produced it.

The convivial ritual also included rules for mixing wine with water, a custom that the Middle Ages inherited from the Greek and Roman worlds and that was habitually practiced even when drinking pure wine (*merum*) had become increasingly more common.[112] In ancient societies of the Mediterranean, the knowledgeable mixture of wine and water, which granted domination over the dangerous drink, was perceived as a mark of civilization, whereas drinking it uncut, thus making oneself a slave of drunkenness, was in itself a mark of ethnic and cultural barbarity.[113] In the Middle Ages, on the contrary, despite many exceptions, the idea of not mixing water with wine reacquired cultural status.[114] In monastic use, *merum* and *mixtum* alternated according to predetermined rules.[115] What remains curious is the use of the same term, *miscere*, to indicate two separate actions—pouring and mixing—as though they were one and the same. Ildemaro's comment in the Benedictine Rule does not fail to emphasize that: "the verb *miscere* can be understood in two ways: in the sense of *ministrare*, as when we say 'pour the wine,' or in the sense of *mittere*, as when we say 'mix water with the wine.' "[116] The symmetry at this point is perfect. Wine is tempered with water to avoid intoxication; water is tempered with wine to reduce the dangers of its coldness.[117]

The pairing continues on the liturgical level: the Eucharist requires wine and water together, and different allegorical interpretations determine the choice. The Old Testament can be seen in water and the New in wine, which, by transforming it, gives it flavor.[118] Or wine is Christ and water his people; therefore, "when water is mixed with wine in the goblet, the people are united with Christ."[119] Or else "wine is the divine nature of Christ and water is human nature."[120] In any case, Rabano Mauro explains, "neither of the two substances should be offered in sacrifice without the other, neither wine without water, nor water without wine."[121] In this pairing, however, the values are unequal. If the two natures of Christ are inseparable, it is clear that the *divinitas* stands above the *humanitas*. Therefore, the first is represented by wine, "long more excellent than water," as Pascasio Radberto wrote.[122]

The multiplicity of functions that wine performed in the Middle Ages—cultural, social, economic, religious, hygienic, and therapeutic—can account for the extremely high level of consumption documented for those centuries. The indications we have are scarce and refer only to religious communities, but the overall picture they trace is unequivocal: during the Carolingian period, daily rations, at the minimum, came to one and a half liters per day per capita (a figure that, according to various calculations, could be more or less doubled).[123] The Benedictine Rule had fixed one *emina* per day,[124] nevertheless foreseeing from the beginning possible increases justified by considerations of place, work, heat of summer, and particular occasions.

Outside of these few data, no calculation is possible, but the condemnation of drunkenness with which medieval literature is obsessed cannot be merely rhetorical. The habit of heavy drinking did not always respect the laws of self-control laid down by ecclesiastic and secular authorities. The repeated prohibition made to priests and monks against frequenting taverns in the company of peasants[125] suggests that this occurred commonly. The appeals made by Carolingian rulers that judges and other public officials not appear inebriated[126] at hearings reveal disturbing situations. The *Life of Gerald, Count of Aurillac* bears testimony to this when his biographer, Odon of Cluny, credits the count with exceptional virtue for never having behaved in this manner.[127]

The condemnation of drunkenness—not only from wine but also from any alcoholic beverage[128]—never took the tone of a crusade, however. The subject was generally approached with generosity and tolerance. Augustine (echoed later by the canonists Ivo and Gratian) insists that drunks be admonished respectfully, "not harshly or violently."[129] Severity should be reserved for more serious crimes, committed by a limited number of people, not for "common social behavior."[130] Drunkenness is condemnable but is not a reason for a major scandal. Furthermore, he recommends distinguishing between occasional drunkenness and chronic drunkenness, between *ebrietas* and *ebriositas*. The same metaphor of *sobria ebrietas* as the highest moment in the contemplation of God, which Ambrose takes from Origen and passes on to patristic and medieval periods,[131] would not be comprehensible without a mental background—inherited by Christianity from the platonic, gnostic, and hermetic tradition and not without suggestions of a Dionysian origin—inclined "always to celebrate the mystery of wine":[132] the mystery of a substance that brightens the spirit and sharpens the mind before confusing it and clouding it and the mystery of nature, which every day replicates itself before our eyes even if we try to make ourselves unaware of it. Men, Augustine observes, are astounded to hear about the miracle at Cana (or, we would add, about the miracles that so many saints contrived to imitate it) and are not aware of the real miracle, the one performed by God day after day, when He transforms water into wine through grapevines: "what else but this happens to rainwater that seeps through the roots of grapevines?"[133]

In this miracle, man also has his part. We started with Augustine, and we return to him: "The grape hangs from the vine like the olive from the tree . . . but the grape does not become wine, nor does the olive become oil, before it is pressed."

CHAPTER XIII

Rich Food, Poor Food

THE HISTORY OF food has a powerful social meaning, which sources reveal with relative clarity. To recognize the differences and dynamics of class in the structure of production, the modality and contrasts of distribution, the typology of daily consumption, and the symbolic values attributed to foods and to eating habits is fairly easy for the most part because all this emerges from the documentation. However, this topic is more difficult to define on more strictly technical grounds—that is, to take into account the way cooking was practiced. The relation between poor food and rich food and the separation between popular culture and elite culture in modes of preparation and in tastes are subjects that would seem to be inaccessible to anyone concerned with the Middle Ages (or any historic period). Because the written culture of those centuries was produced for the upper classes and oral sources are denied to the historian who is not dealing with contemporary matters, only the cuisine of the well-to-do has been documented, albeit in a discontinuous manner, and passed down from archival and literary sources, whereas we are forced to remain silent on the cuisine of the poor or, at best, to propose indirect hypotheses, interpolating texts and working from fantasy.

True? In theory, yes. But a more detailed reading of the sources has convinced me of the contrary. Indeed, written texts never express the culture of the lower classes, and yet they demonstrate it, with greater fidelity than we might have thought. I have reached this conclusion by analyzing cookbooks that began to appear in Italy as of the fourteenth century. As we have already seen,[1] there are two principal families of cookbooks: one of southern origin that has its progenitor in the *Liber de coquina*, from the Angevine court of Naples (presumably based on a Sicilian archetype from the thirteenth century), and that was subsequently copied with additions and variants in various parts of central and northern Italy; the other of Tuscan origin, probably Sienese, which also spread to many regions, with adaptations that also included linguistic ones. When poring over these gastronomic-philological matters in a book written jointly with Alberto Capatti,[2] I extended my interest in such texts to the beginning of the modern era, delving into the rich fifteenth-century cookbook of Maestro Martino and then, going forward and back, into the Renaissance cookbooks by Cristoforo Messisbugo and Bartolomeo Scappi. The latter cookbook was a monument to the Italian art of cooking, a *summa* of gastronomic knowledge gathered by the author over decades of association with the cooking and cultures of different regions, from Milan to Venice, and from Bologna to Rome, the city in which he ended his career at the court of Pope Pius V, to whom he dedicated in 1570 his *Opera*, a modest title for a work of magisterial substance.

There is an abyss between the technical and linguistic expertise of this *Opera* and the first, timid expressions of fourteenth-century texts, at times exasperating in their concision (probably explained by the professional audience to which they were addressed, an audience that needed few directions to understand the basics of its own work). And yet there is a link, in my view, as the Renaissance is no more than the conclusion and perfection of the Middle Ages; despite the opposition invented long after (in the fifteenth and sixteenth centuries—in other words, by the Renaissance itself[3]), this is still commonly accepted, even by specialists. The link is in the approach to the practice of cooking, which evolved without the solution of continuity; the link is in the permanence of flavors and tastes, in the continuous interchange between court cooking—in the Middle Ages, the cooking of the urban upper class as well—and "popular" culture, in the excessively but inescapably vague meaning that a term like this can suggest.

The fact is that the aristocratic mentality of the late Middle Ages and early modern era, although raising insurmountable barriers of social behavior—beginning with food—between the ruling classes and those ruled, did not at all exclude the daily convergence of tastes and customs. The rigidity of symbolic constructs that dramatically separate peasant life from that of the nobility (or city dwellers, in a variant typically Italian) could peacefully cohabit with "peasant" products and flavors in the kitchens of the elite. These constructs could even incorporate it: models of opposition and exclusion representing the utopia of the ruling classes, as organic and coherent as they were, were rejected in practice—in both directions. Social, economic, and juridical constrictions might have determined what was eaten, and thereby might have oriented the diet of peasants away from that of the upper classes (for example, it was possible to deny rural communities access to the forest and to hunting and thereby eliminate game from the peasant table[4]), but to transform constriction into ideology must have been difficult. The peasants did not give up certain foods just because intellectuals considered them ideal for the table of courtiers and urbanites (I have in mind tree fruits and feathered game, which agronomic and dietetic texts of the fourteenth and fifteenth centuries, echoing suggestions of naturalistic thinking from previous centuries, proposed as the exclusive foods of the upper classes[5]). The class war, which literature tried to exorcize (one need only turn to the novella by Sabadino degli Arienti in which a peasant in the Bolognese countryside, rebelling against the orders of his master, is captured and brutally punished for having dared to steal, and eat, a prized peach, reserved in principle for the landowner[6]), was doubtless a daily event—and often a successful one. A myriad of chinks, uncontrolled segments of the processes of production, revealed themselves to the ingenuity of the peasant.

But the inverse also held true. If the peasants were not stopped by ideological barriers that they found intolerable or, more simply, that they ignored, the landowners in turn did not find unappetizing the foods described in literature as "typically peasant" and seen as such in the collective imagination, or at least in the imagination of the upper classes. About this contrast between ideology and reality, and the practical ruses to overcome it, the cookbooks of the early Middle Ages provide formidable and misunderstood evidence.

The oldest cookbook of the peninsula, the *Liber de coquina*, begins with vegetables and does so deliberately: "Wishing to discuss herein cooking and various foods, we shall begin first of all with easy things, that is, with vegetables."[7] There follow ten different recipes for cabbage before going on to spinach, fennel, and "instant leaves" and then to preparations based on legumes: chickpeas, peas, lentils, and beans—all foods that in literature, and in the culinary *ideology* of the Middle Ages, belong to the peasant world. Is this, then, a book of "popular" cuisine? Certainly not. The cuisine of the *Liber* is expressly intended for people of rank: "prepare delicate cabbage for the gentry," we read, or "the fragrant little leaves can be given to the lord."

The discrepancy between "intellectual" food writing and "real" practices is obvious. The contrast is powerful and requires equally powerful *signs* to escape from ambiguity, to reenter the sphere of "ideologically correct" images. The first sign is that of side dishes and modes of use that clarify the social destination of the food item. A humble product is ennobled by making it part of a different gastronomic or symbolic system, such as making it merely one ingredient—not the main one—of a prestigious dish. As we read in Sabadino degli Arienti, garlic "is always a rustic food" but "at times is artificially made elegant if placed in the cavity of a roasted duck." From the moment that garlic is stuffed in a roasted duck, its peasant nature is "artificially" modified. Therefore, *agliata*, a sauce made of garlic crushed in a mortar and pestle, typical of peasant cooking, can also appear in cookbooks for the upper classes: a Venetian cookbook of the fourteenth century proposes that it accompany "all meats." Similarly, the recipe for "delicate cabbage for the gentry" in the *Liber de coquina* makes sure to specify its use as an accompaniment to all meats: "*cum omnibus carnibus.*"

The second sign of ennoblement, aside from the matter of accompaniment, is the enrichment of a humble product with costly ingredients, such as spices. Take, for example, this recipe from a Tuscan volume of the fourteenth century: "Take small turnips, thoroughly cooked in water, and sauté them with oil, onion, and salt; when they are cooked and ready to serve, add spices and put them into bowls."

Take note of the logic of the argument: once spiced, any food is worthy of a lordly table. This implies a shared basis of gastronomic culture, the common use across social classes—beyond symbolic opposition—of alimentary methods and customs, the intermixing of "precious things" and "ordinary" ones. The possibility of choosing the one or the other was deliberately foreseen by the already mentioned Tuscan cookbook, which leaves every choice to the taste of the lord: "In each sauce, savory or broth, one can put *precious things*, such as gold, precious stones, choice

spices, or cardamom, fragrant or *ordinary* herbs, onions, leeks, as you like."
This view was not shared by all. At the end of the fourteenth century a
northern version of the *Liber de coquina* completely eliminated the section
on vegetables. But the general tendency was decidedly the former, as
shown by the major cookbooks of the fourteenth and fifteenth centuries,
which revived and amplified the totally peasant tradition of using vegetables in cooking: cabbage, turnips, fennel, mushrooms, pumpkin, lettuce, parsley, and every kind of herb, as well as legumes such as beans and
peas, are the base of so many of the preparations (soups, pies, fritters)
listed in the fifteenth-century cookbook by Maestro Martino.

If the centrality of vegetables is one of the dominant characteristics of
popular cooking—this is why it is so important to verify their presence in
the cookbooks of the courts—poor foods, par excellence, are the polentas
and gruels made of inferior grains such as legumes and chestnuts, key elements in a cuisine marked by the need to fill the belly so as to assure daily
survival. And yet even this poor cuisine left important traces in recipes
intended for the upper classes.[8] "Crushed broad beans" are none other
than a polenta of broad beans, like the one that occasionally goes by the
name of *macco*, as a vast literature of peasant cooking confirms. This recipe
is utterly simple and poor in its first version (a second one, richer, adds
spices and sugar): "Take broad beans that have been crushed and carefully selected and when you have boiled them and poured off the water,
wash them carefully and put them back into the same pot with a small
amount of tepid water and salt, seeing to it that they are covered by the
water, and stir often with a spoon; once they are cooked, remove them
from the fire and smash them hard with a spoon, then let them rest for a
while and when you put them in a bowl add honey or oil in which onions
have been sautéed, and eat." Equally noteworthy is the *paniccia col latte*
(a gruel of foxtail millet and milk) that appears in the Tuscan cookbook:
a simple "legume" (as it is defined in the text, perhaps assimilating millet
into legumes), carefully washed and crushed, boiled and mixed with milk
and lard. Truly a peasant dish, but for the fact that instead of serving it
as the main dish of the meal—as was the case for the poor inhabitants of
Lucca, who, in the eighth century, received from charity a *pulmentario* of
broad beans and *panico* (foxtail millet)—our *paniccia* was a side dish for
something more substantial: "this dish can be eaten with roasted goat."

Medieval cookbooks also include gruels made with oats, barley, and
millet—at times proposed as food "for the sick," unadulterated, without

added spices, and suitable for that reason—and close to the model of peasant consumption. Spelt, millet, and legumes appear in the recipes of Maestro Martino, and many porridges of inferior grains (barley, millet, and foxtail millet) are found in the pages of Bartolomeo Scappi, always enriched with spices, sugar, and prestigious meats but nevertheless traceable to a cuisine that bears the mark of the peasantry. The author seems perfectly aware of this, as, for example, when he points out, in the recipe for a soup of dried beans, that "this dish is called Macco in Lombardy."

Like *macco*, and having the same etymology (from *maccare, ammaccare,* meaning to grind into flour and knead), *maccheroni*—or gnocchi, in the oldest meaning of the term[9]—was a dish much favored by peasant cooking, and cookbooks of the fourteenth and fifteenth centuries provide the first recipes, ones of the greatest simplicity: flour, or bread crumbs, mixed with cheese, or egg yolks, so as to obtain balls of dough that can be cooked in boiling water. Not even the great court cooks, like Cristoforo Messisbugo and Bartolomeo Scappi, neglect this particular type of "*maccheroni*, called gnocchi" (other *maccheroni*, those of today, will in the meantime have disappeared): "made with refined flour, the crumb of bread, and hot water, on the *gratacascio* [cheese grater], cooked in water, covered with *agliata*," they appear among far more elegant and sumptuous dishes. And in Scappi's *Opera*, there is a gruel of *formentone grosso*, or corn, a product that even peasants had difficulty accepting on their own table.[10]

The *torta* or *pastello*—an ingenious creation, which we owe to the Middle Ages—is a shell of dough, placed in the oven or between red-hot slabs of stone or earthenware, with the dual purpose of containing or cooking a filling and eventually transporting it. It is an edible object that seems made expressly to cross all social lines.[11] Extremely practical, easy to make and keep, apparently within the ability of everyone, and therefore capable of designating a gastronomic civilization in its entirety, it became diversified immediately in its uses. The filling can be more or less complex, more or less prestigious and costly, without ceasing to be recognizable as an element that identifies it as part of a common culture, both urban and rural, both lordly and popular.

In Scappi's pages, even the preparation of fish seems to be one of those magical points of contact between the professional, cosmopolitan cook and the practices of the common people, the culture of the *terroir*. More than once Scappi refers the reader to the simple recipes of the fishermen, to which he would add nothing. Gudgeon [or goby, a small freshwater fish] "has to be cooked fresh, otherwise it goes bad quickly." The fishermen of Chiozza and Venice cook it on embers and also use it in an ingenious fish soup made with malvasia [a sweet white fortified wine that the English call malmsey], water, a little vinegar, and Venetian spices, or fry it in oil like other fish, and serve it hot with orange sauce on top.[12] Similarly, "the fishermen of the Po make soups of barbel [a European freshwater fish], or fry it, or cook it on the grate." And after giving the recipe for turbot *in pottaggio* (fish soup), the source says, "during the time I was in Venice and Ravenna I learned from the fishermen of Chiozza and Venice, who make the best *pottaggi* on all the shores of the sea, that there was no better way to make it than the way I said above." However, he adds, "I think that they make it better than cooks do because they cook [the fish] as soon as they catch it." This is an admission that does not seem inspired by popular thinking. It is rather a question of time: the fish of the fishermen is better than that of "cooks" because it is fresher.

A typical product of poor cooking, which both medieval and ancient cultures associated, above all, with the world of peasants and shepherds, is cheese. In this case as well, it is apparent that in the Middle Ages a process of "ennoblement" occurred, related either to questions of taste or to the image of cheese as a food for fasting, a substitute for meat on days of abstinence on weekdays and the eve of holidays and later, in the fourteenth and fifteenth centuries, also during Lent. If, on the one hand, all this confirmed the status of cheese as a "poor" food that replaces another—meat—regarded as more prestigious and desirable, on the other hand, it also necessarily bestowed an important role in the alimentary system,[13] similar to the one held by fish for the same reasons.[14]

Less significant, perhaps, are the contributions of popular culture to meats, a preeminent symbol of social prestige. But let us at least note that the taste for offal—often regarded as typical of popular taste in that it is what butchers discard (which may justify its curious appellation of "fifth quarter")—crossed all social classes during the Middle Ages and the Renaissance, as demonstrated by cookbooks intended for the upper classes.

Important harmonies (which do not exclude substantial differences) between "rich" and "poor" cuisines can be seen in the sphere of preserves, primarily based on salt, as well as vinegar, oil, and other ingredients. Peasant cooking, above all, counted on preserved products; they kept well throughout the year and constituted the prime assurance of survival in a rural economy that could not rely on a daily market or the caprices of the weather. This is one of the principal distinctions (as imaginary as real) between rich and poor, lord and serf, city dweller and peasant. The former ate fresh food; the latter generally did not.[15] Meat, fish, cheese, and vegetables all arrived on the peasant table monotonously tasting of salt. But the importance of preserved foods in gastronomy is that of having been a fundamental meeting point between popular culture and elite culture. If preserved food is the first defense against hunger, the surplus of labor and culture that results in an abundance of natural products soon makes it possible to leave the ambit of need and enter that of pleasure.

All of this led to important consequences. The first is methodological: it is not true that the culture of the lower classes and the oral tradition that expressed it are irretrievably lost. Both were transmitted elsewhere, in the written texts and by the dominant culture, with formal and substantive evidence drawn from the way the procedures of preparing the dishes are described, and presumably executed. By that, I mean that poor cooking (that of the popular culture) was made more visible in the elite cookbooks of the Middle Ages and Renaissance—as implied in the examples selected—by the particular modes with which the work of a cook was performed. The prevailing mechanism was one of accumulation, which *added* noble products to a simple base or *paired* noble foods with simple ones. This suggests that the point of departure was, by definition, the one more widely shared; diverse elements were added *afterward*. This is emphasized also because it constitutes an important element of diversity with regard to modern culinary practices. For a number of centuries, refined cuisine—that of great families and today of great restaurants—set itself apart not only in the advanced and conclusive phases of procedure but also often in preliminary procedures. The French school of the seventeenth and eighteenth centuries, out of which a large part of contemporary culinary techniques arose, was innovative with regard to medieval and Renaissance traditions in the introduction of precooked bases—fond brun, roux blanc, roux brun, and so on—that conferred on the dish a different character from the outset. For that, too, the cookbook of a star chef is scarcely comparable today to poor cooking. If in some way it expresses or evokes it, it is indirect and hard to decode. If instead we recognize that the point of departure closely mirrors a "common" code of cooking—as seems to me to be the case of medieval and Renaissance cooking—the reliability of upper-class cookbooks becomes decidedly greater.

The second consequence derives directly from the first. If Italian cookbooks of upper-class cooking can lend themselves, starting in the Middle Ages, to restituting an extensive panorama not only of the culture and tastes of the elite classes but also of the culture and tastes of the lower classes, that means that the evolution of a gastronomic patrimony occurred over time in a joint action of all the social components of the country. The key to understanding this phenomenon lies, in addition and above all, in the importance of the cities as the specific site of the production and development of an alimentary culture.[16] The locus of economic, cultural, and social exchanges, the city—with its territory, which in some way the city comprises and represents—is the ideal site for intermixing, hybridization, and contamination. Popular culture and elite culture confront one another on a daily basis, alternately imitating and blending into one another. The cooks who work at courts or for great families, in some cases of noble but more often of popular origin, are doubtless the key figures in this mechanism, which is yet to be explored. The fact remains that cookbooks for the nobility express a socially diffused culture, an *urban* culture that in its turn is *regional* (in that the city dominates and represents a region) and *national* (in that the city comprises a network of its own culture through markets and the circulation of products, people, and ideas).

This, to me, holds the secret of the richness and vitality of Italian cuisine, all the more diversified and articulated—and for that reason interesting— for having developed historically as a place of encounter between different cultures, not only from a *territorial* point of view but also from a *social* point of view. It is also for this reason that we can rightfully talk of a "national" gastronomic heritage[17] because the written tradition, the expression of an elite cuisine, transmitted and represented over centuries a culture in which everyone could recognize fragments of his or her own identity. If the splendor of Renaissance courts represents, still today, a source of pride for the inhabitants of innumerable cities (Mantua, for example, holds up the cuisine of the Gonzagas as the collective patrimony of the city, as does Florence that of the Medici or Rome that of the popes), this is not just to promote tourism and an instrumental use of history but also to reflect a tradition that is an important part of the collective memory and, to a greater or lesser degree, contains the cultures of the entire society. Cooking can therefore be seen as an ideal terrain for conflict but also for the encounters and exchanges between different cultures.

CHAPTER XIV

Monastic Cooking

WAYS OF APPROACHING food play a central role in medieval monastic thinking, endowing the daily problem of nutrition with important cultural values and conferring on it a heavily ritualized character. A remarkable variety, in time and space, distinguishes the ideological and existential choices of individual groups and orders. There are, however, important common traits, mental and cultural attitudes, immediately recognizable as typical of the monastic experience.[1]

One aspect that is totally uniform is alimentary *deprivation*, the *renunciation* of food as a means of mortifying the flesh. The practices of fasting (understood in a primarily quantitative sense: the elimination of the first of the two daily meals) and abstinence (understood in a qualitative sense: the elimination, temporary or permanent, of certain foods from the monastic diet) assume different characteristics according to the greater or lesser degree of ascetic rigor, the material conditions of life, the rituals, and the liturgical calendar. But these are details within a choice that is general and precedential.

It should immediately be made clear that deprivation does not mean absence. On the contrary, one can only deprive oneself of what one has, of what one is accustomed to having: "*privatio praesupponit habitum*," Rabelais ironically remarks.[2] On this, monastic culture is in agreement: there would be no value or merit in a renunciation that was obligatory in some way because of circumstances; it is necessary to renounce an available pleasure so that the choice acquires value and meaning. When Abbot Pacôme (one of the fathers of eastern monasticism) returns to his monastery after a prolonged period of solitude in the desert, he learns to his astonishment that for the previous two months his cook had ceased preparing the traditional dish of vegetables that was served to the brothers on Saturdays and Sundays. Asking the reason for this, he is told that it had become pointless because the monks had stopped eating it, preferring to mortify their bodies by refraining from cooked foods. Surprisingly, Pacôme acquiesces, although harshly disapproving a decision that he does not hesitate to call "satanic"—for "he who abstains only against his will and out of necessity, with no object of desire, abstains in vain and will have no recompense." If food is absent from the table, "temperance has no value." Instead, every day "many dishes should be cooked and placed before the brothers so that by depriving themselves of what has been given to them they can augment their perfection."[3]

It is thus not a paradox to find in the monastic world an intense interest in food, in the search for alimentary resources, and in the careful organization and management of supply systems alongside forms of ideological repulsion. This is not only because the same principle of deprivation presupposes the availability of foods from which to abstain and their destination for other purposes (particularly charity), but also because the alimentary regime of the monks, being extremely selective with regard to the quality of foods consumed, implied a constant effort to rationalize and control resources.

What meanings does monastic culture attribute to the deprivation of food? And first of all, what meanings come out of the abstention from meat, which is the first and most important of those deprivations? The prime purpose of renouncing food, and the simplest and most immediate, is the mortification of the flesh, the rejection (ideological, of course) of that burden of matter that hinders the elevation of the soul toward God. In this sense—according to a play on terminologies that was common in medieval treatises—food for the body was contrasted with food for the soul, earthly bread with celestial bread. The "contempt for the body" is to be understood in a moral, not a theological sense (in the religious context of Christianity, founded on the idea of divine incarnation, this would be inconceivable); but it is not hard to recognize in certain attitudes of monastic culture an echo of dualistic ideologies, always denied and always recurring in the ascetic tension of Christian spirituality.

The rejection of food is therefore the negation of the priority of the body in human experience, and from this perspective, one understands why the very first choice of this "negative regimen" is the rejection (more or less radical, more or less rigorous) of meat. Meat was held, by definition, to be "the nutrition of meat." That ambiguity of the term (*caro nutrita carne*) was part of the ideology that proposed it and found ample support in medieval scientific literature (treatises on medicine and diet) which saw meat as the prime alimentary value, the ideal food for "nutrition."[4] Whether from the vantage point of basic cultural choices or of individual psychological attitudes, the rejection of meat was an elitist choice to distance oneself from the "normal" food of humans. This was an important motive for self-identification on the part of a particular group of individuals, who, for this reason as well, felt themselves closer to God. And more generally, this accounted for an attitude of detachment and renunciation of food.

In this rejection of the world and of meat, there were also subtler concerns. If the consumption of meat was for most people the best kind of nutrition, for some social groups—those who held power, the military aristocracy—it represented something more: it was the symbol of strength and power, the manifestation of a violent mentality that was an integral part of the culture and customs of *potentes*. During the Carolingian period, among the punishments imposed by imperial law for political crimes of singular gravity was the deprivation of meat accompanied by the laying down of arms.[5] For many who entered monastic orders—in large part offspring of aristocracy—the deprivation of meat took on the meaning not only of a generic renunciation of the "world" but also a rejection of *that* particular world from which so many monks had originally come.

Medieval monasticism—above all, that of Cluny, so closely tied to the nobility (although this applies more generally)—was not intolerant of alimentary habits that were too deeply rooted to be abandoned all at once, but the principle of renunciation was irreversible and perhaps all the more rigorous in that its daily practice was so difficult. The biographies of the great reformers (Odo of Cluny, Hugo, and so many others) show them tenaciously struggling with monks so attached to eating meat that they resist all attempts at "moralization." In cases like these, the texts insist on the idea of combatting the sin of gluttony or the question of individual submission, but the heart of the problem seems less a moral one than a social one: the sharing, on the part of the monastic body, of habits and lifestyles common to the world of nobility.

Abstinence from food—and in particular, from meat—was also programmed for another reason, that of a technical nature. Deprivation of food was, in fact, considered one of the principal means of realizing an important objective of monastic status—*virginity*, seen as a privileged condition for approaching God more rapidly and more intensely. The dietary choices of the monks thus appear to be closely related to the repression of sexuality. Abstinence and chastity go together, be it in a metaphoric sense (gluttony and sexuality, the two primary physical pleasures, are images of one another and follow each other in turn) or in a functional sense (this type of diet is seen as a means of facilitating chastity, with implicit or explicit reference to the medical science of the time and the conviction that foods of a "hot" nature encourage sexuality and those of a "cold or dry" nature inhibit it).[6]

Perhaps yet another reason led monks (at least, some of them) to reject meat: the wish to align their own dietary style with the vegetarian model of Eden, as recounted in the book of Genesis and announced by the prophet Isaiah as returning at the end of time. This was a nonviolent alimentary model that avoided killing living creatures. Aspirations like these were never openly declared (although certain passages of monastic literature assure us that they were not lacking) because they were incompatible with Christian doctrine,[7] which, at least in principle, made no distinction between foods (plant and animal), accepting all of them as a gift of divine Providence.

Violence was rejected by certain groups that were labeled "heretical." One need only remember the vegetarian rigor of the Manichean sects, later revived by Cathar philosophy—radical examples whose presence one can readily trace in "orthodox" monasticism as well.

After the rigorous prohibitions of early monasticism, especially in the east, the consumption of meat became the object of discussions, proposals, and choices that changed from one time to another. If a few monastic rules maintained the original rigor (above all, in northern Europe, where the tradition of meat eating was more entrenched and its opposition all the more fierce, as shown, for example, by the Rules of Colombano, which totally excluded meat), others more easily legitimized the consumption of meat (especially in southern Europe, as in the Italian *Regula Magistri*). In the end, a line of compromise won out, which is how the regulations of the Benedictine Rule, for centuries the principal model of western monastic life, might be defined. The Benedictine text, in fact, making mention only of the meat of quadrupeds as being strictly prohibited, allows the consumption of poultry, though not explicitly encouraging it.[8]

This margin of tolerance, which allowed substantial freedom of choice and discretion (*discretio*) to the abbot, and also to individuals and to individual communities, seems to have been motivated either by cosmological considerations (based on differentiated scansions of the times of creation, high medieval culture made a clear distinction between terrestrial animals, on the one hand, and animals of the air and water, on the other) or by medical-dietetic convictions related to the image of greater lightness attributed to birds (the metaphoric notion of flight as lightness is translated into values more specifically nutritional). In turn, the physiological aspect took on ethical meanings (lightening the organism so as to rise closer to God): "The meat of winged creatures," wrote an Italian physician of the sixteenth century, "is much more suited to those who expect more from exercising the spirit than the body."[9] In conclusion, it is possible that what might have influenced monastic regulations—insofar as the meat of winged creatures can generally be considered less rich in blood than the meat of quadrupeds—was the ancient Hebrew taboo against blood, which Christianity had formally rejected but which long persisted in the culture and mentality of the high Middle Ages, as confirmed by penitential books and hagiographic sources.[10]

In any case, it is clear that "*sola quadrupedia, non volatilia* [only quadrupeds, not winged creatures]" were prohibited to the monks—the quotation is from Rabano Mauro[11]—even if the model of total abstention remained the highest aspiration of many. In a famous letter written to Charlemagne by Teodemaro, abbot of Montecassino, the abbot describes the monks of that abbey—surely with some chauvinism—as the most faithful interpreters of the Benedictine Rule, who, only under special circumstances (one week at Christmas and one at Easter), convince themselves to eat the meat of winged creatures; moreover, he adds, many brothers abstain even at those times.[12]

The exclusion of meat from the diet resulted in its programmed substitution by other products that could take its place as "strong" food, as energy foods high in nutritional value. These replacement products—which therefore had great success in the monastic tradition from both an economic and a cultural point of view—were fish, cheese, eggs, and vegetables.

The acceptance of fish as an alternate to meat was not that simple. During the early centuries of the monastic experience, but not only then, more rigorous tendencies did not hesitate to exclude fish, like any other animal food, from the table of the brothers. Others condoned it but cautiously (for example, the Rules of Aurelian and Fruttuoso accepted it only on specific holidays or on other particular occasions, with the explicit authorization of the abbot) or, like Benedict, did not mention it. With time, however, it gained admission to the point that fish became—in contrast to meat—one of the primary alimentary symbols of monastic life. An edifying (and entertaining) tale by Pier Damiani concerns a monk who, invited to dinner by Count Farolfo, yielded to the temptation of a loin of pork. Then a huge pike was brought to the table, and the monk began looking at it avidly. Jokingly, the count said to him: "You who ate meat like a lay person, why do you now examine the fish like a monk?"

The relationship between monastic life and the consumption of fish soon became a commonplace. The presence of streams in which to fish and the construction of hatcheries are presented as indispensable for the founding of a monastery. "Rich in fish," according to the *Cronaca della Novalesa*, was the site of the abbey of Bremen,[13] and the *Life of Saint Odo* of Cluny relates that the marsh near the monastery of Fleury, "which earlier bubbled with frogs," at some point began—miraculously, the author suggests—to abound in fish. And not only is this relationship found in literary texts: hatcheries and artificial fisheries stood beside monastic complexes, and archival sources confirm the keen concern of the monks that they be assured of their right to fish. To this end, the monastery of Bobbio, in the ninth century, exploited its property on the lake of Garda; the monastery of Nonantola had at its disposal a squadron of fishermen who fished in the nearby Po River.[14]

The need to substitute fish for meat is often the subject of miraculous episodes related by hagiographic sources. The *Dialogues* of Gregory the Great relate that Onorato, a monk at Fondi during the first half of the fifth century, having been invited to a dinner with relatives in the mountains of Sannio, refused to eat meat and was derided for it. "Eat!" they said. "How do you expect us to find you a fish in these mountains?"

At that point, there was no more water, and a servant was sent to the spring: "while he was drawing water a fish jumped into the pail and when the servant poured water for the guests, out came a fish that satisfied Onorato for the whole day."[15] An almost identical episode appears in the biography of Count Gerald of Aurillac, who, in the company of the monk Ariberto, found himself in the embarrassing position of not having any fish to offer him. Suddenly, a servant who had gone to draw water "saw on the bank a little fish, still palpitating, that jumped out of the water before his eyes," as though offering itself as a meal. Not only the monk but also Gerald tasted it and found it "most delicious."[16]

Other miracles took place while eating fish. In the *Life of Saint Simeon*, a monk in the monastery of San Benedetto Po, it is written that brother Andrea was sitting at the dining table "when, accidentally, a fishbone got stuck in his throat in such a way that he could neither swallow it nor spit it out." Everyone feared for his life, but Simeon, praying to God, miraculously managed to make him eject the bone.[17]

In truth, the monks were not always champions of abstinence. During the Carolingian era, between the eighth and ninth centuries, they closely followed the lifestyle of the gentry, from which most of them had originated, regularly introducing meat into their daily diet. This is also (and perhaps primarily) why the reformers—going back to the original rigor of the Rule—tried to convince them to give up meat in favor of fish. The *Life of Saint Odo* of Cluny is instructive in its mention of his many attempts (stubbornly thwarted) to reform monastic life: Giovanni, a disciple of Odo's and his biographer, relates that in the Tuscan abbey of Saint Elia "we found monks whom we were unable to keep from eating meat." The same thing occurred at Fleury, but in both cases, the diplomatic skill and patience of Odo succeeded in putting an end to it.[18]

The fish eaten by monks (and also lay people, both peasants and lords) were mostly freshwater fish, caught on the site according to a prevailing view of local production.[19] A good inventory of the species best known and most often consumed (sturgeon, trout, among others) can be found in certain *consuetudini* drawn up at Cluny in the eleventh and twelfth centuries, which, as we shall soon see, codified the gestures used by the monks to indicate them (necessitated by their vow of silence).

Even cheese had a special place on the monastic table, and it has been observed that most of the cheeses eaten today have a link, direct or indirect, real or mythical (but no less meaningful), with some monastic establishment of the medieval period.[20] Eggs seem to be a high-energy food: as a dish in itself or as an ingredient in a variety of dishes, they appeared regularly and abundantly in the daily diet of the monks. Saint Bernard of Chiaravalle accused the monks of Cluny of being too disposed to the pleasures of gastronomy and, furthermore, of knowing too many ways to prepare eggs and make them succulent: "who can determine how many ways eggs can be turned or beaten, how skillfully they are mixed, flipped over, liquified, hardboiled, thickened, served fried, boiled, stuffed, blended or separated?"[21] Another fundamental ingredient in the monastic diet was legumes: beans, peas, chickpeas, lentils, and most of all broad beans were the basis of many dishes prepared in different ways. The broad bean, cooked according to a ritual codified in the minutest detail,[22] which illustrates its prime alimentary importance, was also ground into flour and mixed with grains to make gruel, soup, and polenta.[23]

Legumes and vegetables (the Latin *olera*, produced in great quantity in the large kitchen gardens of monasteries) were the basic ingredients of the *pulmentaria*, another constant presence on monastic tables, as it constituted the main dish of the daily meal, according to Benedictine tradition.[24] As to fats for seasoning and cooking, those preferred were vegetable oils (olive, walnut, seeds) but also lard, which it would seem was not included in the overall prohibition against meat; fats made up a separate alimentary group.[25]

Bread—which Benedict prescribed in the amount of one pound per person, independent of whether it was a fast day or not and whether it was eaten once or twice during the day[26]—was a constant presence in the diet of the monks, more fundamental than related to meanings that transcend the level of food to merge with liturgy and mysticism. Along with bread was wine, the two forming an indivisible pair of obvious symbolic meaning: wine was by far the drink most often consumed by the monks, in spite of the ambiguous halo of suspicion that hovered over it. Wine could certainly bring about sin and indulgence, but the habit of drinking it was so embedded in medieval society that Benedict could not bring himself to prohibit it: "in these times it is impossible to persuade the monks of the contrary," the Rule says, limiting itself to recommending control and moderation, and establishing one *emina* as the daily measure.[27] Important hygienic and medical benefits were moreover associated with wine—and not mistakenly, at a time when the antiseptic qualities of a moderately alcoholic drink doubtless protected the body, defending it against the threat of infection that could come from poorly kept foods and, most of all, from water, often turbid or contaminated.[28] Pure water was therefore rarely drunk, just as pure wine was rarely drunk: the two liquids were normally mixed and flavored with herbs, aromas, and honey. Only in the most northern regions of Europe was the consumption of beer, or cider, widespread—but always subordinate to wine.

The monastic diet oscillated considerably during the course of the week and the year for liturgical reasons (the calendar of fasts and abstentions) or because of the activities of the monks. In the first instance, the direct determinant of food was the feast: major holidays (Christmas, Easter) and important occasions (the birthday of the abbot or of a benefactor) were celebrated symbolically through food, served with uncommon abundance and variety. This "joyful" aspect of food appears more or less clearly according to individual cases: particularly sensitive to this are certain rules, such as those of the so-called Maestro, whereas others show a preference for a link between work and food, as in the case of the Rule of Benedict, which prescribed quantitative and qualitative increases of rations for those monks who were engaged in activities or circumstances that were particularly laborious.[29] The tie was not broken when monastic society, committed to manual labor as dictated by Benedict, progressively moved away from it, concentrating more exclusively on prayer. The monks in Cluny could justify the abundance and variety of their alimentation—seen with disapproval by the Cistercians—precisely because of the effort required by the daily liturgy.[30]

Another connection, essential for understanding the alimentary attitudes and choices of the monk, is the one between food and health: dietary science in its proper sense. On the one side, it teaches that food is the original medicine. On this axiom were founded medical notions and practices inherited from Greek and Latin antiquity and passed on to posterity through the decisive contribution of the monasteries. The use of foods is thus the fruit of this combined knowledge, this science of the "humors" utilized preventively and therapeutically, in addition to its function in such special choices as chastity. In monastic practice, the health of the individual was a fundamental variable for determining the type of diet assigned to him. Only healthy and robust brothers were held to the restrictive norms proposed by the legislator, whereas the sick and the "weak" (a term that at times assumes moral as well as physiological connotations) were allowed relatively broader transgressions: larger quantities, prohibited foods.[31] This was particularly true for meat and broth made with meat, considered the best kind of "strong" foods and the most suited to restoring lost energy. Energy supplements (often based on eggs and possibly on meat) were also foreseen among those foods that were subjected to brining, a form of "purification" regularly practiced in the monasteries, in accordance with medical doctrines of the time.

To estimate with any precision the size of food rations in medieval monasteries is probably a fruitless undertaking for various reasons: the variety of situations in time and space, the imprecision and insufficiency of numerical data sporadically provided by the documents, and the difficulty of relating actual parameters to the units of measure used locally (which varied from one to another—often a lot). It is primarily because of these oscillations that the calculations proposed by scholars resulted in divergent conclusions, often diametrically opposed. Some, like Rouche, thought they could describe foods that were extremely rich and abundant:[32] others, like Hocquet, drastically limited such values.[33] In reality, as demonstrated by Devroey,[34] the presumed theoretics about these calculations are all indemonstrable. Without taking into consideration that needs and consumption are historically variable data, whether from a biological or a cultural point of view, the legitimacy—above any other consideration—of measuring with the criteria of today the caloric needs of those men seems highly questionable, as it attributes to their foods the nutritional values of today's foods.

To avoid any "false precision," let us limit ourselves to pointing out that during the Middle Ages the members of monastic society appear to have been among the consumers best protected from the risk of hunger because they possessed ample resources and great managerial ability and because the tendency to eat and drink heavily, typical of the aristocratic society of the time for reasons of prestige, involved a good part of the monastic world—above all, in central and northern regions of Europe. Between the sixth and ninth centuries, daily rations in general were increased, and those determined in the 816 council of Aix (four pounds of bread and six pounds of wine per person) were judged "cyclopean" by the Lateran synod of 1059.[35] As for the proverbial opulence of the Cluny table, it assuredly did not arise out of the pure imagination of the "inimical" Bernard. Moreover, the primary attribute of abstinence and the incessant urging to mortification of the stomach would be incomprehensible without a widespread condition of well-being.

In conclusion, food is a way of making a community cohesive. To eat together in the refectory was one of the most significant moments in monastic solidarity, symbolic of belonging to a group. Only exceptional circumstances involved isolation. A sick person ate alone, whether as a hygienic precaution or so that the occasional diversity of his diet did not trouble the harmony of the group or perhaps arouse envy or scandal. A monk found guilty of some grave misdemeanor would eat alone, this being the first tangible sign of his "excommunication."[36] A monk who retreats into a temporary hermitic experience also would eat alone. All of these examples are seen culturally as exceptional and outside the norm: the monastic choice is preeminently a convivial choice.

Conversation (preferably not noisy) would seem to be a "natural" attribute of a meal. Plutarch devoted one of his famous "convivial questions" precisely to the subject of what is or is not proper to discuss while eating, which subjects are suited to the table and which are not.[37] Therefore, when medieval monastic rules imposed a strict observance of silence during meals, they came face to face with an anomaly, an unnatural norm that marked a difference between that table and "other" tables, between life in the monastery and life in the "world."

This was hardly a novelty. Already in the pagan world, silence was imposed by certain philosophers, like Pythagoras, on their disciples. Even in the Old Testament, there are numerous exhortations to limit speech. But it is, above all, with Christian monasticism that silence became central to daily life, both as a form of personal mortification and as an external sign of detachment from the habits of the world. Silence, considered an essential condition for meditation and the contemplative life, was imposed for most of the daylight hours; speech and conversation were allowed only for a few moments and only in a few specific places expressly designated for that purpose. The Benedictine Rule prescribes constant silence and, above all, at night and in the refectory—the "natural" place for words; only in this way does renunciation becomes meritorious to the highest degree.

To be silent in the face of food might seem a way of focusing on this gift of God, of appreciating and tasting it to the fullest. Not so: appreciation and enjoyment of food are part of the experience of monks but not of the ideology expressed in the regulations, which, on the contrary, recommend the maximum inattention at the table. Not by chance is the consumption of food always accompanied by edifying texts read aloud in the refectory. The Holy Scriptures, the homilies of the Church fathers, and the edifying lives of the martyrs and saints are a constant and almost obsessive reminder that the material food being consumed is nothing compared with the spiritual food of the word of God. One must therefore listen and be distracted from food; the mind must be used to detach oneself as much as possible so as to avoid the temptation of experiencing it as a pleasure instead of a simple bodily necessity.

In any case, not all monks (and perhaps very few) were inclined to endure the burden of silence. They consequently evolved strategies and stratagems to get around the problem: to maintain the duty of silence but at the same time to communicate. Is it possible to speak without speaking? Clearly, yes: there is no need for speech to speak. They invented signs of every kind—hand gestures, facial expressions, body movements—to tell each other what they wanted to say without disobeying the Benedictine Rule. With time, a veritable "language of silence"—a communication code endowed with its own rudimentary but precise dictionary and an elementary but efficient grammar—evolved. Initially, it had to be practiced secretly and illicitly (somewhat like signals between partners in card games), but later it was accepted as legitimate and was even set down in writing.[38]

We know that already by the beginning of the tenth century, in a monastery in Baume, there was a fixed system of signals that its abbot transmitted to the more famous monastery in Cluny. During the next century, such lists of "signs" seem to have been definitively fixed, so much so that they were listed among the *consuetudini*, the regulations set down from time to time by the abbots to complement the Benedictine Rule, which remained the principal reference for monastic life. A list compiled by the monk Bernard contains some three hundred "signs"; they have been found at Eynsham in England, Saint Jacques in Liège, Saint Victor in Paris (a community not of monks but of canons), and many other places. Even Cistercian monasteries developed their own particular gestural language, different from the traditional one at Cluny.

This did not go without opposition. Certain monastic orders (like the Carthusians) refused to adopt sign language, considering it indecorous and disrespectful. There is no dearth of scandalized description, such as that of Gerard of Cambrai, who, in 1180, visited the Benedictines of Canterbury and noticed that at mealtimes the most absolute silence reigned over the refectory but the monks were "conversing" animatedly among themselves. Gerard relates that he had the impression of being in the midst of a theatrical performance and remarks that the use of the lips would certainly have been more dignified than those ridiculous gesticulations.

What did those signs indicate? Primarily objects (foods, plants, animals, clothing, domestic utensils), a few actions (kneeling, confessing), and a few abstract notions (good, evil, anger, wisdom). Foods constituted the major part of the "dictionary" because there was the need to indicate them in all their varieties and also because the refectory was the place of greatest silence and yet at the same time the place where the need (as well as the desire) to speak was greatest: to select a food, ask for more, pass it on to others, and so on—perhaps also to comment on its quality.[39]

The criteria by which these signs were devised corresponded to certain fundamental models, starting with the rule of imitation: to translate the object visually, describe it with a gesture. For example, a fish was represented by an undulating movement of the hand, held vertically, with the fingers joined, "simulating with the hand the action of the fish's tail in water." The species of a fish was specified with an additional sign: for lamprey, it was suggested to "simulate with a finger on the jaw the spots that this fish has under its eyes." For cuttlefish, "separate the fingers and move them," imitating the movement of the animal in water. For trout, the direction was "to trace a sign with one finger from one eyebrow to the other," the sign for the female, it is specified, "because the female of this species has a band at that spot."

Not all "dictionaries" are in agreement. The pike in the Cluny text by Udalrico is imitated by its exceptional speed in the water, whereas in the text by Hirsau it is described with its typical "spatula-like" face. In every case, the directions reveal an alimentary culture that is attentive and informed (in spite of the ascetic premises of the choice of monastic life) and that possesses a precise and detailed knowledge of the animal and vegetable world. Surprisingly exhaustive catalogs follow one after the other in these texts, meticulously subdividing fish from poultry, vegetables from grains, and beverages from foods, extending all the way to pots, bowls, and jars.

In other instances, it is the specific function of the object that is reproduced. To indicate salt, the movement of the hand salting a food was used: "Join the ends of the fingers to the thumb and holding them together, move them two or three times separating them from the thumb as though sprinkling something with salt." To indicate walnuts, one made a gesture as though cracking them: "Sign of the walnut: stick a finger in your mouth and hold it between your teeth on the right side of the mouth as though you were cracking open a walnut with your teeth." For a pig, one made the gesture of slaughtering: "Hit your forehead with your fist, since that is the way it is killed."

From these few examples, the documentary interest of these "gestural dictionaries" is evident. In their evocation of the circumstances when foods were used or their external appearance, they apprise us of technical details we would otherwise not know. Gastronomic details are also revealed concerning the preparation of foods, such as the types of bread baking (in the oven, under embers, in water, in a frying pan), the various colors of wine, and the ways of cooking eggs. Complex dishes are indicated by their principal ingredients, as in the case of *fladones*, a savory pie with a filling of cheese and other things, typical of medieval gastronomy.[40] "Using the usual signs for bread and for cheese, bend all the fingers of one hand so as to form a cavity and place them on top of the other hand." This mimes the shape of a pie.

There are still other suggestions that allude to the social value of foods, to the symbolic function of their consumption more than to their material appearance. To indicate salmon or sturgeon ("noble" fish much prized in the Middle Ages), one must first make the "general" sign for fish and then add a second sign to indicate how exceptional it is: "Place your fist under your chin with the thumb raised." Indeed, "in this way one indicates arrogance, for it is above all the arrogant and the rich who eat these fish."

Dozens of signs like these offer us precious information about the alimentary and gastronomic culture of the Middle Ages, thanks, paradoxically, to the imposition of silence.

CHAPTER XV

The Pilgrim's Food

A HAGIOGRAPHIC TEXT of the tenth century relates the pilgrimage made to Rome by Odo, abbot of Cluny, along with a young monk, Giovanni, who would later become his biographer. In a passage in the *Life of Saint Odo*, we read that when the two were crossing the Alps on their return from Rome, an old peasant—*pauper*, in the Latin text—came alongside them, and on his back, he carried a sack containing food for his trip: bread, garlic, onions, and leeks. "Pious Odo," Giovanni writes, "no sooner saw that man than he invited him to sit on his horse and put his putrid sack on his own back. I could not bear the stench and moved away from them by falling behind." But the abbot called Giovanni back and said, "Alas, what this poor man eats nauseates you to the point of not tolerating the smell?" With these words, he shamed his disciple, "and by so doing," Giovanni concludes, "he cured my sense of smell."[1]

Beyond the edifying conclusion, this episode vividly illustrates a situation that must be clarified: he whom we commonly call "pilgrim" is an abstraction that should be replaced within concrete dimensions. A pilgrim is none other than a man, but all men are *not* equal—at least, that is how it was in the Middle Ages. There are no "men" in general; there are lords and peasants, monks and city dwellers, rich and poor, powerful and weak. And not all of them eat the same things. The monk Giovanni, accustomed to eating well, to refined smells and flavors, cannot bear the stench of garlic and onion that emanates from the sack of their chance fellow traveler. Therefore, a "pilgrim" does not exist in reality. There is a peasant pilgrim, a monk pilgrim, and a lord pilgrim, each one of whom eats what his social rank proposes or imposes in a world in which food was the principal means of manifesting class differences, prestige, wealth, and power. In medieval culture, there were foods that, by definition, possessed a "social status" of poverty. Greens, herbs, and root vegetables were seen as peasant foods, as opposed to such luxury foods as game and fruit which graced the lordly table.

Now that we understand the need to specify the social identity—and the alimentary identity as well—of the "pilgrim," we can say that when a traveler treads the roads to or from Rome or other sacred places of Christianity, whether on foot (like the *pauper* of our story) or on horseback (like the abbot who invites him to mount), his sack must contain foods that can keep for days or even weeks. This is the basic requirement that unites them, and it is for this reason that bread is the primary item in the traveler's equipment: dry bread, often very dry, to be eaten after being moistened with water or wine. But even when we speak of bread, we are, in fact, referring to products that are essentially quite different from one another. Peasant bread can be imagined as dark, made of inferior grains such as rye, millet, or spelt, basic products in a rural diet throughout the Middle Ages and even in later centuries. Only in the sack of well-heeled pilgrims can we find white bread made of wheat.[2] Other foods of long conservation to eat with bread are cold cuts, cheeses, and dried meats. For drinking, the pilgrim may have some water, but he certainly carries wine, the universal beverage of the Middle Ages, by far preferred to water (even though mixed with water) for reasons of hygiene: water was not always safe to drink, and when it was, it did not stay so for long.[3]

We should not imagine our pilgrim as one who ate only the food he carried on his shoulder. From time to time or even every day, he could stop somewhere for refreshment. Taverns and inns are not modern inventions; even the medieval pilgrim frequently came across them along his way.[4] There is a famous guide for pilgrims going to Santiago de Compostela that dates back to the twelfth century and contains detailed information not only about places of worship and prayer on their itinerary but also about where to sleep and eat.[5] Over the centuries, inns and taverns multiplied in the countryside and the cities. In some urban centers, the owners of such locales at times organized themselves into corporations and imposed statutes on themselves so as to fix rules of activity, modalities and prices of lodging, and types of food to offer travelers. A statute on the art of inkeeping was drafted in Florence in the fourteenth century.[6] Among the particularly delicate problems that its drafters faced was the relationship between the innkeepers and tavern keepers and the vendors of food: To what point was it permissible for the former to sell food to their guests, thereby placing themselves in competition with the shopkeepers? Many chapters of this statute dwell on the problem in order to arrive at an honorable compromise between the conflicting needs of the two categories.

The foods offered by innkeepers—like those that pilgrims carried with them—were either products that could last (bread, cold cuts, dried meat, and cheeses) or prepared dishes that could be quickly reheated or eaten cold, for quick and efficient service. Minestroni, made of vegetables and legumes, and stews were the principle dishes of this simple gastronomy of a clearly popular stamp. An example of such dishes is one for which a recipe appears in the fourteenth-century cookbook by the anonymous Tuscan, reprinted in the nineteenth century by the Bolognese scholar Francesco Zambrini. The recipe is for "jellied fish without oil": "Bring to a boil wine and vinegar, and cook well-rinsed fish in this; once cooked, take them out and place them in another container. Into the remaining vinegar and wine put onions cut crosswise in the amount of one-third the original quantity; then add saffron, cumin and pepper and pour it all on the cooked fish and let it cool. This is *schibezia da tavernaio* (*schibezia* in the manner of a tavern keeper).[7] This is a dish similar to the *carpione* still prepared in Italy, based on fish left to marinate in wine and vinegar after having been fried in oil. The name *schibezia*, of Arabic origin [the dish and the term, still in the Spanish repertory, known as *escabeche*], was not understood by Zambrini, who, in a note, associated it with *schifezza* (something disgusting), as though the writer of the cookbook had meant to define this as "a disgusting tavern dish."[8] This is evidently absurd, for had this been the writer's opinion, he would not have included the recipe.

What is interesting is that a cookbook written in a cultivated society and intended for an aristocratic audience should contain a "tavern keeper's" recipe in the text, a dish suitable for preparation in an inn as a dish that is always ready and at the disposal of travelers who want to eat in a hurry. Not really fast food, but, then, why not? If not the haste of a trip that always took a long time, then perhaps it was the urgency of hunger that asked for it. Significant here is the concurrence of poor food and rich food, road food and home (or court) food. From other sources, we know that no less than an emperor, Frederick II, was avid for this dish.[9]

A recipe "for pilgrims," explicitly defined as such, appears in another medieval Italian cookbook, written in the fifteenth century by Giovanni Bockenheim, a cook of German origin who worked at the court of Pope Martin V. (We should not be surprised by this because German cuisine was much appreciated in the Middle Ages, as French or Italian cuisine is today.) In his cookbook entitled *Registrum coquine* [*Register of cooking*], written between 1431 and 1435, Bockenheim included a broad bean soup for which he gives the following directions: "Take broad beans, rinse them well in hot water and let them soak overnight. Then boil them in cold water, chop them finely and add white wine. Season with onion, olive oil or butter, and a touch of saffron." This dish, he adds at the end, "is good for traveling clerics and pilgrims."[10] This is a strange attribution, like others that our author attaches to every recipe in the collection. The meaning is not easy to interpret, but what is clear is that these dishes of vegetables and greens represent an important part of what was available in the taverns and inns where travelers sought refreshment.

Aside from the food he brought with him or could find for payment in the taverns along the way, the pilgrim had a third option, which was free hospitality that many religious centers offered the traveler. What were called *xenodochia* in medieval documents were places for help and hospitality, largely run by monasteries and occasionally by churches and cathedrals. They were scattered all over Italy and Europe, and here, too, the pilgrim would have found ready-to-eat food, dried meats and preserved fish, cheeses, cold cuts, and bread. The monastic food model also tended to retrace the peasant model, simple and sober, even if here, as elsewhere, the usual signs of social difference were not absent: the abbot's table, at which the most important and high-ranking guests were seated, was separate and different from the common refectory served by its own kitchen. Even in monastic centers, poor pilgrims and rich pilgrims were treated differently. Nor could it be otherwise in a society like that of the Middle Ages, which conceived of food as the ultimate mark of diversity and privilege.

The hermitic community of Camaldoli, which was also prepared to receive and feed guests and pilgrims, regulated its internal life according to norms set down in writing by the abbots during the course of the twelfth century. In the *Liber eremiticae Regulae* we read, on the subject of wine, that the hermits do not drink wine, in theory, but that habit and the weakness of the body are reluctant to eliminate it completely.[11] It is thus admitted, with a few stipulations, that the brothers do drink occasionally, but moderately, and because they drink little, they consume only undiluted wine of excellent quality. Not always, however, does the wine meet this standard. It could be spoiled, sour, or moldy (*corruptum, acidum, macidum*). What to do in such cases? Simple: serve it to others, and for the hermits, find some more suitable wine.[12] This makes me think, with a touch of cynicism, that those "others" were first and foremost those poor pilgrims or, to put it more accurately, pilgrims who were poor.

CHAPTER XVI

The Table as a Representation
of the World

THAT THE DINING table is one of the best places for communication—perhaps the ideal place, where the desire to communicate with one's familiars is expressed with ease and freedom—is so evident and so readily observable in daily life that there is no need for historical confirmation. We shall therefore concern ourselves with the table not as a *place* but rather as a *means* of communication by analyzing some of the forms and modes with which this convivial ritual, this fundamental gesture that guarantees and celebrates daily survival, makes itself the bearer of all kinds of signs and meanings.

This is brought about by the *collective* dimension of this gesture, which for that alone acquires a linguistic and communicative content because every gesture enacts with others, in front of others, affecting its essential nature (in this case, eating), and enriching it with symbols and values of *circumstance*, as Barthes put it.[1] And given the fundamentality of the gesture in question, its primary importance deriving from the preservation of life, the symbols and values it projects are also of primary importance and intensity. The dining table, where life nourishes itself, becomes the perfect means for affirming (or negating) the meanings of life—in particular, those meanings that concern life with others, either confirming or, on occasion, revoking them. Above all, this kind of interpersonal dimension springs out of the convivial ritual, in view of the collective character of the gesture, which seems ingrained in human nature: "We," Plutarch has one of his characters say in his *Table Talk*, "do not invite one another merely to eat and drink, but to eat and drink together."[2]

The *convivio* (banquet table) is thus a metaphor for the identity of a group or of life together—literally, *cum vivere*.[3] Living together does not necessarily imply harmony of intentions or affections, as the reality and terminology of "convivial" are too often misunderstood. The banquet table, like life, is a neutral place where everything, and the contrary of everything, can take place; even tensions and conflicts find their ideal environment, not only because the banquet hall is technically the ideal place for assassinations and poisonings but also because it is metaphorically the most meaningful, the most resonant sounding board for amplifying everything that happens in the order of things and the relationships between people—separations and betrayals, no less than friendships and alliances. It is at the table, for example, that Mauro, son of a nobleman from Amalfi, is betrayed by Gisulfo, duke of Benevento: "At first Gisulfo treated him with honor . . . and had him eat with him. Then, he had him removed from the table and imprisoned in his room."[4]

Although the banquet table expresses the identity of the group, it also expresses, within that context, the underlying relations of strength and power. Further, it expresses the "difference" of those who are not invited. A metaphor of the community, of its internal harmonies and external relations, the banquet table is the place of inclusion, as well as exclusion. Expulsion from the communal table represents the first and most significant form of *excommunication* for the monk who is stained with wrongdoing. To eat in solitude, according to the Benedictine Rule, is a sign of guilt and a means of expiation.[5] For the layperson as well, "excommunication" involves solitude and exclusion from the communal table, and no one can eat with someone who has been excommunicated without himself incurring the same punishment. This, Odo of Cluny relates, is what happened to the King of England for having eaten with two Palatine counts who had been excommunicated by the bishop.[6]

No less evident are the power relations within the group that sits together at the banquet table, as already seen in the modality of participation at the communal table.[7] This can be the symbolic place of collective solidarity in which one participates by virtue of being a part of that group. We see this in the monastic community, in the ritual gatherings of lay corporations and confraternities, or even more simply, within the nucleus of the family, described by certain medieval documents as the collectivity of those who live "by the same bread and the same wine."[8]

In other cases, being at table together is the result of an invitation. Then a differentiating mechanism comes into operation that places on an unequal level the one who invites and the one who is invited. The significance of this gesture has diverse values—and even contrary ones. If the invitation is freely made—that is, voluntarily—it can place the guest in a situation of objective debt and thus of inferiority (a situation that rights itself with reciprocity or a counter-gift, common in the field of anthropology).[9] In this case, to invite people to one's own table is a sign of liberal generosity, of economic well-being, and in the final analysis, of power: an invitation is a gesture of self-affirmation and therefore all the more impressive as the number (or rank) of the people gathered around oneself increases. In the banquet hall of Emperor Frederick II, 18 people were received at his table on a regular basis, but another 162 were seated at tables in a smaller dining room nearby.[10] The table of Henry VI, who "defied the rule of numbers," was described by Pietro da Eboli in song.[11]

The significance of the gesture changes totally when the invitation is not voluntary but obligatory, indicating a situation of dependence, of social inferiority on the part of the host. Such is the meaning of the meals that many peasants were obliged to offer their lord or, more commonly, to his agents when they came to inspect the agricultural operations and the sharing of products, and to ensure correct payment of the rent. Once in a while, one comes across extraordinary documents, such as the lease drawn up in 1266 at Asti between two small farmers and a person significantly titled *dominus Pancia*, who requests the payment of two dinners for two as annual rent—one in January, the other in May—with a menu minutely described in the document.[12] But the more common payment of "donations" (obligatory, however), consisting of food and alimentary products, does not seem to have a different meaning. That, too, expresses an obligation of gratitude—in other words, a state of subordination and social inferiority. It is to this end that flat breads (*focacce*), chickens, and eggs were generally stipulated in agrarian contracts.[13]

The inherent symbolism of those offerings and those invitations, defined from time to time by precise rules of decoding, explains why medieval documentation is so rich in disputes over the payments of dinners and suppers, in which the core of the contention has less to do with furnishing one or two piglets to the presiding individual or institution than with the *significance* attributed to that payment: Was it voluntary or compulsory? A sign of power or subordination? A complicated affair of dinners required but not provided was at the origin of a quarrel in the twelfth century between the Bishop of Imola and the head of the city's cathedral.[14] The monks and canons of the cathedral of Saint Ambrose in Milan were involved in a similar conflict.[15] Yet another dinner was disputed by the priors and clerics of the church of Saint Nicholas in Bari, as we know from an inquest conducted in 1254. Traditionally, priors offered canons a *convivium* (banquet) right inside the church.[16] In the relation between persons or (in these cases) interested parties, the meaning attributed to the offering of food or to the invitation to dine was the decisive factor, and the judges called in to settle the differences found themselves faced with delicate exegetic problems, resolved after careful examination of witnesses.

Social hierarchy and rights of precedence were manifested scenically in the banquet hall and in the arrangement of the tables mounted on trestles that could be set up or removed as needed. Generally kept separated, the tables could be placed side by side to group guests of the same rank and social equality, according to precise convivial logistics. Even in monastic customs, the most decidedly "democratic" in imposing an egalitarian dimension on the refectory, the abbot eats at a separate table in the company of occasional guests who are only provisionally allowed to be part of the group.[17] Around each table, the assignment of places took on significance based on the greater or lesser proximity to the head of table (meaning the man in power), represented through theatrical staging: the elongated rectangular shape of the table, as seen in the iconography, characteristic of the medieval table, lent itself well to designating the central position of the *dominus* (or the special guest) at the center of the long side. We know, for example, about the ceremonial complexity at the court of Byzantium that ruled over placement at the table, determined by the position and prestige of the individual.[18] And we know about the resentment of Liutprando, bishop of Cremona and ambassador of Emperor Otto I, on seeing himself seated at the fifteenth position, much too far (in his view) from the sovereign.[19]

Dante Alighieri apparently had an experience of this kind when he went to Naples to see King Uberto, as Giovanni Sercambi relates in one of his novellas. The king, eager to have the famous poet as his guest so as "to see and hear his good judgment and brilliance," invited him to court. When Dante arrived, he was "dressed in the most ordinary clothes, as only a poet can." It was precisely the hour of dinner, "and having washed their hands and gone to the table, the king and the other barons took their seats, and Dante was finally placed at the end of the table," which is to say the seat farthest from the king. Offended by such mistreatment (although the king, seeing his grubbiness, never imagined it could be Dante), the poet ate his portion and "immediately left . . . to return to Tuscany." The king, after some time at the table, asked for Dante and wanted to know why he had not presented himself; he was told it was that grubby individual at the end of the table who had already left in haste.

Distressed by the confusion, the king sent a servant after him; finding Dante not far off, the servant handed him a letter of excuse. Turning around, Dante returned to Naples, but this time he presented himself to the king "dressed in a splendid robe." Uberto "at dinner had him placed at the head of the first table, right beside him." As the food and wine began to arrive, the poet astounded the noble company with his bizarre behavior. "Taking the meat, he rubbed it all over his clothes, and the wine as well. 'That one must be a ruffian,' commented the king and the barons, seeing him pour wine and broth on his clothes. The king said to Dante, 'What is it that I have seen you do? For someone presumed to be so wise, how could you do such ugly things?'" Dante's reply, at this point foreseeable, was a severe moral admonishment: "Your majesty, I am cognizant of this great honor that you bestowed, but you bestowed it on my clothes. I therefore wanted them to enjoy the dishes that were served." There was general embarrassment, but the king recognized the supreme honesty and sagacity of the poet "and honoring him, made him remain at court so as to hear more from him."[20]

Even serving dishes contributed to expressing prestige and power: utensils and dishes of great value distinguished the royal and princely table from the common one. Not wood or pewter or earthenware (the last being the most widely used material at that time for table service[21]) but gold and silver were displayed on lordly tables, along with precious glass and crystal. The idea was to impress the guest, overwhelm him, subjugate him with the host's wealth. The banquets of Roger II "inspire admiration in the other princes"[22] (a noteworthy pairing of two seemingly incongruous terms: an "admiration" that is "inspired," like awe or fear). In fact, those who reclined at the table (the term *discumbere*, used here by the chronicler, seems to indicate the retention, still in the twelfth century at least in the kingdom of Sicily, of the Roman custom of reclining while eating, generally abandoned in the early centuries of the Middle Ages) were astonished by the abundance and variety of foods and beverages and by the "incredible opulence of the service": everyone was served in "cups or plates of gold and silver"; even the servants were luxuriously dressed in pure silk.

The mania of ostentation could extend to the kitchen as well. Roger of Wendover wrote that Empress Isabella (sister of Henry III of England, third wife of Frederick II of Sweden) had not only goblets for wine and plates of purest gold and silver but also—and this is what was most shocking, excessive, and to say the least, superfluous—cooking utensils made of precious materials: "all the pots, large and small, were made of purest silver."[23]

Even at the most sumptuous of tables, wine cups and eating utensils were never intended to be used by only one person but by at least two at the same time. Cups were passed from hand to hand;[24] bowls (for liquid foods) and cutting boards (for solid foods) were placed between two guests. None of this can be interpreted as a shortage of utensils in view of the fact that this was common to the tables of both the very rich and the very poor. Rather, we may discern in this once again the expression of the sense of community (sharing food as a means of and a metaphor for living together) that deeply permeated medieval culture. This indisputable fact gave rise to so many comic episodes in the fiction of the thirteenth and fourteenth centuries, in which the seating side by side of incompatible guests, of differing behavior at the table (different speeds of consumption, different abilities to swallow hot foods), led to occasions of unwelcome fasting for the less vigorous and audacious.[25]

There were, however, rules of etiquette that imposed a certain uniformity on dining behavior. European literature, especially at the start of the thirteenth century, produced numerous manuals of "good manners" that instructed gentlemen (and ladies) and their offspring how to behave at the table.[26] One should not wipe one's hands on one's clothes but on the tablecloth (napkins having yet to be invented); one should wipe one's mouth before drinking (also out of respect for the dining companion who drinks out of the same receptacle); one should not slurp from the plate, not bite into bread and then put it back in the basket, not put one's fingers into sauces, not spit or pick one's nose, and not clean one's teeth with the point of a knife—these and other rules came to be set down and codified for the primary reason of raising a boundary, fencing in a protected area of privilege and power by distinguishing its usages from those "outside" of it. And those "outside" meant peasants, the "rustics" who precisely then, from the thirteenth century on, began to be considered and designated as the negative pole of an urban or aristocratic society that became increasingly more rigid about its privileges and separateness.[27]

"Good manners" (urbane and courtly) were the formal means of this process of enclosure, and the table, once again, serves as the locus of identity and exclusion. The increasing formality of the convivial ritual did not, however, eliminate the physical, material dimension of the relationship with food typical of medieval sensibility. An example is the diffidence toward the fork, seen only exceptionally on the tables of the period; the hands were long preferred, thereby assuring a direct, tactile contact with food.[28] In this instance the books of good manners limit themselves to suggesting the use of only three fingers, not the whole hand, "as peasants are wont to do."[29]

During the high Middle Ages, rules of dining behavior were established within the monastic society for the purpose, here, too, of defining and marking its own identity and a lifestyle different from that of "others." Particularly important is the Benedictine vow of silence,[30] to be practiced at all times in daily life and thus also during meals. This would seem unnatural for a place (the table) that is geared by its very nature to discussion and communication. But it is precisely this that reveals the will to remove oneself from the world and its logic, to remain outside the noise of the worldly banquet[31] so as to establish another kind of communication, with God and with the divine teaching that one receives from the readings during meals. Not to speak, but to listen—this is a model of behavior that even a man as powerful as Charlemagne imitated, according to his biographer Eginardo,[32] having Augustine's *City of God* read to him at the table (at other times, it would seem he preferred the deeds of legendary heroes, such as those of King Arthur,[33] which he is said to have loved). As for the monks, it is amazing to see how the rule of silence led to the invention and codification of a gestural language entrusted to the hands, the tongue, the eyes, and to some degree, the whole body to describe and indicate (while respecting the rule) all the foods and dishes that appeared on the table and could become a subject of discussion.

This we learn from the *consuetudini* of the abbey at Cluny dating from the eleventh and twelfth centuries.[34]

Even the quality and forms of food provided the motivation for communicating during meals. If the monastic diet can be characterized primarily by its renunciation of meat (for the most part), the substitute foods—vegetables, cheese, eggs, and above all, fish—became its symbol. To eat fish or in any case to give up meat during Lent and fast days was not so much a gastronomic humiliation (there is ample documentation on the opulent banquets built around fish that were enjoyed by the ecclesiastic hierarchy throughout the Middle Ages) as it was a sign of identification with a very specific religious community. The practice of fasting (in the technical sense that medieval precepts gave to the term, meaning to eat once during the day, after sunset) was imposed on everybody during certain liturgical celebrations and on the monks during extended periods of the year as well. "Witnesses affirm that he did not fast when the king was fasting"—this explains how, according to an Arab chronicle of the twelfth century, it was possible to recognize that the emir of Palermo, Filippo di Mahdia, "was really a Muslim" and why the Norman King Roger II had him condemned to the stake.[35]

Beyond these very general images, it was the nature and quality of individual foods that determined the social identity of the person who consumed and offered them. Durable foods (dried meat and fish, cheese, and products like grains, legumes, or chestnuts that can last throughout the year) necessarily had a "poor" image that evoked the problem of survival. Fresh foods (meat, fish, and fruit) suggested instead images of luxury. Another important differentiating element was seasonal food and local food (the great myth of present-day culture), which the Middle Ages tended instead to devalue, seeing them as a mark of poverty or, at the very least, of mediocre normalcy. While ordering for his sovereign the best products of every region, Cassiodoro, minister of Theodoric, king of the Ostrogoths, observes in a letter that "the opulence of the royal table is of not inconsiderable importance to the State since it is thought that the master of the house is only as wealthy as the rare dishes on which one dines at his table. Only the common subject is satisfied with what the territory provides. The table of a prince must offer all kinds of things and arouse amazement merely to look at it."[36]

The ability to bring together on one's own table foods from various sources was therefore an important indication of wealth and power. Noteworthy is a passage from John of Salisbury, who condemned the excessive ostentation of the tables of his time (with quotations from Macrobius and ancient anecdotes), in which he described a visit he made to Puglia—probably between 1144 and 1156 in the retinue of Pope Adrian IV—and a dinner to which he was invited by someone identified only as "a rich man from Canosa." He apparently kept his guests at the table from three in the afternoon until six the next morning, drowning them in foods from every part of the Mediterranean: "delicacies from Constantinople, from Babylon, Alexandria, Palestine, Tripolitania, from Berber regions, Syria, Phoenicia"—as though (John remarks) Sicily, Calabrua, Puglia, and Campania were not enough to enlighten a "sensitive guest."[37]

It was not only through the substance of food that the language of power and wealth was transmitted. Equally important were the forms in which it was presented, the "gastronomic architecture" that constituted the inevitable complement of convivial architecture. However, the medieval period was not yet the era of the dazzling scenic inventions, of the astounding creations that amazed the guests of princely courts[38] between the fifteenth and sixteenth centuries, transferring to the realm of spectacle a large part of the convivial experience, alternating between visual illusions and gustatory deceptions. Nevertheless, here, too, there was no lack of attention to the forms and theatricality of the food. One need only recall the "armed castrato," a large ram or billy goat slowly cooked on a spit and then "decorated" with sausages woven around the horns before being served "on a great table." This is a recipe from a fifteenth-century cookbook, compiled in southern Italy.[39]

The special attention given to color in the preparation of dishes is made clear in these texts. Also noteworthy is how the chromatic concerns of medieval cooking, unlike those of today, developed autonomously in the art of flavors. If the color of a food is understood today to be a proof of its freshness and its "nature," in the Middle Ages, on the contrary, the food was "colored" with foreign substances to give it an artificial and almost unnatural appearance. Various ingredients (above all, herbs and spices) were used to color foods, and many sauces that accompanied meat dishes were known by their color: white sauce, camelline sauce (from its characteristic camel color), green sauce, black pepper sauce, and many others, for which the cookbooks offer numerous recipes.[40]

Directions are often quite explicit: "color with the yolk of an egg" in the recipe for a meat pasty;[41] "color with saffron [*colora del safferano*]" in the recipe for the broth known as "martino";[42] "color with saffron [*colora de zaffarno*]" in the recipe for a pasty of lamprey;[43] "color with saffron" for a pasty of shrimp;[44] and for an herb pie, "give it color and as much saffron as you can [*dalli colore et çaffarano al meio che poy*]."[45] The taste for yellow (achieved by extensive use of egg yolk and saffron and by techniques of frying and browning) made a clamorous return in the cookbook of Maestro Martino, which speaks of "coloring" yellow a great many dishes[46] and constitutes a distinguished treatise on medieval gastronomy, a kind of gastronomic companion piece to the golden backgrounds so typical of the painting of that period. The origin of this kind of predilection was the solar image of gold, symbol of an indestructible eternity,[47] an image that was normally realized by alternative products because gold, even more than inedible, was unattainable by most. In fact, real gold was used at times in the preparation of food, and we know how the search for that "potable gold" was central to the work of alchemists.[48] Still today there are cooks who like to adorn their dishes with gold leaf (risotto alla milanese topped with a leaf of gold is one of the history-making dishes of Gualtiero Marchesi, the most famous Italian chef of the twentieth century).

Along with yellow, there was also much use of white, symbol of purity,[49] particularly indicated for Lenten foods. To some degree, all colors appeared on the table in a multicolored play about which I would like to offer a final example, the tricolored Lenten pie made of almonds, ground and boiled, divided into three parts; mint, parsley, and marjoram (accounting for green) are added to the first part, saffron to the second, and white sugar to the third.[50] Among the colors most common to us today, the rarest on the medieval table was assuredly red, which finally gained recognition because of the popularity of tomato sauce—but not before the eighteenth and nineteenth centuries.[51]

Manners of cooking and preparation also contributed to accenting this "unnatural" character of medieval cuisine, against which the moralists railed, invoking frugality and simplicity. John of Salisbury, mentioned earlier, deplored the custom of stuffing the meat of one animal with the meat of another so as to render it unrecognizable by the smell—a technique, John reminds us, already in use in the Roman era with the *porcus troianus* (meaning a pig stuffed with other meats, recalling the Trojan horse). But at least, he remarks, at the time of the Romans, people were amazed by such inventions, served only exceptionally, whereas today they seem to have become the norm and no one is surprised by them any longer: "many things that no longer amaze us, because they have been used and abused, aroused admiration and astonishment in our ancestors: the Trojan pig, today domesticated."[52]

In conclusion, the decisive moment in the convivial framework for defining and representing the structures of power is the division and distribution of food. As is known, both the Celtic-Germanic tradition and the Greco-Roman tradition attributed fundamental importance to the portioning of meat.[53] The quality of the cuts assigned to guests (the appreciation and rules varying with the culture) served to recognize the hierarchy between individual guests, whether confirming it, destabilizing it, or overturning it. The acquisition of the "best piece" was often at the heart of furious contests of power, regularly acted out in the banquet hall with a more than evident symbolic and metaphoric finality.[54] No less important (especially in Celtic and Germanic traditions) was the quantitative aspect of the challenge: power fell to the one who could eat the most, the one who, by ingurgitating enormous quantities of food, succeeded in demonstrating his purely physical and animal superiority over his peers.[55]

Medieval culture is deeply ingrained with this tradition. The image of the powerful one who eats a lot (who eats a lot because he is powerful and is powerful because he eats a lot) permeates the literature and is also seen, in contrast, in the obsessive insistence of monastic views on the need to humble oneself by moderating the appetite. In the high Middle Ages, the primordial image of the powerful man as one who eats and drinks more than others, thereby demonstrating his strength and legitimizing his position of power, appears to have been extremely vivid and active. An example is the episode of Guido, duke of Spoleto, who, according to Liutprando of Cremona, was rejected as king of the Franks because it was discovered that he ate little.[56] In this perpetuation of the anthropological significance of food as a sign of power in a society dominated by the fear of hunger, important modifications took place over the course of time.

Later, the quantitative aspects of consumption in this "dietetics of power" partially disappeared (although present in chivalric literature), increasingly replaced by a qualitative character: how to select food, distinguishing between refined food and rustic food, seems to have been an essential part of noble behavior as it developed in courtly ethics.[57] Exquisite wines and pure white bread, delicate meats and perfumed Oriental spices[58] created a new idea of luxury, no longer determined by the priority of quantity. Quite the contrary, we come across a figure like that of Frederick II, who, to maintain his health, ate abstemiously and only once a day. And it should be mentioned, to emphasize the irreligious character of the emperor, that he did this for his body, not his soul: "not for divine reward but to preserve his physical health," as pointed out by Johann von Winterthur.[59] No one would have written anything like that about Charlemagne. A prisoner of the social customs and obligations of his culture, Charlemagne would never have allowed himself to be concerned about his health; though suffering from gout, he continued to load his table with enormous quantities of spit-roasted meats.[60]

The concept of heavy eating did not disappear entirely. Let us say that with the passage of time it changed meaning, placing itself more on the level of potentiality than of reality. No longer a matter of enormous consumption, the new way of showing off power in noble society during the early and high Middle Ages was to provide a great variety of food on one's own table, lavishly offered to the largest possible number of guests. We might say, paraphrasing Bloch, that the progressive transformation of the ruling class from a de facto nobility to a de jure nobility[61] found its perfect correlative in eating styles: even heavy (and good) eating transformed itself in a way from a de facto reality into a de jure reality. The concept thus underwent a change: a man of power was not someone who eats a lot (who can and must eat a lot) but someone who has the right to eat a lot—that is, to have many kinds of food at his disposal. At that point, the question of the right to eat—more immutable and inviolable as the nobility became closed within itself and stood on its own privilege—may no longer have corresponded to reality. A lord in the late Middle Ages was no longer necessarily a great eater but more than anything a great director who manifested his power in convivial spectacles during which food was indeed eaten—but most of all looked at.[62]

The *right* to eat (which replaced the *obligation* to eat) in the society of the late Middle Ages was expressed in forms increasingly stereotyped and ritualistic. The *Ordinacions* of Peter IV of Aragon (1344) prescribed that each guest at the table of the king be served in keeping with his status: "since in serving it is proper that certain persons be honored above others in accordance with the level of their status, we want that in our platter there be enough food for eight; food for six will be placed in the platter for the royal princes, archbishops, and bishops; food for four, in the platters of other prelates and knights who sit at the king's table."[63] In the nineteenth century, at the Bourbon court of Naples, a similar dining code was still observed: during the reign of Ferdinand IV, the king could have ten courses, the queen six, and the princes four.[64]

At the beginning of the fourteenth century, the progressive rigor of standards of consumption as the status symbol of noble privilege found expression in "sumptuary" laws, aimed at defining alimentary and dining models of the different social classes and confining them within a predetermined scheme.[65] The prohibition against exceeding certain limitations on the number of guests, courses, and dishes was always justified by such moral motivations as the condemnation of waste and the recommendation of moderation in consumption. What nonetheless remained substantive was the desire to normalize lifestyles, to prevent behavior unsuited to the "obligations" of one's social status and disrespectful of hierarchies. For this, above all, excessive manifestations of wealth and of power centered on food and dress were condemned and prohibited.

For example, the *Ordinationes generales et speciales*, proclaimed in 1308 in Messina by Frederick III, prohibited public banqueting (*generalia convivia*) for weddings—that is, transforming a perfectly legitimate celebration into a pretext for forging agreements and alliances in the midst of a family event. During the period of a wedding, Frederick decreed, one could organize a banquet to last only one day, exclusively for first- and second-generation relatives of the bridal couple and for those who came from distant places.[66] Another law prohibited all functionaries and local representatives of the monarchy ("counts, barons, soldiers, squires") from entertaining guests "from outside the territory of their residence," which would indicate their intention to enlarge their own legitimate sphere of influence. In addition, the cost of a banquet could not exceed one-third of their daily budget.[67]

Restrictive laws of this kind reveal the tendency on the part of the ruling classes to construct and consolidate relations of fealty and alliance around festive tables, in accordance with an anthropological model that surely recalls the primordial image of the leader who, after having accumulated loot and riches, redistributes them to his men, thereby legitimizing the power invested in him. The same principle of redistribution, transposed by Christian culture into a moral and religious key, reappears in the exhortation to the rich and powerful to practice charity, a genuine social obligation expressed first and foremost in the form of meals and food offered to the poor, immediately perceptible in its symbolic signifi-cance.[68] To feed the *pauperes* (in the dual medieval sense of "weak" and "indigent" and with all the ambiguity possible in a culture that identified as "professionally poor" a large segment of the ecclesiastic and monastic corps) was a duty that no person of power could neglect. Moreover, it assured the salvation of the soul, and from that point of view, the needy were the best possible medium for establishing a cordial relationship with heaven. This accounts for the provisions, in the life or death of testators, to feed a certain number of poor people at a given festivity or anniversary; the richer and more powerful the donor, the more gener-ous he was obliged to be. A chronicler relates that in 1233 Frederick II magnificently celebrated his own birthday in the public square of San Germano: "more than five hundred poor people ate and were well sated with bread, wine, and meat."[69]

In connection with the idea of the poor as a possible key to heaven., we must look at ethnographic and anthropological studies, focused on southern Italy, that set apart the figure of the poor person (a weak link and marginal factor in the social order) as the "vicar of the dead," mean-ing the image and counter-image of the dead, and thus a means of mak-ing contact with their world.[70] From this, it would be easy to arrive at the theme of the funeral banquet, the meal to honor the dead, perhaps even set up at their tomb as a means of communicating with them and as the symbolic representation of the uninterrupted solidarity and identity of the group.[71]

Even in the case of charity to the poor, the fundamental notion of food as a mark of social and economic identity remained operative. In the already cited *Ordinacions*, Peter of Aragon states that all leftovers should be given to the poor. "Whenever wine spoils in our cellar . . . the cellarer dili-gently offers it to our alms."[72] And again, "when bread in our bakery hap-pens to go bad . . . the baker makes a point of solicitously getting it to our charity," along with bread left over from dinner.[73] Also, "every time fruit and cheese go bad they are immediately distributed to the almoners."[74] Moreover, the Rule of the Camaldoli monks had already established that spoiled, acidy, or moldy wine was not to be served in the refectory but should go to outsiders: to the poor and pilgrims stopping by.[75]

The "poor" thus also had a place, and one of primary importance, in this game of abundance and ostentation—not only because they themselves were the means and the object but also because their poverty (a social and economic situation that was so widespread it could be called "normal") constituted the only true motive for which a rich and generous table could be the site and symbol of privilege and power. The system was structurally integrated in its contrasting elements: only a situation of widespread hunger (or precarious conditions of life) could justify so intense and so deep a symbology of food. The "poor" themselves shared the culture of abundance and ostentation: that is, the *real* poor, not those who, having made a profession of poverty, could allow themselves to sublimate values and to choose renunciation, abstinence, and hunger as the ideal model of life. The *real* poor—whose alimentary style so many monks and hermits and bards of joyful poverty pretended to re-create for themselves—aspired instead to fill their bellies, and as copiously as possible, conforming in every way to the model of the way the powerful ate.

Only for the latter was abundance a daily practice; for the poor it was a dream, an exceptional event. The Land of Cockaigne, that great popular myth of full bellies and sated appetites that spread throughout Italy and all of Europe in the early twelfth century,[76] was the utopian obverse of a frustrated wish, the mirage of an oasis to which only a few were allowed access, whereas most were excluded. The poor also shared the culture of abundance, elevating it to their favorite dream and in some cases translating it into reality when certain recurring rituals (Christmas, Easter, the feast of a patron saint, a family wedding) imposed on the celebration the plenty and ostentation that characterized the daily banquets of princes. In medieval culture it was indeed the abundance of food that distinguished a holiday, as though it were a propitiatory gesture to exorcize the fear of hunger (but the subject has a broader and more general meaning).

The same ecclesiastic culture (which for a long time regarded the food miracle—or more precisely, the proliferation of food—as one of the important signs of sainthood) saw in the festive banquet a logical and symbolic priority that took precedence over any other form of celebration. Most of the gifts of food or meals offered to monasteries and churches were on the occasions of major religious holidays. Monastic laws and ecclesiastic precepts rigorously forbade practices of fasting or abstinence on feast days,[77] and there is no room for doubt about this.

When Christmas happened to fall on a Friday, the disciples of Saint Francis (as related by Tommaso da Celano in the second biography of the saint) heatedly discussed among themselves whether to give precedence to the obligation of abstaining from meat and of moderate eating on Fridays or to the obligation of celebrating the recurring holiday of Christmas with a generous banquet. In their uncertainty, they turned to their master and sent Brother Morico to ask the question. "You are sinning, brother," was the brusque reply of Francis, "to call the day the Child was born for us [a day of abstinence]. On a day like that I would like even the walls to eat meat, but since that is not possible, let them at least be spread with it." Francis, the biographer continues, "wanted poor people and beggars to be fed to satiety by the rich, and oxen and donkeys to be given a more generous portion of food and hay than usual." And once, it seems, he said to his companions, "If I could speak to the emperor I would beg him to decree by a general edict that all who have the means should scatter wheat and grain on the streets so that on a day of such celebration the birds, and particularly our sister larks, have food in abundance."[78] The particular devotion that Francis felt for Christmas made him want to set a great banquet in which all men, rich and poor, could take part along with the animals, the birds in the air, and the walls of the houses, were it possible.

CHAPTER XVII

The Fork and the Hands

CUTLERY IS NOT a necessity. Many people in many parts of the world prefer taking food with their hands, thereby enjoying a more direct, immediate, physical rapport with it. During the Middle Ages, this was the custom in Europe as well, but a new table culture slowly grew, a new way of perceiving the relations between diners and food and between diners themselves.

The first manuals of etiquette, which appeared in the thirteenth century in various European countries, took for granted that the only utensil available was the spoon, used for liquid foods. This was the only utensil deemed indispensable for obvious practical reasons. A knife and large fork served to cut meat on the common cutting board but not as individual utensils. The medieval diner was imbued with a deeply ingrained collective sense, and that is how one must interpret the practice of using the same utensils, the same drinking cups, and the same board or platter on which food was placed (as a rule, serving at least two people).

There may have been a few exceptions: an eleventh-century miniature portrays a great lord with a fork in hand (but this was probably the common fork, shared with the dining companion sitting opposite him).[1] In the same century, Pier Damiani refers to the strange custom of a Byzantine princess whom he met in Venice, who "did not touch food with her hands . . . but raised it to her mouth with a small two-tined fork"[2]— an exception indeed at that time.

The hands were the real players in the alimentary performance, and it was to the correct use of the hands that twelfth-century manuals on etiquette devoted their attention; for example, they insist on the use of only three fingers to grasp food—not five, like "rustics." This is the origin of the special importance given to cleaning the hands before a meal: "I hear it said about many people," relates a text on *Hofsucht* (manners) compiled in thirteenth-century Germany and attributed to someone by the name of Tannhäuser, "that they are wont to eat without having washed. If that is true, I find it disgusting, and may their fingers be paralyzed!"[3]

As for utensils, the only rules concern the use of the spoon. "*No sorbiliar dra boca quand tu mangi con cugial* [do not suck through the mouth when you eat with a spoon]" is the sixteenth of the *De quinquaginta curialitatibus ad mensam* [Fifty table manners] by the Milanese writer Bonvesin de la Riva, who lived between the thirteenth and fourteenth centuries. Also, "Do not slurp when eating with a spoon," for "the man or woman who sputters between spoonfuls behaves like an animal."[4] As for the *Hofsucht* mentioned above, it declares that "a man of nobility should not share a spoon with another person."[5] This is a noteworthy injunction, as it reveals a cultural change taking place, a desire to put greater emphasis on the identity of the individual and the distance between guests. This "privatizing" also increases the distance between guest and food with the technical aid of individual utensils: first, the multiplication of spoons and then the appearance of forks.

Aside from these cultural movements, reasons of practicality must also have favored the introduction of individual forks. If they appeared earlier in Italy than elsewhere, it is perhaps because of certain alimentary uses—in particular, pasta, which, already in the late Middle Ages, characterized Italian gastronomy as compared with that of the other side of the Alps.[6] It is true that in the eighteen and nineteenth centuries Neapolitan "macaroni-eaters" were still portrayed in paintings and prints holding in their hands spaghetti just purchased from street vendors. But in general, spaghetti and macaroni require utensils, especially if hot (as they should be), well buttered (as was the usage in the Middle Ages), and covered with grated cheese. It is thus not by mere chance that one of the oldest literary references to the fork involves a pasta eater: the already mentioned Noddo d'Andrea, who, in one of the *Trecentonovelle* [Three hundred stories] by Franco Sacchetti, "starts to take up the macaroni, surround it with his mouth and wolf it down." Noddo was famous for the speed with which he managed to ingest food, even when boiling hot. In fact, he had already swallowed six mouthfuls of that "scorching macaroni," while his table companion "still had his first mouthful on his fork."[7]

Other documents attest, fortuitously for the most part, to the spread of a new "culture of cutlery" in twelfth- and thirteenth-century Europe. For example, the Franciscan Guillaume de Rubruk, when describing the eating habits of the Tartars (among whom he had been on a diplomatic mission for the King of France), comments on the way they distributed pieces of mutton to guests "with the tip of a knife or with a fork . . . similar to those we use to eat pears and apples cooked in wine."[8]

It is therefore toward the end of the Middle Ages that cutlery makes its entrance into table customs, albeit discontinuously and with important regional differences in usages and in choices. In the treatise *De civiltate morum puerilium* (1526–30), Erasmus of Rotterdam does not mention the fork at all but limits himself to evoking the rules of using the hands according to medieval tradition: "Country people plunge their hands into sauces"; "It is uneducated to dig one's hands into the bottom of a plate"; "Whatever you cannot take with three fingers you would do well to leave in the plate."[9] A few decades later the French writer Calviac dedicated a page of his treatise on good manners (*Civilité*) to the diversity of habits in each country, with the warning that precisely because of that diversity, "the boy [to whose education the treatise is dedicated] will have to conform to the place and manners of those among whom he finds himself." In particular, he singles out in Europe a region of the spoon (more conservative) and a region of the fork (more innovative)—Germany and Italy, respectively: "Germans use spoons for eating soups and all liquid dishes," whereas Italians prefer the fork whenever possible. France was seen as a region of mediation between the two cultures: "The French use the one and the other [spoon and fork] according to which one seems better suited and more convenient for them." Calviac goes on: "Italians in general prefer to have one knife for each person. Germans consider it so important that they are very annoyed if their knife is taken or is requested by others. The French, on the contrary, for an entire table of diners use two or three knives without seeing any problem if it is asked for or taken, and proffer them when requested."[10]

Naturally, we are dealing here with elite customs. During his trip to Italy in 1581, Michel de Montaigne did not come across many knives on the tables where he was a guest. Only in Rome, at the table of the Cardinal of Sens, was "each person offered a towel to wipe his hands [after washing them], and to those to whom they wish to pay special honor, seated beside or opposite the master of the house, they present large squares of silver that bear a salt-cellar. . . . On top of that is a napkin folded in four; and on that napkin, bread, a knife, a fork, and a spoon."[11]

Among the dining customs of the sixteenth century, still of great importance—for reasons similar and contrary to those that slowed the spread of individual cutlery—were the large knives and forks with which the "carver" divided and apportioned meats: the office of carver was one of great ceremonial and political significance, around which a veritable art developed, as the carver was equipped with differentiated and sophisticated instruments like those shown in Bartolomeo Scappi's *Opera* (1570) or, in even more detail, in *Trinciante* by Vincenzo Cervio (1581).

Between the sixteenth and seventeenth centuries, the increasing presence of individual cutlery and plates ran parallel to the growth of an individualistic mentality, which bourgeois culture was largely responsible for spreading. The distress caused by this change—cultural even more than technical—was apparent first among such nostalgic representatives of the "old order" as the Marquis de Coulanges, who shortly after the middle of the seventeenth century wrote these heartfelt verses: "Once, soup was eaten from a common bowl without ceremony, and often one wiped the spoon on the boiled hen. Then, one often dipped one's fingers and bread into the stew. Today, everybody eats soup in his own plate; one has to serve oneself politely with a spoon and a fork, and from time to time a servant goes and washes them at the buffet."[12]

The lament over those great days, when one could *feel* food with one's hands and when fingers were dipped into the sauce (this brings to mind "Efemeride" by Ausonio, who told his cook to "shake the scalding pots, quickly stick your fingers into the boiling sauce and lick them with a wet tongue, rolling it back and forth"[13]), has a primarily social and political flavor. What is mourned is not so much the way one ate as the period in which the aristocracy was solidly in power, with its traditional values of pedigree, of clan, and of family cohesion. What is noteworthy is that all this appears in treatises on convivial behavior, recalling the robust physicality of a relationship with food that mirrors perfectly the virile and war-like culture of ancient nobility. Cultures are slow to die, as demonstrated by the voices of dissent, which even in Italy—the country earliest to be conquered by the fork—were raised against the use of the new utensils.

Most interesting is the testimony from the latter half of the seventeenth century of Vincenzo Nolfi, author of a book of etiquette for ladies that includes a chapter entitled "*Del ritrovarsi a banchetto* [On finding oneself at a banquet]." After having reminded his readers that "liquid dishes such as soups, broths and the like . . . are eaten with a spoon," he concedes that other dishes, meaning solid foods, can be taken up with a fork. In every instance, however, he regards it preferable "for the fingers to bring [food] gently to the mouth," and he expresses the opinion that by then the fork had had its day because "the hands of a person are less disgusting than a piece of silver."[14] Nolfi's point of view would have little future, but it nonetheless indicates the persistent hostility to utensils mediating between food and mouth and to their "taste of metal."

Eighteenth-century manuals of etiquette expatiate in minute detail on the way to handle spoons, forks, and knives. "When spoons, forks or knives are dirty, or greasy, it is unpleasant to lick them and not at all acceptable to clean them with the tablecloth," we read in the French text by La Salle (1729). Further: "When the plate is dirty avoid scraping it with the spoon or the fork to clean it, or cleaning it with the fingers" (making clear the equation fingers/utensils and the fundamental interchangeability of the two in the view of many). In addition:

> When at the table, it is not polite to keep the knife in one's hand the whole time; one takes hold of it only when it is needed. It is equally rude to bring a piece of bread to the mouth with the point of a knife. This same rule applies when eating an apple or a pear, or any other fruit. It is against good manners to hold a fork or a spoon with the whole hand, as though grasping a broom. . . . One should not use a fork for liquid food. . . . It is quite polite always to use a fork for bringing meat to the mouth, insofar as proper behavior does not allow one to touch greasy food, or sauces, or even syrups with the fingers.[15]

In the meantime, between the eighteenth and nineteenth centuries, on the tables of the wealthy middle class, service "à la russe" (each course served in sequence and presented to each seated diner—the style still in use today) began to replace the traditional service "à la française" (all the courses brought at the same time, guests serving themselves out of common platters—still alive in the style of the buffet).[16] This marked at the same time the decisive blow to the medieval system of conviviality and the definitive victory of individualism—and gave rise to an unprecedented gastronomic egalitarianism because the new system proposed the same dishes to all, whereas the portioning of the Middle Ages and early modern era was based on the principle of difference and hierarchy. This transformation also favored the increase in the number of pieces of flatware and their progressive differentiation: each type of food—for those who could afford it—required flatware of different shapes and dimensions, predetermined according to the succession of courses. During the nineteenth century, flatware came into general use and conquered new social spheres, thereby losing the elitist character that had distinguished it for centuries.

At the end of this long and tormented history, flatware finally became a commonplace; its presence could perhaps be discussed from an esthetic angle, but its right to exist could no longer be questioned. And yet even today, the manuals of etiquette continue to repeat rules and warnings not too dissimilar to those in the treatises of the fourteenth, fifteenth, and sixteenth centuries, implying that for many, the use of flatware has remained a problem, not only because masters were unable to teach or students to learn, but also because of a residual resistance to accepting these objects that simultaneously simplify and complicate our use of hands. The fact is that flatware tends to distance us from a childhood (individual and collective) that was marked by a more spontaneous and "animal" relation with food, and childhood, as we all know, is the ideal period for nostalgia and regrets in adulthood. Is this not also what explains, along with many other reasons, the success of certain kinds of eating, seemingly "modern" but in reality highly regressive on the level of behavior, such as sandwiches and hamburgers?

At other times, a return to the use of the hands was proposed in more explicit terms as a conscious demand for physicality and a more immediate, "vital" contact with food. This brings to mind the *Manifesto della cucina futurista* [Manifesto on futurist cooking], published in 1932 by Filippo Tommaso Marinetti, who, among the eleven rules of the "perfect meal," included in the fourth rule "the abolition of the fork and knife for the sensorial experience that can be derived from a tactile pre-labial pleasure."[17] Beyond its provocative and exaggeratedly intellectual context, the proposal is not without a certain appeal because it goes back to ancient sensations, deep-seated habits, and probably indelible needs of *homo edens*. Against this dynamic between "nature" and "culture," between spontaneity and artifice, between the hand and the tool, the history of our flatware—and in fact, of our entire civilization—is played out.

CHAPTER XVIII

The Taste of Knowledge

THE ORGAN OF taste is not the tongue but the brain. Better yet, it is the brain that directs and judges the sensations of the tongue. What the tongue perceives is flavors. In the nineteenth century, four fundamental flavors were codified: sweet, bitter, salty, and sour, each of which activates receptors located in specific zones of the tongue—sweet in the front, bitter in the back, salty on the right, and sour on the left.[1] But if the tongue perceives these flavors, it is the brain that recognizes them and judges them "good" or "bad" according to criteria of evaluation that someone taught it: criteria that are passed on and learned, criteria that are variable in time and space. What in a given period is deemed good may in another seem bad; what in one place is considered a delicacy may in another be regarded as disgusting. The social stratum, the professional group, or the family can also develop particular tastes and transmit them to its members. For this reason, taste is an element that constitutes human culture.[2] The tongue represents its biological foundation. The brain, determined by culture and society (and thus by history), decodes and interprets messages related to taste.

All this biologists now take for granted, but it was already perfectly evident to ancient scientists and philosophers and to medieval thinkers and treatise writers as well.[3] Augustine, basing himself on Aristotle, had explained that corresponding to the five "external" senses, there was an "internal" one that analyzed and evaluated information, leading it toward the spirit.[4] In these complex mechanisms, the brain is the "supreme judge,"[5] responsible for the conclusive and synthetic evaluation of the gustatory experience. Taking up the theories of Greek and Hellenistic physicists, Augustine, the founder of medieval science, defined the nervous system as a sensory path (*via sentiendi*) that connects the sensory organs to the brain.[6] He goes so far as to locate the exact part of the brain (anterior, he claimed) that presides over such mechanisms of sensory transmission.[7] "It is the brain, by means of the five senses, that discerns," repeats Gregory the Great,[8] another great father of medieval culture, referring back to Augustine. It is the brain that stores sensory data "in the belly of the memory" (a superb metaphor for someone working on food). Thus, the mouth feels, but it is "the spirit that tastes through the mouth."[9]

Among the five human senses,[10] taste has had a singular history. On the one hand, it was elevated to a means of knowing reality—the *prime* means of knowing reality. On the other, it was disdained, placed in a "low" position on the overall scale of values. In the history of Western culture, beginning in antiquity, a hierarchy arose among the five senses that distinguished the "high" senses (sight and hearing) from the "low" (touch and taste), with smell in an intermediate position. On one side are the "clean" senses—the "intellectual" ones, so to speak—that maintain the distance between subject and object; on the other are the "dirty," "material" senses, which provide physical contact with the object, to varying degrees. We are still today prisoners of this hierarchy when we attribute to the arts of sight and hearing (the figurative arts and music) a position of indisputable high value, whereas we have a hard time granting the same status to such arts as engineering and cooking, based on the "material" senses. True, today many speak of cooking as an art—but rarely without a patronizing smile.

At the origin of these difficulties and this hierarchical ladder is the ancient prejudice against the body, typical of Western culture at least since Plato. This prejudice was reinforced and consolidated by Christianity, which, after inventing the idea of sin, attached it to the physical nature of man, to his material dimension, constructing a utopia of spiritual man freed from his instincts and his body, insofar as possible.

Jerome, one of the Church fathers, the first ideologue of medieval monasticism, explains that the five senses are like so many "windows" that acquaint man with vice.[11] Others use the metaphor of the door.

The senses are seen as the occasion and the vehicle of sin because they lead man into an awareness of his body—and of the physical (and also intellectual) pleasures that it can provide. From this viewpoint, all the senses are dangerous. But one of them, taste, is more dangerous than the others, for it is the only one we cannot do without: without vision, without hearing, without touch, without smell (Jerome explains), we can live, theoretically; without taste, no, because we must eat. And it is precisely through the inescapable experience of eating that man has his first occasion to experiment with pleasure, venturing onto a path that will be hard to leave.

This holds, Jerome declares, not only for individual human beings, who learn from childhood to taste flavors and in this way become attached to the material side of life. It also holds true for humanity as a species, as progeny: our progenitors, Adam and Eve, fell into sin because of a gluttonous temptation, failing to resist tasting the forbidden fruit. Jerome interprets original sin not (or at least not only) as a sin of intellectual arrogance but (perhaps also) as a sin of the flesh, a yielding to gluttony and, immediately after, to lust. Once Adam and Eve ate the forbidden fruit, they discovered their nudity. This kind of interpretation, not justified by the biblical text but accepted and repeated throughout the Middle Ages by a host of biblical commentators, mirrors the Christian obsession with the body, with pleasure, and above all, with that pleasure (gluttony) for which taste, "the window of taste," is the vehicle. This explains the centrality of abstinence and fasting in the rules of monastic life, as well as the obsessive insistence of Christian regulations on penitential and Lenten practices.[12]

Another founding father of western monastic culture, Giovanni Cassiano, introduced an important variant into this reasoning, further qualifying it:[13] among human vices, there is a precise hierarchy because they do not all arise at the same time; instead, they follow each other like a chain reaction. The first—because it is unavoidable, tied as it is to the need to eat—is the vice of gluttony. From this is born the love of the body and consequently lust. This love of the body and of material things leads to avarice, that is, to the love of possession; to anger, if someone contests what we want; to sloth, if we do not succeed in obtaining what we want; and so on. Finally, even arrogance is related in a way to gluttony. This happens, paradoxically, when one seeks (as do the best among monks, along with ascetics and hermits) to forget the body, to raise oneself up to

God by means of fasting. One then considers oneself superior to others, and that is the sin of arrogance.

If this is what the founders of medieval Christian thinking wrote, it would seem to leave little room for a positive view of the sense of taste. And yet that same culture, in the field of science and especially medicine, developed a notion of taste—going back to ancient ideas of the Aristotelian mold—that entrusted to that very sense man's highest cognitive capacity for apprehending the external world. Only taste, we read in certain medieval scientific texts, allows one to know the true essence of things.

Of particular interest is an anonymous text of the thirteenth century (which collected widely held opinions) entitled *Tractatus de quique sensibus sed specialiter de saporibus*, or, more simply in another manuscript, *Summa de saporibus*.[14] The text begins by saying that the nature and properties of things can be known in three ways: by color, by smell, or by taste—in other words, by eyes, nose, and tongue. Through hearing, such knowledge is impossible because the sounds emitted by a thing are not part of its "substance" (the Aristotelian distinction between "substance" and "accident" is one of the constant points of these theories).[15] Touch, however, is deceptive, always at risk of perceiving the nature of things in an altered way, as demonstrated by two examples: hot water is felt as hot, whereas its true nature is cold; ground pepper is perceived as cold, whereas its true nature is hot. The properties of things (*proprietates rerum*) are determined in reference to the physics of Aristotle and the medical theories of Hippocrates, reorganized and developed by Galen. The nature of things derives from the combination in varying degrees of the four fundamental qualities of hot and cold, dry and moist, determined in turn by the four constituent elements of nature—earth, water, air, and fire. Any scientific reflection, from antiquity to the seventeenth century, turns around this basic concept.

So then, to return to our text, hearing and touch are excluded a priori as senses suited to knowing the nature of things. At this point, one turns to sight and admits that in some measure it is capable of transmitting knowledge. But even sight can be mistaken: for example, we see something white and believe it is cold (whiteness being *filia frigiditatis*). Instead, it could be hot, as in the case of garlic. Sight, in reality, captures only colors, shapes, and other "external" properties (*exteriores*), which are not substantial but "accidental" with regard to the nature of things. Smell is somewhat more accurate, often allowing us to know the properties of things—but not always, and not perfectly (*non perfecte*). A strong aromatic fragrance invariably convinces us of the hot nature of the thing, which can instead be cold, as in the case of camphor.

Conclusion: among the five senses, taste is the best suited to acquiring reliable knowledge of exterior reality. Only taste, the anonymous author of the *Tractatus* tells us, is "intended, properly and principally, to investigate the nature of things." Through taste, we can "fully and perfectly" (*plene et perfecte*) identify the "complexion" of something for the simple reason that taste *enters* into the thing, absorbs its properties, and blends into it completely (*ei totaliter admiscetur*). Not by chance, the *Tractatus* explains, do six *lacerti* (we would call them nerve conduits) reach the tongue from the brain, allowing us to penetrate the nature of the object, thoroughly assimilate it, and make it ours (not only on the tongue but in the brain itself). Smell—which is the most effective detector after taste—has only two *lacerti*. How does the sense of taste function? How does it succeed in discovering the properties of things and transmitting them to the brain, which then evaluates them? By means of flavors. "Let us then speak of flavors," our author declares, having arrived at the therefore of his reasoning. Not without reason does this work discuss flavor, as the title indicates: *de saporibus.*

Flavors, the author explains, are of two types, depending on whether the thing to be tasted, the *res gustando*, is capable of inducing a feeling in the senses of the one who tastes it. There is no feeling when the "composition" of the things tasted is too simple—that is, too close to the nature of the four basic elements of creation (water, earth, air, and fire). This is why water does not provoke sensations (*gustum non immutat*). Things of complex composition, however, are first rank, all of them generated by basic elements: herbs, fruit, food, drinks, and the like; the second rank consists of the "humors" generated by these same foods and drinks; and in the third rank are the sensory organs and all the parts of the body. If water does not stimulate taste, it is because simple things do not act on complex ones.

Complex compositions produce sensations (*infert passionem*) by means of eight fundamental flavors, which act in different ways: two of them, sweet and unctuous (*dulcis et unctuosum*), act "with delight [*cum delectatione*]"; that is, they produce a reaction of immediate pleasure. The other six (*salsus, amarus, acutus, acetosus, ponticus,* and *stipticus*) act "with revulsion [*cum horribilitate*]," meaning that they produce a reaction technically defined as physical discomfort—leaving aside the greater or lesser level of appreciation that the taster experiences. This discomfort can stem from two contrary physical actions: either the "dissolution and separation of the joined parts" (a kind of laceration of the taste buds) caused by flavors of a "hot" nature, such as salty, bitter, and sharp, or by a "cold" nature, such as vinegar; or the "wrinkling and shrinking of the parts" (a kind of contraction of the taste buds) caused by a sharp (*pontico*) or astringent flavor.

With respect to the notion of flavor, it was eighteenth-century science that identified four canonical flavors (sweet, bitter, salty, and sour). But medieval science, in the wake of ancient Aristotelian thinking, had an ampler notion of flavor that also included sensations of a tactile nature, such as those that precede the perception of spicy (*acutus*), astringent (*stipticus*, but also *ponticus*, which describes a somewhat less astringent flavor than *stipticus*), and fat (*unctuosum*). Today's scientists are trying to recover this broader dimension, rethinking the notion of flavor as a complex ensemble of diverse sensations, unequally distributed in different receptors of the palate, that blend together taste and feel—and even smell.[16] A fifth flavor, typical of Asian taste (the Japanese *umami*, a "flavor of meat" or glutamate[17]), has now been added to the canon, and even fat (*unctuosum*) is on its way to being recognized as a genuine flavor, whereas "hot" and "cold" (as in the heat of a chili pepper and the cold of mint) are bringing physics into chemistry, and tactile sensations are being placed among molecular mechanisms. The direction all this is taking seems to be the overturning of the eighteenth-century theory of four flavors and the resuscitation of premodern theories that were mistakenly thought to be buried.

The eight flavors of the treatise we have been examining can be found, with few variants, in ancient scientific texts (Aristotle was the first codifier of this[18]) and in other texts of medieval tradition.[19] In some cases, the number changes. For example, the "Regimen sanitatis" of the Salerno school of medicine identifies nine, adding *insipidus* (the flavorless flavor, the taste of water[20]) and subdividing them into three groups: "hot" (salty, bitter, and spicy), "cold" (vinegary, astringent, and sharp), and "temperate" (fat, sweet, and insipid—the best because they are the ones least in need of correction).[21] But aside from differences of detail, the primary interest of ancient and medieval thinkers in flavors lies in the fact that certain qualities (cold, hot, and so on) in the *flavors themselves* correspond to the nature of the *res gustanda*. Flavor (to echo Aristotle) is not accidental but substantial. Flavor expresses and reveals the essence of things.

For this, the term *flavor* was normally used, in cookbooks as well as books on dietetics, in connection with sauces, recommended as "correctives" for the foods they accompanied. For a certain type of meat or fish, prepared in a certain manner, a certain sauce was recommended so that the quality of the first would be "tempered," or compensated by the quality of the second, to achieve a balanced dish. For example, with a meat that is hot and moist, one should serve a sauce that is cold and dry.[22] This kind of precept, found both in texts on dietetics and in cookbooks, plays on the term *sapores*, which indicates, contextually, the *flavor* and the *nature* of the culinary preparation. The nature of the thing (and thus its ability to exercise influence on the level of nutrition) manifests itself directly through its flavor.

Knowledge of things (edible, not edible, partially edible, edible on condition of being modified and "adjusted") is acquired through the sense of taste, which belongs to humans, and the perception of flavor, which belongs to the thing. The act of eating is what produces the contact that activates the sense of taste, making it recognize the flavor and, behind it, the essence of the thing. Flavor *reveals* that essence and thereby becomes an instrument of knowledge. The play on words *sapore/sapere*,* very much in fashion (in Italy) today and used and abused even on the levels of journalism and publicity, in reality is much more than wordplay. It expresses—for those in the Middle Ages who spoke Latin and for those who today speak a language derived from Latin—the profound identity that medieval culture postulated between the two notions. Let us say it once again: flavor, by means of the sense of taste, reveals the essence of things.

But there is more. Medieval dietetic thinking, expressed in fundamental treatises and in small compendiums for daily use, was governed by a basic certainty that we can explain very simply this way: *ciò che è buono fa bene* (or, loosely, what tastes good is good for you).[23] In this way, pleasure becomes the infallible guide to health "because," wrote Aldobrandino of Siena in the thirteenth century,[24] "as Avicenna said, if man's body is healthy, all those things that taste good in his mouth will nourish him best." The words of the Milanese doctor Maino de' Maineri, in the following century, were also very clear: "by means of condiments [foods] become tastier and *as a result* are more digestible. In fact, whatever is more pleasing is better for the digestion."[25]

---

*Alas, not possible in English, but meaning flavor/knowledge.—Trans.

Conviction of this kind, diffused, shared, almost taken for granted, arose precisely out of the logical route we have traced: on one side, there are humans, endowed with a sense of taste; on the other, there is food, endowed with flavor, which reveals its nature. If the encounter between taste and flavor is positive for me—if, in other words, eating a particular thing arouses a pleasurable sensation—that means (medieval doctors thought) that this thing, its particular nature revealed to my senses by its flavor, corresponds to my desire to eat it. In turn, that desire is the expression of the organism's need. Therefore, if my sense of taste finds something to be good, that means that its nature (revealed by its flavor) is suited to my need (revealed by my desire). Generally speaking, finding a flavor pleasurable is the sign of a physiological need, and it is precisely the *desiderium* (the appetite, the desire to eat) that is the revelatory symptom of that need: "from the desire you will surely know it" because "that is the sign to which you should entrust your diet." These words are from the Salerno "Regimen."[26]

This presupposes that I am capable of listening to my body, its demands, and its reactions and that I am not influenced by other suggestions that could orient my choices differently. In the Middle Ages, as today and always, food choices did not depend exclusively on hearing one's body but were also based on considerations that, by their nature, are extraneous to the act of nutrition, such as social conventions, prestige and power (eating certain things because they are a status symbol and refusing others seen as vulgar), faith (a given religious faith can require or prohibit certain foods), reasons of hunger or the market (giving preference to a food because it is more economical or available), intemperance (why not?), and so on. In a world like ours, dominated by alimentary publicity, it is not hard to understand how choices can be influenced by considerations and sentiments unrelated to hearing the body. This may indicate that the picture drawn by medieval doctors was utopian. But who would deny the importance of utopias as the engine of history?

What is good is good for you. This great utopia of medieval scientific thinking coexisted and conflicted with the other great utopia, Christian morality, which taught exactly the opposite: what is good—that is, what arouses pleasure in the body—is bad (for the spirit) because it distracts you from "true knowledge," that of otherworldly reality. On the one hand terror of pleasure, on the other the idea that pleasure can be a guide for life. They seem to be two separate cultures, ostensibly irreconcilable.

Instead, we are dealing with the very same culture, declined in different ways. The same condemnation of physical pleasure presupposes the idea that such pleasure, and the sense of taste that induces it, is the intermediary of a privileged relationship with the world, which should be negated or, better still, transferred to another plane.

Even in Christian texts, pleasure and taste appear (metaphorically) as instruments of perfect knowledge—of a different and truer reality. Augustine, in his commentary on the Psalms, wrote that one cannot speak of the sweetness of God if one has never known him, just as it is impossible to affirm the sweetness of a food if one has never tasted it.[27] The same image recurs when Gregory the Great writes that "the food of knowledge" cannot be known merely by hearing about it; it has to be tasted thoroughly, savored "all the way to the marrow."[28] Gregory the Great, again—to describe the patriarchs of the Old Testament who intuited the coming of Christ but evidently could not know him—used a metaphor that brings us back to the heart of the scientific ideas from which we started. The ancient fathers, he wrote, prophesied the mystery of the incarnation and managed to smell its fragrance: they were "like ships that transport fruit"; they could enjoy the perfume of those fruits but not experience their flavor because they were carrying them to others. "That fruit which they could smell while waiting, we can see, we can pick, we can eat to satiety."[29] The metaphors on divine reality, although seemingly opposed to the science of the body, only confirm it, based as they are on the certainty that for humans, taste is the prime means of knowing the world. To taste is to experiment: *sapore è sapere* (flavor is knowledge).

The idea of taste transmitted by medieval culture was that of an instinctive, "natural" taste. If the experience of pleasure was determined by the satisfaction of an individual physiological need, each taste was a thing in itself and not open to question. The refined scholastic disputations did not include the evaluation of flavors because *de gustibus non est disputandum*. But, in fact, that created problems for the ideological system constructed during the Middle Ages by the ruling classes and by intellectuals (philosophers, physicians, and scientists) who saw food as being an instrument of social difference and therefore as reflecting various qualities that were "objectively" determined. With a bit of forcing, the problem was resolved by superimposing the theme of social difference on that of instinctive knowledge, redesigning—with an obvious conceptual oxymoron—the notion of individuality in a collective key. The idea that emerged was that because knowledge is instinctive and because people are different (socially different), different things are *naturally* pleasing to each of them: the taste of a peasant is not the taste of an aristocrat.

This conviction lasted way beyond the Middle Ages, the elite continuing to lull themselves with the idea that the peasant *would not like* refined food—his body would reject it, or he would end up like poor Bertoldo, forced against his will to eat courtly food, which is precisely what caused his death in the tragicomic story by Giulio Cesare Croce, and we are now in the seventeenth century.[30] In the meantime, however, things got more complicated because the idea of instinctive taste, which opens the door to knowing the world and its rules, was overtaken in the first centuries of the modern era by another idea, that of *good taste*—in other words, a knowledge that is not instinctive but cultivated, filtered by the intellect.

This is not a new idea. It already existed in medieval culture, where it cohabited with the idea of instinctive knowledge (the two had always lived side by side). But at a certain point, between the sixteenth and seventeenth centuries—first in Italy and Spain, then in France and other countries—this idea of cultivated taste, initially limited, took hold and became prevalent. Moreover, it lent itself to a whole series of figurative uses: the ability to (learn how to) evaluate applied not only to the choice of foods—to the sense of taste, literally speaking—but also to everything that makes daily life "beautiful" and "flavorful"—filling the senses of seeing, hearing, touching, and smelling, metaphorically speaking, with emotions that only someone with rigorous intellectual training could appreciate.

According to Vercelloni, who examined this mechanism in a recent book,[31] this transference of images presupposed the "liberation" (or release) of the idea of taste from the specific sphere of alimentation. This kind of emancipation, the appearance of a metaphoric use of the idea of taste, was the condition for the passage of an exclusively alimentary notion to a notion at the same time more ample and more intellectual, defined culturally rather than instinctively. Only in a second stage, by then on the threshold of the contemporary world, did this change make it possible to "redefine retroactively the original meaning of the term," assigning a cultural character to taste in the palatal sense.

But the argument can be turned around, thanks to the fact that the connection between the idea of taste and the sphere of knowledge seems deeply rooted in medieval culture—which is why I do not find improbable a different route, to some degree opposite. It is not the metaphoric and figurative use of the idea of taste that made possible its release from the alimentary sphere; on the contrary, the early development of this idea *in the field of gastronomy* would have favored at a certain point its extension into other fields. This is a hypothesis suggested with great prudence and in a different perspective by Flandrin, who was a pioneer in the history of taste. Although admitting the possibility that "the metaphoric use favored . . . the appearance in the alimentary field of the idea of good taste," he asked himself "how an idea like this [of 'intellectual taste'] could have been created and cultivated . . . by a society that was indifferent to the refinement of cooking and to the sensitive perception of food." It is indeed hard to establish "if the idea of good taste—or bad taste, which is its obverse—was born in the alimentary world or in the artistic and literary world," but it is the first hypothesis that seems more appealing to him.[32]

A qualification is necessary at this point: by itself, the notion of good taste does not at all exclude instinct. Even the faculty of intellectual evaluation contains a spontaneous, intuitive dimension (Voltaire would define taste, in the meaning of good taste, as a kind of "immediate discernment, *like that of the tongue and the palate*"[33]). But the idea of good taste that ultimately prevailed in the modern era is that of a mediated knowledge, a taste "culturally remodeled," as noted by Vercelloni. "What is good is what pleases" will no longer be true, as medieval doctors and philosophers had thought; instead, "what pleases (or what one has to like because is has been deemed good by connoisseurs) is what is good." The medieval adage *de gustibus non est disputandum*, which granted equal legitimacy to all, determined by the natural instinct of each individual, in modern times faced a "progressive loss of verisimilitude," while the idea that not all tastes have the same value and that some people more than others—the so-called experts—are competent to judge them gained acceptance. Taste in this way became a "device for social differentiation." It always was, but in the Middle Ages, people deluded themselves into thinking (or pretended to believe) that this "device" functioned "naturally." In the Renaissance, as Hauser wrote referring to artistic taste, the argument had a wider range: the idea was to create a "culture reserved for an elite from which the majority was to be excluded."[34] This is the cultural mechanism that Flandrin calls "distinction by means of taste"—an idea that had long been unthinkable, even if there was no need to wait until the seventeenth century (as Flandrin maintains) to see it appear. In Italy, as in Spain, it could have been anticipated at least a century earlier.[35]

The shift of the idea of taste to that of good taste had contradictory consequences. It is true that as taste moved away from the paradigm of natural spontaneity, it assumed a more aristocratic and elitist character. But it is also true that as taste became a matter for connoisseurs, based on the notion of training, no one, at least in principle, could be excluded a priori. As Flandrin acutely remarks, literature in the modern era insists on the "spontaneity" and "naturalness" of the "sense of taste," reserving it for the happy few. But it is noteworthy that "no one, in these reflections on taste, ever put forward the idea that it could be hereditary and belong only to persons of noble origin."

With the new notion of good taste, the perspective changed. The ideology of difference no longer rested on an immutable "ontological" given but on the ability (aided perhaps by instinct) to learn. This doubtless heralded the development and affirmation of bourgeois culture. Even the hypothesis that a peasant might enjoy upper-class food (which would destabilize the "natural" order of society) was no longer improbable. In view of this, it became more urgent to deny knowledge to those not socially worthy. To reveal to peasants the secrets that could refine taste, transforming them into gentlemen, would be neither appropriate nor desirable. The concept was already enunciated in the fifteenth century by Gentile Sermini regarding the flavor of sweetness, then considered a mark of social difference: "see that the [peasant] not taste sweet, but sour, yes: for, as a rustic is, so let him remain."[36] Between the fifteenth and sixteenth centuries, a full-scale campaign of propaganda, supported by poets, writers, and philosophers, was created around certain products—in particular, fruit and, above all, the pear—calling forth images of nobility, which were incompatible with peasant taste. I reconstructed this topic in a recent book dedicated to the birth, in those decades, of the proverb *"Al contadino non far sapere quanto è buono il formaggio con le pere* [do not let the peasant know how good cheese is with pears]."[37]

Once again, *sapere* (knowledge) is linked to *sapori* (flavors) and to the mechanisms that form taste. The argument has now been overturned with regard to the Middle Ages, but that is where the roots of this mutation lie.

Notes

1. MEDIEVAL NEAR, MEDIEVAL FAR

1. On the decisive importance of the work and intuitions of Jean-Louis Flandrin regarding recent developments in the history of food, see Montanari 2005b.

2. See chapter 2 this volume.

3. For this mechanism, see Montanari 2004, pp. 147–151.

4. Montanari 2004, p. 75.

5. On this subject, see chapter 18 this volume.

6. Montanari 1993, pp. 146–147; Redon, Sabban, and Serventi 1994, pp. 33ff.

7. See chapter 9 this volume.

8. On this subject, see chapter 17 this volume.

9. On the modalities of service and the way they changed over the centuries, see Capatti and Montanari 1999, pp. 145–183.

10. Montanari 1993, pp. 105ff.

11. Grieco 1987, p. 94. For a detailed analysis of the foods served at the Priors' table, see Frosini 1993.

12. Flandrin 1992, p. 48.

13. Flandrin 1984, pp. 77–78.

14. Montanari 1993, p. 83.

2. MEDIEVAL COOKBOOKS

1. On the subject of recipe manuscripts from medieval Europe, see Lambert 1992, and Laurioux 1997c.

2. Montanari 2004, pp. 109–116.

3. Capatti and Montanari 1999, pp. x–xi.

4. Montanari 2010.

5. Messedaglia 1942–44, p. 406.

6. Capatti and Montanari 1999, pp. 9ff, for what follows in the paragraph.

7. Rebora 1996, pp. 68–69.

8. Flandrin 1984, pp. 80–81.

9. Capatti and Montanari 1999, pp. 10–13.

10. Martellotti 2005.

11. Mulon 1971.

12. Sada and Valente 1995, p. 21.

13. Laurioux 1997b, p. 210.

14. Laurioux 1997b, pp. 210–212.

15. Ibid.

16. Capatti and Montanari 1999, p. 12.

17. Montanari 1993, pp. 1–82.

18. See chapter 1 this volume.

19. Montanari 1989, p. 45 (see G. Sermini, *Le novelle*, XXIX, ed. G. Vettori, Rome, Avansini and Torraca, 1968, 2 vols., pp. 483–496).

20. On the cooking at the court of Savoy, see Salvatico 1999.

21. Capatti and Montanari 1999, p. 29; Montanari 2010, pp. 37–38.

22. On Maestro Martino, see Benporat 1990; Capatti and Montanari 1999, pp. 13–15; Ballerini and Parzen 2001; and, above all, Laurioux 2006, pp. 503ff.

23. Curt F. Bühler Collection, B.19, New York, Morgan Library and Museum.

24. Benporat 1996, pp. 42–43.

25. Laurioux 1997b, pp. 213–215.

26. The first is by Benporat 1996, p. 72; the second is by Laurioux 1997b, p. 215.

27. Faccioli 1987, p. 141.

28. See the analyses offered by Laurioux 2006.

29. Faccioli 1985, p. 141 (in the recipe for blancmange).

3. THE GRAMMAR OF FOOD

1. Rabano Mauro, *De universo*, PL 111, c. 527.

2. Giovanni Italico, *Vita Sancti Odonis*, PL 133, c. 64. See chapter 15 this volume.

3. Liutprando da Cremona, "Relatio de legatione constantinopolitana," in *Liudprandi Opera*, ed. J. Becker, Hanover, Hahn, 1915, pp. 196–197.

4. The analogy of food and language was first proposed in an organic fashion by Lévi-Strauss (1958). More systematically, in the first three volumes of *Mythologiques* (Lévi-Strauss 1964, 1966, 1968), he designed a structural framework of alimentary systems, parallel with and analogous to linguistic systems. Also important with regard to methodology is a short article (Lévi-Strauss 1965) devoted to methods of cooking as a culturally significant baseline of culinary practices.

5. For an analysis of these questions of categories, see Montanari 1993, pp. 46–47.

6. Galloni 1993.

7. Montanari 1990b, pp. 282ff.

8. Ibid., pp. 300–301.

9. On this subject, see Montanari 1979.

10. Montanari 1997b, p. 219.

11. Montanari 1979, pp. 289–290. The greater attention to "internal" resources was naturally related to their territorial dimensions and to the need to define the modalities of exploitation in relation to territorial rights. But it is also a matter of cultural perspectives.

12. Montanari 1979, pp. 111–112, 113 (table).

13. Montanari 1979, p. 161.

14. Capatti and Montanari 1999, pp. 47–48; also pp. 106–107 for the role played by the Arabs in the domain of alimentary culture.

15. Montanari 1979, pp. 366–369.

16. Ibid., pp. 301–303.

17. Montanari 1988a, pp. 124ff.

18. Montanari 1979, pp. 296ff. On the diffusion and importance of the chestnut in the Middle Ages, see chapter 10 this volume.

19. Montanari 1988a, p. 88 (referring to the *Consuetudines* of the Hirsau monastery, where the chestnut is defined as *peregrina* [wandering]).

20. Montanari 1997a.

21. Essential to this subject are the remarks of Flandrin (1994).

22. Hagen 1995, p. 180.

23. AS, *Apr. III*, p. 354.

24. Sancti Chrodegangi, *Regula canonicorum*, XXIII, ed. W. Schmitz, Hanover, Hahn, 1889, p. 15: "si vero contigerit, quod vinum minus fuerit et ista mensura episcopus implere non potest . . . de cervisia consolacionem faciat."

25. The picture is more detailed in the *Exerpta* placed in the appendix of Apicius's text (the celebrated cookbook of imperial Rome, preserved in a manuscript of the fourth century, in which only pepper is mentioned). Presented as "extracts" of the same text, the *Exerpta* was really written a century later (between the fifth and sixth centuries) by a certain Vinidarius, probably an Ostrogoth living in northern Italy. Here, alongside pepper new spices appear—in particular, ginger and saffron, the latter for the specific purpose of a color that became typical of medieval cooking, *propter colore*. New aromas and flavors abound during the high Middle Ages, including cloves, cinnamon, and *galanga*. For all this, see Laurioux 1983.

26. Montanari 1988a, pp. 23ff.

27. Ibid., pp. 63ff.

28. Capatti and Montanari 1999, pp. 101ff.

29. Ibid.

30. For the symbolic meanings of roast and boiled meats, the obligatory reference is Lévi-Strauss 1965.

31. Montanari 2004.

32. Eginard, *Vita Karolis Magni*, 24, ed. G. H. Pertz, Hanover, Hahn, 1863, p. 24.

33. Montanari 1988a, p. 45 (with a reference to Beck Brossard 1981).

34. For all this, see Capatti and Montanari 1999, pp. 145ff.

35. Anastasii Bibliothecarii, *Historia de vitis Romanorum Pontificum*, XCVII, 3270238, PL 128, cc. 1183–1184.

36. Montanari 1979, p. 158. The document appears in L. Schiaparelli, *Codice diplomatico longobardo*, II, Rome, Senate Printing Office, 1933, p. 186, n. 194.

37. Carnevale Schianca 2011, p. 540.

38. Montanari 1990b, pp. 303–304.

39. *Regula Magistri*, XXVI, 1, in *La Règle du Maître*, ed. A. De Vogüé, Paris, Le Cerf, 1964, p. 136: "*et tertium quodcumque fuerit crudum cum pomis.*" This does not refute that *pulmentum* is, by definition, a cooked dish: see the episode of Gaudenzio, disciple of

Romualdo, who asks permission *pulmenta dimettere* so as to satisfy his desire for water, *pomis quoque sive crudis boleribus*. Petro Daniani, *Vita beati Romualdo*, LVII, ed. G. Tabacco, Rome, Istituto Storico Italiano per il Medio Evo, 1957, p. 98.

40. Bianchi 2001, pp. 101 (*Regola di Cesario*, ch. 22), 128–129 (*Regola di Aureliano*, ch. 59), 320 (*Regola di Isidoro*, ch. 9), 344 (*Regola di Fruttuoso*, ch. 3).

41. Cremaschi 2005, p. 63 (ch. 71).

42. Ibid., p. 155 (ch. 10). See PL 88, c. 1062 (with the title *Regula cuiusdam fratris ad vergines*).

43. Montanari 1990b, p. 305.

44. Ibid.

45. Sancti Chrodegangi, *Regula canonicorum*, XXII, p. 15.

46. Carnevale Schianca 2011, p. 230.

47. See chapter 1 of this volume.

48. Such as the *Ordinaciones de la Casa Real* of Pedro III of Aragon, ch. IV, 8; cf. Montanari 1993, p. 107.

49. F. Sacchetti, "Il Trecentonovelle," CXXIV, in *Opere*, ed. A. Borlenghi, Milan, Rizzoli, 1957, pp. 387–390. See Montanari 1989, pp. 401–402.

50. Gregorii Turonensis, *Miracula et opera minora*, MGH, SRM, I, 2, pp. 541–542 (*Liber in gloria martyrum*), 79.

51. Ibid., pp. 147–148.

52. Isidore of Seville, *Etymologiae*, XX, 11, ed. W. M. Lindsay, Oxford, 1911, p. 15: "panis dictus, quod cum omni cibo adponatur."

53. As an example of the conjunctival use of the two terms as integrated elements of a parallel discourse, see in chapter 7 of *Vita di Columbano* the prodigious supply of food given to Colombano and his companions by a man who appears with a provision of bread and *pulmenta* carried by horses: "virum quendam, cum panum supplimento vel pulmentorum acquos oneratos." Giona di Bobbio, *Vita di Columbano e des suoi discepoli*, ed. I. Biffi and A. Granata, Milan, Jaca Book, 2001, p. 44.

54. Whether in normal times or times of fasting, "*panis libra une propensa sufficiat in die.*" When there are two meals, bread is then divided into two parts (two-thirds at lunch, one-third at dinner). When there is only one meal—that is, on the evening of fast days—the entire ration is reserved for dinner. *Regula Benedictii*, 39, in *La Règle de Saint-Benoît*, ed. A. De Vogüé and J. Neufville, Paris, Le Cerf, 1972.

55. Sancti Chrodegangi, *Regula canonicorum*, XXII, p. 15.

56. *Historia Francorum*, VII, 45, MGH, SRM, I, 1.

57. *Historiae*, IV (Rodolfo il Glabro, *Cronache dell'anno Mille*, ed. G. Cavallo and G. Orlandi, Milan, Valla/Mondadori, 1989, p. 218).

58. Bonnassie 1989, p. 1045.

59. Gaufredi Malaterrae, *De febus gesti Rogerii Calaabriae et Siciliae comitis et Roberty Guiscardi fratris ejus*, I, XXVII, RIS2, V, 1, ed. E. Pontieri, Bologna, Zanichello, 1925–28, p. 21: "*fluvialibus carectis et quarundam arborum corticibus cum castaneis et quercinis sive ilicinis nucibus, quas glandes dicimus, porcis subtractis, et mola post exsiccationem tritis, panes facere, modico milii admixto, tentabant.*"

60. Cited by Bonnassie 1989, p. 1045.

61. For a general discussion of this point, see Montanari 1979.

62. Montanari 1984, pp. 191–200 (medieval society faced with famine).

63. Bianchi 2001, p. 454 (ch. 22).

64. Ardonis seu Smaragdi, *Vita Sanctis Benedicti Anianensis*, PL 103, c. 361: "*Carnes etiam armentorum oviumque dabantur per singulos dies, lac etiam vervecum praebebant auxilium.*"

65. Examples appear in Montanari 1979, pp. 433–434.

66. Montanari 1993, pp. 51ff. Fumagalli (1970) earlier stressed the "compulsory" nature of this change.

67. *Chronicon Novaliciense*, III, 21 (*Cronaca di Novalesa*, ed. G. C. Alessio, Turin, Einaudi, 1982, pp. 169–171).

68. Montanari 1993, pp. 31–32.

69. Montanari 1989, p. viii.

4. THE TIMES OF FOOD

1. Montanari 2004, pp. 5–10. See chapter 5 this volume.

2. Goffredo di Monmouth, "Vita Merlini," 146, in *Historia regum Britanniae*, ed. I. Pin, Prodenone, Studio Tesi, 1993, p. 222.

3. Montanari 1979, p. 172.

4. *Inventari altomedievali di terre, coloni et redditi*, Rome, Istituto Italiano per il Medio Evo, 1979, p. 20.

5. Ibid.

6. Ibid., p. 204.

7. Montanari 1979, pp. 233, 236.

8. Montanari 1993, pp. 51ff.

9. Mane 1983, pp. 222ff.

10. Montanari 1984, pp. 191ff.

11. Braudel 1982, p. 45.

12. Rouche 1973.

13. Montanari 2004, pp. 20–22.

14. Montanari 2004, p. 20.

15. Ibid. (and for the text that follows).

16. Montanari 1988a, pp. 175–182 ("Il sale e la vita dell'uomo [Salt and human life]").

17. Ibid., p. 182.

18. Capatti and Montanari 1999, pp. 114–119.

19. Lévi-Strauss 1965.

20. *Capitulare de villis*, c. 70, MGH, *Leges*, CRF, I, p. 90.

21. Montanari 1979, pp. 109ff.

22. Montanari 1984, p. 198.

23. Le Goff 1977, pp. 3ff.

24. Cassiodoro, *Variae*, XII, 4, CC, *Series latina*, 96, p. 467.

25. Montanari and Sabban 2002, II, pp. vii–viii, regarding the following discussion in this chapter.

26. See chapter 2 this volume.

27. On monastic cuisine, see chapter 14 this volume.

28. On the "social" contrast between roasted and boiled, see Montanari 2004, pp. 57–61.

29. Redon, Sabban, and Serventi 1994, pp. 30–31.

30. Ibid., p. 37.

31. *Regula Magistri*, XXV, in *La Règle du Maître*, ed. A. De Vogüé, Paris, Le Cerf, 1964, pp. 132–134. See Montanari 1990b, p. 318.

32. Montanari 1988a, p. 84.

33. Capatti and Montanari 1999, pp. 59ff.

34. Ibid., p. 62.

35. Little has been written on the subject of mealtimes. A good starting point might be Flandrin (1993) for a multifarious view from a historical-anthropological optic.

36. There are no specific studies on this subject. Mazzetti di Pietralata (2006) is not generous when it comes to documented historical information.

37. Montanari 1979, pp. 184–186.

38. Montanari 2004, pp. 105–108.

39. Donizone, *Vita di Matilde di Canossa*, I, X, vv. 795ff, ed. P. Golinelli, Milan, Jaca Book, 1984, p. 85.

40. Montanari 2004, p. vii.

41. "Regimen sanitatis," in *Flos medicinae Scholae Salerni*, ed. A. Sinno, Milan, Mursia, 1987, p. 28.

42. Herodotus, *Histories*, II, 77.

43. Pucci Donati 2007.

44. "Regimen sanitatis," pp. 28–44.

45. For example, the reflection of the dietary culture developed in medical texts and apparent in many proverbs. Flandrin (1997a, pp. 392–394) has pointed out the "complicity" between written and oral culture, scientific thought and popular perception.

46. Capatti and Montanari 1999, pp. 82ff.

47. Le Goff, 1977.

48. Faccioli 1987, p. 170.

49. Ibid.

50. Ibid., p. 174.

51. Ibid., p. 183.

52. Ibid., p. 188.

53. Capatti and Montanari 1999, pp. 64–66.

54. *The "Sallazzo" and the "Saporetto" along with other rhymes by Simone Prudenzani of Orvieto*, Giornale della letterature italiana, suppl. 15, ed. S. Debenedetti, Turin, Loescher, 1913, p. 134 (*Liber Saporetti*, 80).

5. THE AROMA OF CIVILIZATION: BREAD

1. Montanari 2004, pp. 9–10.

2. Ibid.

3. Ibid., p. 8, with a reference to Braudel 1982.

4. Kaplan 1976.

5. For all information concerning ancient Rome, see André 1981.

6. Soler 1973.

7. Montanari 1993, p. 25.

8. Ibid.

9. Montanari 2005a (discussing the famous theses of Henri Pirenne).

10. Montanari 1993, pp. 25–26.

11. Ibid., pp. 62ff.

12. Ibid., pp. 130–135.

13. Bautier 1984, p. 33. See chapter 3 this volume.

14. Gregory of Tours, *Liber in gloria confessorum*, 30, MGH, SRM, I, 2, p. 316.

15. Antimus, *De observantia ciborum*, I, ed. M. Grant, Blackawton, Prospect Books, 1996, p. 50.

16. *Statuta Adalbardi*, in *Le Moyen Age*, 2ème siècle, IV, ed. L. Levillain, 1900, pp. 351–386, in particular pp. 357–358.

17. Montanari 1989, p. 485. The chronicle of the banquet appears in C. Ghirardacci, *Historia di Bologna*, RIS2, XXXII/I, ed. A. Sorbelli, Citta di Castello, Lapi, 1932, pp. 235ff.

18. According to Vogel (1976, pp. 228–230), the gospel accounts should be interpreted differently, and multiplication of food (in reality, a eucharistic sharing) is a false reading. If this were the case, the success of the passage with *that* meaning would be even more significant.

19. On "breads of famine," see chapter 3 this volume.

20. Bolens 1980, pp. 470–471.

21. Montanari 1993, p. 127. Texts such as these proliferated in the modern era, particularly in periods of extreme famine, as in the sixteenth or eighteenth and nineteenth centuries. In 1591, there was the *Discorso sopra la carestia, e fame* by Giambattista Segni; in 1801, there was the treatise *Della ghianda e di altre cose utili a cibo e coltura* by Michele Rosa. Even the potato, which spread through Europe in the second half of the eighteenth century as a means of preventing famine and hunger, was initially proposed—by agronomists like Parmentier in France and Battarra in Italy and even by public authorities—as a new product for making bread, a proposal that turned out to be illusory. Ibid., p. 173.

22. Bautier 1984, pp. 132–134.

23. Rabano Mauro, *De universo*, PL III, c. 590.

24. Montanari 1988a, p. 144 (n. 80).

25. Ibid., p. 134.

26. Gregory of Tours, *Vitae Patrum*, VII, 2, MGH, SRM, I, 2, p. 237.

27. *Vita S. Radegundis*, I, 15, MGH, SRM, II, p. 369.

28. Gregory of Tours, *Historia Francorum*, IX, 21.

29. *Vita S. Eligi episcopi Noviomagensis*, I, 21, MGH, SRM, IV, p. 685. See Bautier 1984, p. 37.

30. Ibid., and n. 65.

31. *Statuta Adalhardi*, p. 354; *Consuetudines Corbeienses*, in *Corpus Consuetudinum monasticarum*, I, ed. J. Semmler, Siegbury, 1963, p. 372.

32. Rouche 1984, p. 292.

33. Davies 1971, p. 124.
34. *Vitae Patrum*, V, IV, 10, PL 73, c. 865. This is merely an example.
35. See chapter 15 this volume.
36. *Vitae Patrum*, V, IV, 56: an old man who is visited by another old man tells his disciple *"infunde nobis panem"*; ibid., 58: a monk, after the daily fast, at the sixth hour *"infundit panem"*—both in PL 73, c. 871.
37. Bautier 1984.
38. Montanari 1990b, p. 318. The text is in *Regula Magistri*, XXV, in *La Règle du Maître*, ed. A. De Vogüé, Paris, Le Cerf, 1964, pp. 132–134.

6. HUNGER FOR MEAT

1. Montanari 1993, pp. 12–17; 2004, pp. 5–10.
2. For these texts see Montanari 1993, p. 15.
3. Ibid., pp. 19ff.
4. Ibid., pp. 20–21.
5. Ibid., p. 16.
6. Aulo Cornelio Celso, "De medicina," II, XVIII, in *Della medicina libro otto*, trans. A. Del Lungo, Florence, 1904, p. 104.
7. Aldobrando of Siena, *Le régime du corps*, ed. L. Landouzy and R. Pépin, Paris, Champion, 1911 (and Slatkine Reprint, Geneva, 1978), p. 121: *"Vous devés savoir ke sour totes coses qui nourissment dounent, doune li chars plus de norissement au cors de l'homme, et l'encraisse, et l'enforce* [You must know that of everything that gives nourishment, meat gives more nourishment to the body of man, and fattens him, and strengthens him]."
8. Montanari 1988a, pp. 63–92 (monastic diets).
9. Ibid.
10. On ancient vegetarianism see Haussleiter 1935.
11. See Montanari 1988a, pp. 64, 91–92.
12. Ibid., pp. 66–67.
13. André 1981.
14. Montanari 2002a.
15. Montanari 1993, p. 206.
16. Ibid., pp. 19–23.
17. Montanari 1988a, p. 47.
18. Galloni 1993.
19. Hilton 1973; see Montanari 1993, pp. 59–60.
20. Montanari 1993, pp. 118–120.
21. Baruzzi and Montanari, 1981.
22. Montanari 1993, pp. 67–71.
23. Ibid., pp. 96–97, and following paragraph.
24. Ibid., pp. 113–114, and following text as well.
25. Grieco 1987, pp. 159ff. For the symbolism of fruit (in particular, the pear), see also Montanari 2008.

7. THE AMBIGUOUS POSITION OF FISH

1. For Flandrin's insistence on the social and cultural dimensions of products (their "status"), see Montanari 2005b, pp. 375–378.

2. Ibid., pp. 98–103.

3. See chapter 6 this volume.

4. Haussleiter 1935.

5. For this, see Zug Tucci 1985; Montanari 1993, pp. 99–100.

6. See chapter 14 this volume.

7. Zug Tucci 1985, p. 303.

8. Montanari 1993, p. 101.

9. Montanari 1979, pp. 292–294 (and also for references to documents below).

10. The advice of Abelard to Heloise appears in Letter VIII, known as "Rules," in Peter Abelard, *L'origine del monachesimo e la Regola*, ed. S. Di Meglio, Padua, EMP, 1988, pp. 217–218.

11. Anthimus, *De observantia ciborum*, ed. M. Grant, Blackawton, Prospect Books, 1996.

12. See chapter 2 this volume.

13. Capatti and Montanari 1999, p. 85.

14. Ibid.

15. Zug Tucci 1985, pp. 303–305, 310–212, 316, for this and further documentary references (Albertus Magnus, Thomas Aquinas, and Thomas de Cantimpré).

16. Braudel 1982, p. 190; see ibid., pp. 190–194, for information about herring and later cod fishing.

17. Zug Tucci 1985.

18. On the subject of dried and salted sturgeon, see Messedaglia 1941–42.

19. Montanari 1993, p. 103.

20. Flandrin 1994.

8. FROM MILK TO CHEESES

1. "All the doctors concur in the opinion that milk [. . .] generates a lot of blood—as though it were blood expressed from the breast," wrote the humanist Bartolomeo Platina in his famous work *De honesta voluptate et valetutdine* [On guiltless pleasure and good health]; see in Faccioli 1985, pp. 49–50. See Camporesi 1985, p. 70.

2. Vogel 1976.

3. Naso 1990a, p. 67.

4. Camporesi 1985, p. 59.

5. Jordanes, *Getice*, LI, 267. See Montanari 1993, p. 15.

6. Harris 1990, pp. 128–152 (milkophiles and milkophobes).

7. Montanari 1993, pp. 12–19.

8. Ibid., pp. 223ff.

9. Isidore of Seville, *Etymologiae*, XII, I, ed. W. M. Lindsay, Oxford, 1911. See Montanari 1988a, p. 41.

10. Faccioli 1985, p. 50 (as well as the quotations that follow).

11. Panthaleonis de Conflentia, *Summa Lacticiniorum*, in Naso 1990a, pp. 122–123 (a translation into Italian was made by Emilio Faccioli: Pantaleone da Confienza, *Trattato dei latticini*, Milan, 1990). See Camporesi 1990, pp. 89–117.

12. Naso 1990a, p. 66, and the text following.

13. Ibid., p. 72.

14. Faccioli 1985, p. 51 (and for the quotations that follow).

15. Ibid.

16. "Regimen sanitatis," in *Flos medicinae Scholae Salerni*, ed. A. Sinno, Milan, Mursia, 1987, p. xxxvii: "*si post sumatir, terminat ille dapes.*"

17. Regarding medieval proverbs about food, Cunsolo 1970; Antoniazzi and Citti 1988; Pucci 2012.

18. Flandrin 1997a, pp. 392–394.

19. On the controversial relations between Platina and Maestro Martini, see Laurioux 1996, pp. 41ff; 2006, pp. 503ff.

20. Faccioli 1987, p. 186.

21. Naso 1990a, pp. 140–141: "*Pauperes* [. . .] *et quos ad quottidianam casei commestionem impellit necessitas regulis superioribus asttringuntur, cum cogantur et in principio et in medio ac fine comestionis ipsorum caseum manducare.*"

22. Columella, *L'arte dell'agricoltura* [The art of agriculture], VII, 2, 1, ed. C. Carena, trans. R. Calzecchi Onesti, Turin, Einaudi, 1977, p. 498.

23. Montanari 1993, pp. 98–103. See chapter 7 this volume.

24. Moulin 1988, p. 70.

25. Montanari 1979, pp. 248–249.

26. Ibid.

27. Naso 1990a, p. 77.

28. Ercole Bentivoglio, *Le satire e altre rime piacevole* [Satires and other pleasurable rhymes], Venice, 1557, c. 16r. See Camporesi 1990, pp. 95–97.

29. Faccioli 1987, p. 290 (*Libro novo nel qual s'insegna a far d'ogni sorte di vivande* [The new book that teaches how to prepare every kind of food], Ferrara, 1549).

30. Montanari 2008.

31. Faccioli 1985, p. 50.

32. Anonimo Toscano, *Libro della cocina*, in Faccioli 1087, pp. 58–61, 64–65.

33. Ibid., pp. 66–67.

34. Ibid., pp. 175–176 (Maestro Martino, *Libro de arte coquinaria*).

35. Ibid., pp. 172ff.

36. Ibid., p. 187: "*Habi de bono caso frescho, et un poco di bon caso vecchio . . .* " (recipe for "*frictelle de fior de sambuco*").

37. Ibid., p. 192.

38. Ibid., pp. 193–194.

39. Naso 1990a, pp. 47–48.

40. Ibid., p. 47.

41. "*Numquam did hominem, qui ita libenter lagana cum caseo comederet sicut ipse.*" Messedaglia 1943–44, pp. 384–385.

42. Giovanni Boccaccio, *Decameron*, VIII, 3.

43. Faccioli 1987, pp. 157–158, 160.

44. Celio Malespini, *Novelle*, ed. E. Allodoli, Manciano, 1915, nov. VII, p. 64.

45. Camporesi 1980, p. 102.

46. Cavalcanti, *Cucina teorico-pratica,* Naples, 1839 (first ed. 1837). See the passage in Faccioli 1987, p. 809.

47. Faccioli 1985, p. 51.

48. Naso 1990a, p. 46. In certain regions, such as those of Parma and Ferrara, new breeds were introduced.

49. Ortensio Lando, *Commentario delle più notablii & mostruose cose d'Italia & altri, luoghi,* ed. G. Salvator and P. Salvator, Bologna, Pendragon, 1994 (revised from the Venice edition of 1553, but first published in 1548).

50. Naso 1990a, pp. 45–46, 59 (n. 2).

51. Pantaleone da Confienza, II, 1–2, in Naso 1990a, pp. 114–115. To the "samples," whose excellence is accepted by all, Pantaleone added (for evident reasons of chauvinism) a third: the *robiole* from the Langhe in Piedmont, "small cheeses" (*parvi casei*) little more than a pound, generally made of ewe's milk, even if some add cow's or goat's milk; *bona copia* is made in the nearby Lomellina. Pantaleone da Confienza, II, 3, in Naso 1990a, pp. 115–116.

9. CONDIMENT/FUNDAMENT

1. J. L. Huillard Bréholles, *Historia Diplomatica Friderici II*, Paris, 1852–1861, v. IV, t. 1, p. 383: "in the exercise of royalty it is necessary to increment the prestige of the administration, legislation and arms [*officia, leges et arma*] with the condiment of science [*necessaria fore credimus scientiae condimenta*]." (Enciclica ai maestri dello Studio bolognese, a. 1232.)

2. Febvre 1938, p. 124. See Hémardinquer 1970b, p. 254.

3. *Annales d'Histoire Sociale,* XVI, 2, 1944, p. 32.

4. Hémardinquer 1970a.

5. Stouff 1970, p. 261.

6. Such as Knibiehler 1981, pp. 167–168 (contested by Flandrin; see the following note).

7. Flandrin 1984, p. 32.

8. Hémardinquer 1970a, p. 271 (n. 2).

9. Pliny the Elder, *Naturalis historia,* XXVIII, 133: "*E lacte fit et butyrum, barbararum gentium lautissimus cibus divites a plebe discernat.*"

10. Ibid., XI, 239: "*Non omittendum in eo* [butter] *olei vim esse et barbaros omnes infantesque nosros ita ungui.*"

11. Strabo, *Geografia,* III, 3, 7.

12. Flandrin 1994, pp. 56ff.

13. Cato, *De agricultura,* 79, 80, 121. See André 1981, pp. 184–185.

14. André, p. 183.

15. On this subject, see also Montanari 1993, pp. 12–13.

16. Polibius, *Storie,* II, 15; Strabo, *Geografia,* V, 12, 218.

17. Mazzarino 1961, pp. 217ff (also Corbier 1989, p. 121).

18. Montanari 1993, pp. 19–23. On the importance of the pig in the economy of the high Middle Ages, see Montanari 1979, pp. 232–244; Baruzzi and Montanari 1981.

19. Antimus, *De observantia ciborum*, ed. M. Grant, Blackawton, Prospect Books, 1996. See Montanari 1988a, pp. 206–208.

20. Montanari 1979, p. 232.

21. Ibid., pp. 243–244.

22. Montanari 1988a, pp. 79–80.

23. For the construction during the early centuries of the Middle Ages of a new "alimentary language," created from the joining of Germanic and Roman values, the latter articulated in turn in Christian culture, see Montanari 1993, pp. 12ff.

24. Montanari 1979, p. 158. See chapter 3 this volume.

25. See above, p. 118.

26. "Fragmentum historicum de Concilio Aquisgranensi" (a. 816), in MGH, *Concilia aevi karolini*, I, p. 832: "*Et uia oleum non habent Franci, voluerunt episcopi, ut oleo lardivo utantue.*" See Hémardinquer 1970a, p. 267.

27. MGH, *Concilia aevi karolini*, I, p. 832.

28. Flandrin 1994, p. 38.

29. Ibid., pp. 59, 79 (n. 108).

30. *Capitulare de villis*, XLIV, MGH, *Leges, CRF*, I, pp. 82–91: "*De quadragesimale duae partes ad servitium nostrum veniat per singulos annos, tam de leguminibus quamque et de piscato seu formatico, butirum. . . .*"

31. Hildegard of Bingen, *Subtilitatim diversarum naturarum creaturarum libri novem*, III, 16, PL 197, cc. 1229–1230: "*se comeditur, nauseam provocat, et alios cibos comedendo molestos facit.*"

32. The disgust that the flavor of olive oil aroused in northern lands is demonstrated, according to Flandrin, by the fact that in the sixteenth century, as soon as the Protestant reform rejected the Lenten rule of the Roman papacy, the inhabitants of those lands immediately returned to their traditional use of butter, or else (like the French who remained Catholic) they paid heavily for a papal dispensation to use it during Lent. The building of the "Tower of Butter" on the Rouen Cathedral seems to have been funded by a bishop armed with these dispensations. See Flandrin 1994, p. 57.

33. Liutprando da Cremona, "Relatio de legatione constantinopolitana," 41, XI, in *Liutprandi Opere*, ed. J. Becker, Hanover, Hahn, 1915, pp. 181–182: "*turpi satis et obscena, ebriorum more oleo delibuta.*" Regarding this episode, see Koder and Weber 1980, pp. 85ff; Montanari 1988a, p. 154.

34. *Regula Isidori*, 11, PL 83, c. 881; *Regula Fructuosi*, 18, PL 87, c. 1108; see *Reglas monasticas de la Espagna visigota*, ed. J. Campos Ruiz and I. Toca Melia, Madrid, 1971. Even the *Regula Magistri*, 53, 6–7, suggested that one could do without oil as a condiment, to which end it was not used directly in the preparation of food but added in separate plates so that those who wished to do without could do so. *La Règle di Maître*, ed. A. De Vogûé, Paris, Le Cerf, 1964. According to Cassiano, perpetual abstinence from wine and oil is one of the practices that can be voluntarily observed, if desired, without jeopardizing the monastic profession. *Collationes*, XVII, 28, SC 54, p. 281. The deprivation of oil, like wine, is prescribed in the Byzantine liturgy during days of abstinence (unless they happen to fall on major feast days). Parenti 2003, p. 457.

35. Oil was a great alimentary luxury for those hermits who practiced the more severe abstinences, as seen from Simeone, hermit and later monk in the monastery of

Saint Benedict Po: "only the dish of vegetables which was eaten on the major holidays could be seasoned with bit of oil [*modico ungebat oleo*]." See Montanari 1979, p. 402.

36. On the subject of oil from the Puglie, see Iorio 1985.

37. For all of this, see Cherubini 1984b, pp. 184–188 (and the ample bibliography he provides).

38. Ibid. As of the twelfth century, oil from Apulia was exported to Constantinople. In the fourteenth and fifteenth centuries, oil from the Marches reached Constantinople, Salonika, Cania, and Cyprus. In addition to Italian ships, those from Dalmatia were actively involved in the sale of oil to the Levant.

39. Melis 1984, p. 131.

40. Ibid., p. 132.

41. Bertolotti 1991. An extensive bibliography is found in Ciappelli 1997.

42. *La battaglia di Quaresima e Carnevale*, ed. Lecco, Parma, 1990, pp. 58 (vv. 235–236: "*Charnage . . . voit venir les pois au lart*"), 68 (v. 414: "*pois a l'uile*" threaten Carnival), 58 (v. 258: "*Li burres vient trestout devant*" in aid of Carnival), 71 (v. 488: "*l'uile se combat au saïn*"), 74 (v. 538: "*tuit s'acordent a fere pes*").

43. Ibid., pp. 76–78 (vv. 557–574).

44. See the Veronese case in Brugnoli, Rigoli, and Varanini 1994, pp. 30, 38.

45. Flandrin 1994, pp. 45, 53.

46. Ibid., pp. 36–37 (table 4).

47. Ibid., p. 57.

48. Ibid., p. 61 (see Montanari 1993, p. 147).

49. Flandrin 1994, p. 52.

50. Published in Laurioux 1988 (later reprinted in Laurioux 2005, pp. 57–109).

51. Ibid., pp. 740–741 (n. 61, 63).

52. Ibid., p. 737 (n. 42).

53. Ibid., p. 736 (n. 38).

54. See chapter 2 this volume.

55. Faccioli 1987, p. 158 (Maestro Martino, *Libro de arte coquinaria*).

56. *Libro novo nel qual s'isegna a far d'ogni sorte di vivande* [New book which teaches how to prepare all kinds of dishes], Ferrara, 1549.

57. *Opera*, Venice, 1570.

58. Celio Malespini, *Novelle*, ed. E. Allodoli, Lanciano, 1915, nov. VII, p. 64.

59. Capatti and Montanari 1999, p. 60.

60. See in the appendix to Ortensio Lando, *Commentario delle più notabili & mostruose cose d'Italia & altri luoghi* [Commentary on the most notable and most amazing things in Italy and other places], ed. G. Salvatori and P. Salvatori, Bologna, Pendragon, 1994 (revised from the Venetian edition of 1553, but first published in 1548).

61. *Cronaca modenese di Tommasino de'Bianchi detto de'Lancellotti*, Parma 1862–84, t. VII, 1539, pp. 176ff (quoted in Basini 1970, p. 14). See also Camporesi 1980, p. 102.

62. Faccioli 1985, p. 52 (II, 41). For the relations between Maestro Martino and Platina, see Laurioux 2006, pp. 503ff.

63. Michele Savonarola, *Libretto di tutte les cosse che se magnano, Un'opera di ditetica del sec. XV*, ed. J. Nystedt, Stockholm, 1988, p. 148 (and for what follows). Geremia Simeoni, a fifteenth-century doctor from Friuli, recommends avoiding "milk and its derivatives,

of whatever kind," beginning with butter. *De conservando sanitate, I consigli di un medico del Quattrocento*, ed. M. D'Angelo, Cassacco, 1993, p. 69. For the overall diffidence of ancient and medieval doctors toward dairy products, see Camporesi 1985.

64. Montanari 1993, pp. 103–115.

65. Savonarola, *Libretto*, pp. 128, 160.

66. Ibid., p. 159.

67. Montanari, p. 160.

68. Ibid., pp. 105–108 (and for what follows). See Flandrin 1994, p. 10, and chapter 6 this volume.

69. Montanari 1993, pp. 118–120.

70. Images of poor valley people who ate butter can be found in travel literature, a fine example being Gillet 1985, pp. 60–62 (Jouvin de Rochefort's stop in Alto Adige).

71. Naso 1990b, p. 201.

72. G. Carbonelli, "*De sanitatis custodia*" *di maestro Giacomo Albini di Moncalieri con altri documenti sulla storia della medicina*," Pinerolo, 1906, p. 84.

73. Panthaleonis de Conflentia, *Summa lacticiniorum*, II, 11, in Naso 1990a, pp. 122–123 (a translation into Italian was made by Emilio Faccioli: Pantaleone da Confienza, *Trattato dei latticini*, Milan, 1990). See Camporesi 1990.

74. See chapter 8 this volume.

75. *Summa lacticiniorum*, II, 11, in Naso 1990a, pp. 122–123.

76. Ibid., II, 12, in Naso 1990a, p. 125.

77. Ibid., II, 14, in Naso 1990a, p. 126.

78. Ibid., II, 13, in Naso 1990a, p. 126.

79. Ibid., III, 1, in Naso 1990a, p. 128.

80. Flandrin 1994, p. 33 and notes.

81. *Summa lacticiniorum*, II, 13, in Naso 1990a, p. 126. "I do not remember eating good cheese [because of the passion for butter] in all of Flanders, not in Brabant nor in Hainaut or in Artois."

82. Flandrin 1994, pp. 38, 71–72 (n. 49) for the quotation from Champier.

83. On the question of the cultivation of olives in the Middle Ages, see Cherubini 1984b; Pini 1990; Pasquali 1972; Varanini 1983; Iorio 1985.

84. Ibid., pp. 302–303.

85. Dufourcq and Gautier-Dalché 1983, p. 153.

86. Pliny the Elder, *Naturalis historia*, XXIII, 88.

87. Ibid., XXIII, 79: oil for medicinal use should be "*tenue, odoratum quodque non mordeat* [thin, fragrant but not biting]," unlike the one "*cibis eligitur* [used for food]." See André 1981, p. 182.

88. Flandrin 1994, p. 42.

89. Gillet 1985, p. 136.

90. Ibid., pp. 135–136. See Flandrin 1994, pp. 42–44.

91. Flandrin 1994, p. 42. Evelyn's treatise *Acetaria, A Discourse of Sallets* was printed in 1699 (see Montanari 1993, p. 145).

92. Flandrin 1994, p. 41.

93. Brugnoli, Rigoli, and Varanini 1994, pp. 57–58.

94. *Capitulare de villis*, 35, p. 86. See Montanari 1988a, p. 40.

95. Montanari 1992, pp. 96–97. See chapter 6 this volume.

96. See above note 9.

97. Vincenzo Tanara, *L'economia del cittadno in villa*, Venice, 1665 (first edition published in Bologna in 1644), pp. 14–175 (see Camporesi 1985, pp. 71–72).

98. See chapter 1 this volume.

99. Flandrin 1994, p. 28. On this "revolution of taste," see Pinkard 2009 and chapter 1 this volume.

100. Bartolomeo Stefani, *L'arte di ben cucinare*, Mantova, 1662, p. 54.

101. Brugnoli, Rigoli, and Varanini 1994, p. 43.

102. Pellegrino Artusi, *La scienze in cucina e 'arte de mangiar bene*, ed. A. Capatti, Milan, Rizzoli, 2010, p. 209 (recipe).

103. See Camporesi 1970; Montanari 2010.

104. Artusi, *La scienza*, passim.

105. Hémardinquer (1970a, p. 261) has brought to light this phenomenon with regard to France. For Italy, equally up-to-date studies are lacking. Nevertheless, on the evolution of Italian food choices during the past century, see Capatti, De Bernardi, and Varni 1998; Sorcinelli 1999.

10. THE BREAD TREE

1. This definition (the chestnut as "acorn" or "walnut") frequently recurs in works by all the Latin agronomists and even in texts on dietetics, like the one by Galen, which will be quoted below.

2. Columella, *De re rustica*, IV, 33.

3. Pliny the Elder, *Naturalis historia*, XV, 25.

4. Grant 2005, p. 145 (*On the properties of foods*, book II).

5. Montanari 1979, pp. 38–42.

6. *Edictus ceteraeque Langobardorum leges*, ed. F. Blühme, Hanover, 1989, p. 301.

7. Montanari 1993, p. 5.

8. For this and what follows, see Cherubini 1984a.

9. Comba 1983, p. 51.

10. Bruneton-Governatori 1984.

11. Bonvesin de la Riva, *De magnalibus Mediolani*, ed. M. Corti, Milan, 1974, IV, p. 98.

12. Cherubini 1984a, p. 157.

13. Castor Durante da Guido, *Il tesoro della sanità*, Rome, 1586, ed. E. Camillo, Milan, 1982, p. 113.

14. Cherubini 1984a, p. 154.

15. Giacomo Castelvetro, "Brieve racconto di tutte le radici, di tutte l'erbe e di tutti i frutti che crudi o cotti in Italia si mangiano," in *Gastronomia del Rinascimento*, London, 1614, ed. L. Firpo, Turin, Utet, 1973, p. 165.

16. Piero de'Crescenzi, *Trattato della agricoltura*, traslato della favella fiorentina, revisto dallo 'Nferigno accademico della Crusca, Bologna, 1784, I, p. 199 (v. 6).

17. G. A. D'Herrera, *Agriculture viewed by various ancient and modern writers*, trans. (into Italian) Manbrino da Fabriano, Venice, 1568, p. 107. Quoted in Gasparini 1988, p. 9.

18. Vincenzo Tanara, *L'economia del cittadino in villa*, Venice, 1665 (first printed in Bologna, 1644), p. 507.

19. Salimbene da Adam, *Cronica*, ed. G. Scala, Bari, Latanza, 1966, II, p. 846.

20. Cherubini 1984a. The expression "plant of civilization" is used by Fernand Braudel to indicate the central role that certain plants (wheat, rice, corn) played in the productive and symbolic system of entire regions of the world and their historic development. See Montanari 2004, p. 8.

21. Zagnoni 1997, pp. 49–50, 56 (app. 2).

22. Agostino Gallo, *Le vinti giornate dell'agricoltura e de'piaceri della villa*, Venice, 1593, p. 117.

23. Columella, *De re rustica*, op. cit.

24. Tanara, *L'economia*, p. 506.

25. Zagnoni 1997, pp. 53–54.

26. de'Crescenzi, *Trattato della agricoltura*, pp. 297–298.

27. Gallo, *Le vinti giornate*, p. 117.

28. Cherubini 1984a, p. 154.

29. Bruneton-Governatori 1984, pp. 281–321.

30. Montanari 1979, pp. 148–150.

31. Montanari 2004, pp. 23–25.

32. Cherubini 1984a, p. 157.

33. de'Crescenzi, *Trattato della agricoltura*, p. 298 (v. 6).

34. Ibid.

35. Gallo, *Le vinti giornate*, p. 118.

36. Cherubini 1984a, p. 162.

37. Tanara, *L'economia*, p. 506.

38. Castelvetro, "Brieve racconto," p. 165.

39. Cherubini 1984a, p. 160.

40. Tanara, *L'economia*, p. 507.

41. Cherubini 1984a, p. 154.

42. Ibid., p. 167.

43. Ibid., pp. 160–161.

44. Cagnin 1988, p. 41.

45. "Bononia manifesta," in *Catalogo dei bandi, editti, costituzioni e provvedimenti diversi, stampati del XVI secolo per Bologna e suo territorio*, ed. Z. Zanardi, Florence, Olschki, 1996 (n. 2539).

46. Tanara, *L'economia*, p. 507.

47. Castelvetro, "Brieve racconto," p. 165.

48. Durante, *Il tesoro della sanità*, p. 113.

49. Tanara, *L'economia*, p. 505.

50. Ibid.

51. Durante, *Il tesoro della sanità*, p. 113.

52. P. A. Mattioli, *I discorsi nelli sei libri di Pedacio Dioscoride Anazarbeo della materia medicinale*, Venice, 1568, p. 229.

53. Tanara, *L'economia*, p. 505.

54. Bartolomeo Platina, *Il piacere onesto e la buona salute*, ed. E. Faccioli, Turin, Eindaudi, 1985, p. 187. On the relations between Platina and Maestro Martino, see Laurioux 2006, pp. 503ff.

55. Bartolomeo Scappi, *Opera*, Venice, 1570, II, CLXXXVII, p. 71; V, CXX, p. 365.

56. See chapter 13 this volume. See also Montanari 2010, pp. 23–32.

57. Pérez Samper 1998, p. 232 (III, 8).

58. "Le confiturier françois," X, in *Le cuisinier françois*, presented by J.-L. Flandrin, and P. Hyman, Paris, Montalba, 1983, p. 481.

59. Tanara, *L'economia*, p. 507.

60. Mattioli, *I discorsi*, pp. 228–229; Durante, *Il tesoro della sanità*, p. 113.

61. Tanara, *L'economia*, p. 508.

62. Bonvesin de la Riva, *De magnalibus Mediolani*, IV, 14, p. 98.

63. *Codex Astensis*, ed. Q. Sella, IV, Rome, 1880, pp. 43–44 (n. 1022). See Montanari 1989, pp. 318–319.

11. THE FLAVOR OF WATER

1. Guillelmus de Sancto Theodorico, *Liber de natura corporis et animae*, I, 46, ed. M. Lemoine, Paris, 1998: *"Visus enim igneae esg naturae, auditus aeriae, odoratus fumeae, gustus aquosae, tactus terrenae."*

2. *Navigatio ancti Brendani abbatis*, 16, ed. C. Selmer, Notre Dame, Indiana, 1959.

3. Ibid., p. 26.

4. The expression is from Roche (1984). In developed countries, the "conquest of water" does not precede the nineteenth century, see Goubert 1986. Useful suggestions are found in Sorcinelli 1998.

5. Cassiodorus, in his letters, speaks of those of Paria and Ravenna. *Variae*, VIII, 30; V, 38 (CCL, XCVI).

6. The first example is Saint Anthony, who, in the Egyptian desert, on at least two occasions made water gush up to slake the thirst of men and animals. Anastasius, *Vita Antonii*, 54, 1–5; 59, 1–5, ed. G. J. M. Bartelinl, Milan, Valla-Mondadori, 1974 (*Vite dei santi*, ed. C. Mohrmann, I), pp. 45, 48; the original Greek text is in PG, XXVI, cc. 919, 927. In the first instance, it is Anthony himself, visiting places of prayer of some hermits with only a camel to help him transport bread and water, who remained without water along with his companions. Having stopped to pray, he asked God to make water gush out, thereby restoring the animals as well and filling the empty water skins. In the second instance, two hermits on their way to Anthony finished their water supply. One of the two died from thirst; the other was saved by Anthony who, illuminated while praying, sent other hermits to help him (the hagiographer asks why both were not saved and then replies that the option of life or death is not up to Anthony but to God).

7. Numbers 20:2–11 (Moses makes water gush out of the desert rock to slake the thirst of the Israelites).

8. One example among many appears in *Vita Willibrordi*, XVI, 9, MGH, SRM, VII, p. 129: the saint, to relieve the shortage of water, prays to God *"qui populo suo in desertis aquam produxit de petra."*

9. *Vita Carileffi*, 4, AS Iulii I.

10. On the substantial "nonexistence" of the topos, too often invoked by scholars, which in any case refers to an extratextual truth, a well-defined environmental and cultural *context*, I refer the reader to considerations I proposed in Montanari 1988b. On the relationship text-context and the possibility/necessity of leaving the first

to arrive at the second, see the fine methodological pages in Ginsburg 2000, pp. 44–49.

11. Montanari 2003.

12. Gregory the Great, *Dialogi*, II, ed. A. De Vogüé, SC, 261–265.

13. Ibid., III, 16.

14. Giona di Bobbio, *Vita di Colombano e dei suoi discepoli*, I, 9, ed. B. Krusch, Hanover, 1905.

15. *Vita Gualtieri auctore Marbodo*, AS, *Maii* II, p. 702.

16. *Vita Leufredi*, AS, *Iunii* V, p. 95.

17. Saint Venanzio makes water flow from a rock, and this leads many to convert. *Acta Apocrypha S. Venantii*, AS, *Maii* IV, p. 141.

18. This example, among others, is taken from Gregory of Tours, *Liber in gloria martyrum*, 36, MGH, SRM, I/2, p. 61: in the territory of the city Lemovicina, a spring that watered the fields changed course and ended in a swamp, making it unusable for irrigation; Saint Clement miraculously turned it back to normal.

19. An example in *Vita Walfridi*, AS, *Feb.* II, pp. 843–844.

20. *Via Sentiae in Tuscia*, AS, *Maii* VI, p. 72.

21. Cassiodorus, *Variae*, IV, 31.

22. Muzzarelli 1982.

23. Augustine, *Confessioni*, X, 31, 44.

24. Squatriti 2008, pp. 593–594.

25. *Vita Livini Flandrensis*, PL 87, c. 337.

26. *Vita patrum lurensium*, II, 2, MGH, SRM, III, p. 144.

27. Gregorii Turonensis, *Vitae Patrum*, I, 2, MGH, SRM, I, 2, p. 665.

28. *Vita S. Emani presbyteri*, AS, *Maii* III, p. 597.

29. Palladio, *Storia Lausiaca*, 39, 3, ed. G. J. M. Bertelink, Milan, 1974, p. 205.

30. Guillelmus de Sancto Theodorico, *Liber de natura corporis et animae*, I, 16.

31. Tommaso da Celano, *Vita prima sancti Francisci*, I, 51: "*octa cibaria . . . saepe aut conficiebat cinere aut condimenti saporem aqua frigida extinguebat*." See Bonaventura, *Legenda maior sancti Francisci*, V, 1: "*condimenti saporem admixtione acquae ut plurimum reddebat insipidum*."

32. See chapter 18 this volume.

33. "Regimen satitatis," in *Flos medicinae Scholae Salerni*, ed. A. Sinno, Milan, Mursia, 1987, p. 84.

34. Palladi Rutilii Tauri Aemiliani, *Opus agriculturae*, I, 17, ed. R. H. Rodgers, Leipzig, B/G. Teubner, 1975, p. 21.

35. Ermini Pani, 2008.

36. Walter Map, *De nugis curialium*, II, ed. C. N. L. Brooke and R. A. B. Mynors, Oxford, Clarendon, 1983: "*non bibes aquan veterem que de se rivum non facit*."

37. On techniques of purifying water, see Lorcin 1985; Moulin 1988, pp. 120–121.

38. Pucci Donati 1007, pp. 131–133.

39. André 1981, pp. 172–173.

40. Matthew 27:48: "Suddenly one of them ran and took a sponge and after soaking it in vinegar, speared it on a stick and gave it to him to drink." That this "vinegar" was the *posca* of Roman soldiers seems fairly plausible (some translators see in this "stick" the standard issue javelin), just as it can be seen as a charitable gesture. See also John

19:28–29: "Jesus, knowing that all things were now accomplished, that the scripture might be fulfilled, saith, I thirst. Now there was set a vessel full of vinegar: and they filled a sponge with vinegar and put it upon hyssop and put it to his mouth." Only Luke 23:36 describes the gesture as malevolent: "And the soldiers also mocked him, coming to him, and offering him vinegar." This reading of this episode probably recalls Psalms 69:22: "They put poison in my food and when I was thirsty they gave me vinegar."

41. See chapter 12 this volume.

42. Hippocrates, *De dieta*, II, LII, 1.

43. Only at the start of the seventeenth century did the idea make headway that the digestive process was related to chemical rather than physical reactions. Flandrin 1997b, pp. 540–546.

44. "De observantia ciborum," in *Traduzione tardo-antico del Perì diàites pseudoippocratico*, I, II, ed. I. Mazzini, Rome, G. Bretschneider, 1984, ch. 96, p. 7. The dietary-gastronomic treatise by Antimus (sixth century) also insists from the very beginning on the need, for the purpose of digestion, for a thorough "cooking" of the food in the stomach and on the resulting pernicious consequences of anything (such as too much water) that might cool it. Anthimus, *De observantia ciborum*, ed. M. Grant, Blackawton, Prospect Books, 1996, p. 46.

45. "Regimen sanitatis," V, 6 (*Potus aquae*), p. 82. See De Renzi, *Collectio salernitana*, Naples, 1852, I, p. 452, pp. 246–247: "*Potus aquae sumptus fit edemti valde nocivus, / Hinc friget stomachus, crudus et inde cibus.*"

46. "Regimen sanitatis," V, 1 (*De potu*), p. 76: "*ut digestio fit tibi pocula sint bona vina.*"

47. Quoted from Lorcin 1985, p. 263: "*vinum etiam pose eas [aquas] potatum est illi aliquod remedium.*"

48. This usage, widely practiced in Roman times, was particularly common in the region of Byzantium (Kislinger 2003, pp. 141–142), but also in the West mention of it is found: cups of wine heated with water (*caldellos*) are mentioned in *Regula ad virgines* by César of Arles, *Recapitulatio*, XVI, PL 67, c. 1120; see Archetti 2003, p. 220.

49. "*i jungas aquam moderanter corpora nutrit,*" the *Flos medicinae* declares regarding wine. "Regimen sanitatis," V, 1, p. 76.

50. Gregory 2008, p. 1.

51. Prospero 2007, pp. 300–310.

52. Ibid., pp. 302–303 (commentary on *De sensu et sensato* by Aristotle).

53. Guillaume de Conches, *Dragmaticon [Dialogus de substantiis physicis]*, V, 10, 3, ed. G. Gratarolus, Strasbourg, 1576, reprinted Frankfurt am Main, 1967.

54. Cassiodorus, *Variae*, III, p. 53.

55. See the case of Piero de'Crescenzi, recalled by Squatriti 2008, pp. 584–585.

56. See some examples in Flandrin 1990, pp. 161–162.

57. Augustinus Hipponensis, *Sermones*, 4, ed. RB 79.

58. Hyeronimus, "Commentarii in propheti minores," 76, in *Amos*, II, 5, SL 76, ed. M. Adriaen, 1969. See Isidorus Hispalensis, *De natura rerum*, XXXIII, 1, ed. J. Fontaine, Bibliothèque de l'école des chartes, 28, 1960; Beda Venerablis, *De natura rerum liber*, 32, SL 123, ed. C. W. Jones, 1975.

59. Rupertus Tuitiensis, "Commentarium," in *Apocalypsim Iohannis apostoli*, II, 3, PL 169, cc. 825–1214.

60. For example, Gregorius Magnus, *Registrum epistularum*, XII, 43, SL 140, ed. D. Norberg, 1982.

61. "What tastes good is good for you" is what medieval doctors think and write: see chapter 18 this volume.

62. "*Liber III Ippocratis . . . de cibis vel de potum quod homo usitare debet*," in V. Rose, *Anecdota graeca et graecolatina, Mitteilunged aus Handschriften zue Geschichte der griechischen Wissenschaft*, Ii, Amsterdam, Hakkert, 1963, p. 154.

63. Cassiodorus, *Variae*, V, 38.

64. *Itinerarium Egeriae seu Peregrinatop ad loca sancta*, 11, SL 175, ed. P. Geyer and O. Cuntz, 1965.

65. Rose, *Anecdota graeca et graecolatina*, p. 199: "*munda, perspicua sine aliquo odore vel sapore, pondere levi et quae cum requieverit, nullum ex se humi sedimen dimittat.*"

66. Pliny the Elder, *Naturalis historia*, XXXI, 37: "*aquarum salubrium sapor odorve nullus esse debet.*"

67. Gaudentius Brixiensis, *Tractatus XXI*, 11, 4, CSEL 68, ed. A. Glück, 1936.

68. Cassiodorus, *Variae*, VIII, 30.

69. Maximus Taurinensis, *Collectio sermonum antiqua*, 65, SL 23, ed. A. Mutzenbecher, 1962: "*sicut aqua nullius saporis nullius odoris, nullius est praetii, nec sufficiens ad usum nec delectabile ad reficiendum, nec tolerabilis ad servandum.*"

70. Galbertus Brugensis, *De multro, traditione et occasione gloriosi Karoli comitis Flandriarum*, 73, CM 131, ed. J. Rider, 1994.

71. Ambrosius Mediolanesis, *Expositio Evangekii secundum Lucam*, 6, SL 14, ed. M. Adriaen, 1957: "*dum aquam minister infundit, odor transfusus iebriat, color mutatus informat, fidem quoque sapor haustus adcumulat.*"

72. Maximus Taurinensis, *Collectio sermonum antiqua*, 101: "*ex illa vili aqua vini optimi saporem voluit gustare convivas.*" The adjective appears elsewhere in the works of Maximus: when Jesus was baptized, he instituted the sacrament of baptism, and "*humanum genus velut aquam in aeternam substantiam divinittis sapore cincertit.*" Ibid., 65.

73. *Tractatus in evangelicum Iohannis*, 8, 9–12; see Tombeur 1989, pp. 265–266.

74. Balduinus da Forda (Cantauriensis), *Tractatus de sacramento altaris*, II, 1.

75. Godefridus Admontensis, *Homilias festivales*, 17.

76. Beda Venerabilis, *Homeliarum Evangelii Libri II*, I, 14, SL 122, ed. D. Hurst, 1955.

77. Alcuinus, *Commentaria in sancti Iohannis Evangelium*, ep. Ad Gislam et Rodtrudam.

78. Maximus Taurinensus, *Collectio sermonum antiqua*, 103: "*et ut aqua in vinum versa sapore rubore calore conditur, ita scienti quod erat in his insulum accepit saporem, quod pallen gatiae sumpsit colorem, quod frigidum incaluit immortalitatis ardore.*"

79. "Vita Lidewigis virginis," I, 6, in Thomas Hemerken a Kempis *Opera omnia*, VI, ed. M. J. Pohl, 1905.

80. See chapter 18 this volume.

81. Gaudentius Brixiensis, *Tractatus XXI*, 9, 37, CSEL, 68, ed. A. Glück, 1936.

82. Eusebius Gallicanus, *Collectio homiliarum*, SL 101, ed. F. Glorie, 1970, hom. 6: "*Aquis intra hydrias permanentibus idem liquor sed non idem sapor.*" See *Homiliarium Veronense*, hom. 2: "*Aqua enim intra idrias permanens, cum in vini saporem vertitur, idem licor sed non idem sapor.*"

83. *Chronica monasterii sancti Michaelis Clusini*, XV–XVI, MGH, SS XXX/2, p. 967. See Montanari 1988a, pp. 89, 102–103 (n. 193).

84. Archetti 2003, p. 286 (n. 242).

85. "Vita sancti Iohannis cumfesoris," ed. G. Sergi, *Bulletino dell'Istituto Storico Italiano per il Medio Evo*, 81, 1969, p. 168: "*ex modico ampule illius mero . . . mira largitate superhabundanti omnes recreatos.*"

86. Also proposed by Sergi 1970, p. 208.

87. *Chronica monasterii,* op. cit.

88. A single example: Aldegonda has a vision of Saints Peter and Paul, and "*am imo terrae venam fontis scaturire.*" *Vita Aldegundae,* AS, Ian. II, p. 1049.

89. Balduinus da Forda, *Tractatus de sacramento altaris,* III, 2, SC 94, p. 564: "*sitim aquae tam aquae quam vini potio refrigerare potest, altera juxta votum, altera supra votum.*"

90. *Vitae Patrum* IV, Exc. ex Sulp. et Cass., XXXVI, PL 73, c. 838: "*ipsus aquae tanta penuria constringuntur, ut tali diligentia dispenserint, quali nemo facit pretiosissimum vinum.*"

91. The canon of the eight flavors is in *On the soul,* II (B) 10–11, 422b. The reduction to seven is in *Sense and Sensibilia,* 4, 442a.

92. This is documented for the first time in the eleventh century in the treatise on dietetics by Ibn Butlan; see Grappe 2006, p. 77.

93. Laurioux 1997a, pp. 360–361.

94. Guillaume de Conches, *Dragmaticon,* V, 10. 1.

95. Grappe 2006, p. 77 (table).

96. "Regimen sanitatis," p. 104.

97. De Renzi, *Collectio salernitana,* IV, p. 323.

98. Salimbene de Adam, *Cronica,* I, ed. G. Scalia, Bari, Laterza, 1966.

12. THE CIVILIZATION OF WINE

1. Augustine, *Enarationes en Psalmos,* 83, 1, 22, 16–20, CC, SL, 39: "*Uva pendet in vitibus, et oliva in arboribus . . . et nec uva vinum est, nec oliva oleum, ante pressuram.*" See Tombeur 1989, pp. 236, 237–248 (for the symbolism of the press).

2. On the economic and technologic aspects of wine production in antiquity, see the synthesis by Brun (2003).

3. Cicero, *De Republica* 3, 9, 16: "*transalpinas gentes oleam et vineam serere non sinimus, quo pluris sint nostraeque vinear.*" See Cogrossi 2003, p. 501.

4. Paolo Diacono, *Historia Langobardorum,* II, 23: "*Dum enim vinum degustassent ab Italia delatum, aviditate vini inlecti ad Italiam transierunt.*" Pliny the Elder, *Naturalis historia,* XII, 5, also included oil and dried figs among the desires of the Gauls. The motive is already in Livy, *Ad urbe condita libri,* V, 33.

5. Caesar, *Bellum gallicum,* II, 15: the Nervii, a people of northern Gaul near Belgium, "*nihil pati vini reliquarumque rerum ad luxuriam pertinentium inferri, quod his ebus relanguescere animos eorum virtutemque relitti existimarent*"; the Suebi (Swabians) "*vinum ad se omnino importatri non patiuntur, quod ea re ad laborem ferendum remollescere homines atque effeminari arbitrantur.*" See Cogrossi 2003, pp. 501–502 (who interprets these measures as protectionist with regard to the local production of beer, although the text does not seem to suggest such a reading).

6. Suetonius, *De vita Caesarum, Domititianus* 7, 2. See Dion 1959, p. 129.

7. *Historia Augusta, Probus* 18, 8: "*Gallis omnibus et Hispanis ac Britannis hinc permisit, ut vites haberent vinumque conficerent.*"

8. Among the various texts that mention this ordinance (Vopiscus, Eutropius, and others), the *Chronology of Eusebius* associates it with the decisive victory over the barbarians (Dion 1959, p. 148). Cogrossi (2003, p. 502) writes that despite the edict of Marcus Aurelius, even a century later, Valentius and Gratian prohibited the exportation of wine to the barbarians. But the text cited (*Codex Iustiniani* 4, 41, 1) speaks only of *liquamen*, a term that in the Roman era specifically applied to fish sauce. In point of fact, this is the medieval gloss of Bartolomeo da Saliceto that interpreted *liquamen*—mistakenly, in my opinion—as the generic meaning of "liquid," thus including wine and oil.

9. Dion 1959, p. 128.

10. Montanari 1993, p. 24.

11. *Sermones*, 28, 3, 70: "*Vinum, oleum, panis sunt vitae alimenta firmissima.*"

12. *Confessiones*, 5, 13–23.

13. Archetti 2003, pp. 301–301 (n. 286).

14. In the fifth century, the Lateran basilica alone used 8,730 lamps; see Arnaldi 1986, p. 43.

15. Dion 1959, pp. 171ff.

16. Unwin 1993, pp. 146–147.

17. Matheus 2003, pp. 92–98.

18. Unwin 1993, pp. 92–98.

19. Younger 1966, p. 234.

20. Archetti 1998, p. 14.

21. Ibid., p. 481.

22. Fumagalli 1976, p. 159.

23. Ibid., pp. 14–16.

24. Branca 2003.

25. Incmaro of Rheims, *Vita Remigii episcopi Remensis*, 19, MGH, SRM, III, p. 311: "*bibit inde rex ac regalis familia et numerosa turba.*"

26. Pescennio is said to have replied, "Shame! Those who defeated you drink only water!" This appear in Elio Sparziano; see Branca 2003, p. 167.

27. Alcuin, *Epistolae*, 7, MGH, *Epistolae Karolini Aevi*, II, pp. 33–34: "*quia nos non habemus, tu bibe pro nostro nomine . . . saluta fratres nostros in Baccho.*"

28. Gautier 2004, p. 437.

29. On the sale of wine by Frisians in northern lands, see Matheus 2003, pp. 95–96.

30. Gautier 2004, p. 437.

31. Alcuin, *Camina*, XXVI, v. 49, MGH, *Poetae litini medii aevi*, I, p. 256.

32. Theodulf, *Carmina*, XXV (*Carmen ad Carolum regem*), vv. 193–194, MGH, *Poetae latini medii aevi*, I, p. 488: "*Aut se, Bacchem tui, aur Cerealis pocla liquoris / Porgere praecipiat, fors et utrumque vlet. . . .*"

33. In the *Life of Colombano* I, 27, pagans of Swabian ancestry celebrate a "*sacrificium profanum*" around a cauldron of beer that the saint destroys. Giona di Bobbio, *Vitae Columbani abbatis discipulorumque eius*, I, 27, ed. B. Krusch, Hanover, 1905, pp. 213–214. The Bishop Vedast blesses with the sign of the cross the containers of beer to be served with the meal, but some of them, "*gentili ritu sacrificata*," leak, and the beer drips to the ground. Giona di Bobbio, *Vita Vedastis episcopi Atrebatensis*, 7, ibid., pp. 314–316. Beer therefore, as is evident, is not "pagan" in itself but only when it is used as a sacred drink, replacing wine as the protagonist of a religious ceremony. Surely for this reason as well, ecclesiastic

legislation prohibited the consecration on the altar *"pro vino siceram."* See the canon of Reginone, quoted by Bellini 2003, p. 378.

34. Gautier (2004, p. 441) points out how this definition—through wine—of a religious and cultural identity, in no way antinational, differs radically from the one apparent in twelfth-century England when, after the Norman invasion, local authors undertook the defense of beer against wine precisely to protect their national identity.

35. Archetti 2003, p. 309 (*Consuetudines Floriacenses antiquiores*).

36. Dion 1959, p. 171.

37. Ibid., p. 190. See Lachiver 1988, p. 54.

38. Devroey 1989, p. 16.

39. Ibid., p. 18: "Dion has perhaps insisted too much on the role, in his view decisive, played by the aristocracy in the origin and continuity of the medieval vineyard" (as he overemphasized the role of the ecclesiastic and monastic aristocracy); see above.

40. Ibid.

41. Ibid., p. 19.

42. *Vita Carileffi abbatis Anisolensis*, 7, 9, MGH, SRM, III, pp. 391–392. Carileff's wine was the fruit of a vine he had secretly planted himself in the woods of a royal estate. When the king was about to leave, his horse stood stock still as though under a spell. Childebert turned to Carileff, kneeled before him, and asked him, *"pro benedictione de vino quod prius promiserat."* As soon as he drank that humble wine, the spell was broken, and the horse regained his movement.

43. *Capitolare missorum Niumagae datum*, 17, MGH, *Leges*, CRF, I, p. 132: "Quicumque . . . tempore messis vel tempore vindemiae non necessitate sed propter cupiditatem comparat annonam et vinum . . . hoc turpe lucrum dicimus."

44. Montanari 1979, p. 456.

45. *De moribus ecclesdiae catholicae et de moribus Manichaeorum*, 2, 29. In the *Enarrationes in Psalmos*, 62, 10, 5, Augustine declares that without wine *"durare non possumus."* Both passages are quoted by Tombeur (1989, p. 268). See the *Benedictio vini* of the eighth century, in which God is thanked for *"hanc creaturam vivi, quam ad substantiam servorum tuorum tribuisti."* Dell'Oro 2003, p. 438.

46. At least until the tenth and eleventh centuries, there is no record of presses belonging to noblemen: wine making was "decentralized" on individual peasant farms. Devroey 1989, p. 44.

47. Pasquali 1974, pp. 228–231; Montanari 1979, p. 380.

48. Flandrin 1992, pp. 141ff (*Le statut des aliments*). It is precisely Flandrin who coined this expression. See also chapter 7 this volume.

49. On miracles of wine, see Tomea 2003.

50. Dion 1959, p. 190.

51. An example is found in ibid., p. 188. Donato, *Vita Ermelandi abbatis Antrensis*, MGH, SRM, V, p. 697: in the seventh century, Abbot Ermelando of Antresis is traveling with his disciples in the region of Coutances. A local nobleman, Launo, wishes to invite him honorably, but he has almost emptied his wine barrels. Miraculously, the little that was left increased so that he was able to receive his guest with dignity. Also in Tomea 2003, p. 343.

52. Dion 1959, p. 189. Childebert II, king of Austrasia, is the guest of the Bishop of Verdun, who multiplies the wine for the occasion.

53. Pini 2000, p. 370. During the communal period, Pini continues, referring in particular to Italy, the locality of the wine miracles moved into an urban setting, always leaving out the peasants, who would continue "not to drink it" (ibid., p. 372). Conclusion: "If drinking wine was the equivalent until the eleventh century of identifying someone as a nobleman or a churchman, in the twelfth century it served to identify a "burgher" or, more broadly, a "city person" (ibid., p. 373). This statement, in both its parts, seems to me amply contradicted by documents, as we shall soon see.

54. Tomea 2003, p. 347. Miracles around wine "concern a use, no longer reserved for eminent classes, to celebrate a holiday or anniversary, in connection with special events in which the entire community participates or simply in relation to charity."

55. *Vita Odiliae abbatissaw Hohenburgensis*, 21, MGH, SRM, VI, p. 48.

56. *Vita Chrotildis*, MGH, SRM, II, pp. 346–347. See Tomea 2003, p. 352.

57. *Dialogi* I, 9, SC 251.

58. As in the case of Launo, located in the region of Coutances in northwest France, recounted in Donato, *Vita Ermelandi*. Even in the south, wine can be lacking, but the serenity with which Benedict directs the monks not to complain if the *necessitas loci* were to reduce the daily ration (*Regula Benedicti*, 40, 8: "*Ubi autem necessitas loci exposcit ut nec suprascripta mensura* [the daily serving prescribed in the Rule] *in veniri possit, sed multo minus aut ex toto nihil*") seems informed, aside from a precise moral commitment, by the psychological security stemming from the regular provision of wine. "Here we have wine in abundance," writes Theodemarus, the abbot of Montecassino, to Charlemagne to justify the supplementary rations distributed to the monks: "Theodomari abbatis Casinensis epistula ad Karolum regem," in *Initia consuetudinis benedictinae, Consuetudines saeculi octavi et noni* (*Corpus consuetudinum monasticarum*, 1), Siegburg 1963, p. 166. See Archetti 2003, p. 238.

59. Significant is the case of the region of Rheims, examined by Devroey (1989), where the exchanges seem to be "closed within a local or regional framework," as evidenced by the play of offer and demand in periods of overabundance or scarcity; the fall of prices, when wine was plentiful seems to indicate "that there were few or no external replacement markets capable of absorbing excessive quantities" (p. 124).

60. Gregory of Tours, *In gloria confessorum*, 5, MGH, SRM, I, 2, p. 752.

61. Devroey 1989, p. 31.

62. Diploma of Adalberone in *Historia monasterii Monomensis*, MGH, SS, XIV, p. 163: "*ne indigentia vini satis vos coangustet.*"

63. Matheus 2003, p. 95.

64. Reginone of Prüm, *Chronicon cum continuatione Treverensi*, MGH, SS, in us. sch., 50, p. 75. See Matheus 2003, p. 98.

65. Giona di Bobbio, *Vitae Columbani*, I, 16, p. 179.

66. In gratitude for this divine intervention, the count gives the monks of Saint-Sauveur de Redon rights to the island. The text is in Tomea 2003, p. 347.

67. Crodegango of Metz, *Regula canonicorum*.

68. MGH, *Concilia*, II, p. 401.

69. "Collectio capitularis Bernedicti Levitae," in *Initia coInseutudinis benedictinae*, pp. 547–548: "*ubi vinum non est.*" See Archetti 2003, p. 308.

70. Flandrin 1992, pp. 153–167 (Le bon pain).

71. *Allegoriae un universam Sacram Scripturam*, PL 112. cc. 1078–1079. See Tombeur 1989, pp. 252–253.

72. *De clericorum institutione*, I, 31, PL 107, c. 316: "*quasi ipsa fructus terrae dignitate praecellant, et pretiosiores omnibus fiant.*" See Tombeur 1989, p. 260.

73. Tombeur 1989, pp. 201–202. Why did this just man, Noah, seek the voluptuary over the necessary? Ambrose's reply is surprising: precisely because he was just, he was concerned with secondary things, leaving to God to provide the necessary.

74. *Tractatus in evangelium Iohannis*, 8, 3, 9–12: "*sapientes nos fecit; sapimus enim fidem ipsius, qui prius insipientes eramus.*" Tombeur 1989, pp. 265–266.

75. See chapter 18 this volume.

76. Tombeur 1989, p. 203.

77. Gregory 1989, p. 154.

78. Tombeur 1989, p. 203.

79. The custom of beginning a meal with a sweet and syrupy wine is documented from the early Middle Ages (Verdon 2005, p. 205) into the modern era (Flandrin 1989, p. 299).

80. Venanzio Fortunato, *Vita sancti Martini*, MGH, AA, IV, 2, pp. 316–317.

81. Sidonio Apollinare, *Carmina*, XVII, vv. 13–18, ed. A. Loyen, Paris, 1960, I, pp. 125–127; also in *Tituli Gallicani*, XII, MGH, AA, VI /2, XXIII, vols. 5–10, pp. 195–196. See Tomea 2003, p. 356.

82. Gregory of Tours, *Historia Francorum*, VII, 29, MGH, SRM, I, 1, p. 190.

83. Tomea 2003, p. 356 (n. 35) (with reference to a work by Gualandri).

84. Ibid., p. 359, counted eighteen *Vitae* from the high Middle Ages that speak of Falerno.

85. Archetti 1998, p. 161 (with reference to the research of E. Brouette and G. Guadagno). This was also the opinion of Dion 1959, p. 172.

86. Tomea 2003, p. 361 (and what follows).

87. Grappe 2006, pp. 102–104.

88. Andreolli 1994, pp. 29–30.

89. Grappe 2006, p. 101.

90. Anthimus, *De observantia ciborum*, 25, ed. M. Durant, Blackawton, Prospect Books, 1996. See Deroux 1998, pp. 369–370.

91. Ferreolo, *Regula ad monachos*, 39, PL 66, c. 75; but see the critical edition by V. Desprez, "Regula Ferriolo," in *Revue Mabillon*, 40, 1981–84, pp. 117–148: monks should not drink wine because it keeps them from the precepts of penitence; however, because it is impossible to ignore Paul's recommendation, "they will have to be satisfied with whatever wine is available in their monasteries." The passage evokes in its rhetoric the regulation in the Benedictine Rule, which allows wine in moderation "since the monks could not be persuaded to do without"), but in Ferreolo's text, unlike Benedict's, the exception was made in the name of hygiene.

92. 1 Timothy 5:23.

93. See chapter 11 this volume.

94. Pier Damiani, *Epistolae*, 18, 5, in Archetti 2003, p. 288.

95. According to the chronicle attributed to Alexander VI, in the fifteenth century the monks of Monte Oliveto decided to cease drinking wine, and they cut down the vines and destroyed the barrels. After a few years of drinking water, many among them began to fall sick and to complain of stomach pains. They understood at last the meaning of Paul's recommendation to Timothy and resigned themselves. Archetti 2003, p. 289.

96. *Vita Athanasii episcopi,* AS, Iul. IV, p. 80: "*de vini potatione primo abstinere se voluit, sed propter aegritudinem carnis non potuit.*"

97. *Vita Ursi,* AS, Feb. I, p. 946. The relationship between the therapeutic efficacy of wine and virtue related to its consecration also appears in Egidio, *Vita Hugonis,* I, 31, ed. E. H. J. Cowdrey, in *Studi gregoriani,* XI, 1978, pp. 76–77: "a novice in the monastery of Berzé, having taken sick with fevers and being totally wasted, was made to drink a fortified wine in the goblet of the Mass, upon which the fevers disappeared."

98. An example appears in *Vitae Audomari, Bertini, Winnoci,* 19, MGH, SRG, V, pp. 765–767: the wine, blessed by the saint, healed someone who was near death.

99. *Vita Anstrudis abbatissae* [of Laon], 29, MGH, SRM, VI, p. 76; a nun took as medicine a spoonful of dust from the tomb of the Virgin diluted in *vino calido.*

100. Among the wines from "hillsides," Pardulfo suggests, with a precision that would seem to come from experience, those "from localities known as 'Monte di Ebbone' in Epernay, *ad Rubridum* in Cormicy, in Rheims, Merfy, and Chaumuzy." See Devroey 1989, pp. 27–28.

101. This keen observation was made by Grappe (2006, p. 31).

102. Arnaud de Villeneuve, *Le régime tresutil et proufitable,* I, 1, ed. A. Henry, p. 125, in Grappe 2006, p. 154.

103. As Grieco (1994) commented, the variability of the "humors" of wine is atypical within the context of Galenic dietetics, which normally, assigned to vegetable products a single and well-defined nature.

104. *Pedagogo,* II, 19; the entire quotation appears in Archetti 2003, p. 211.

105. Verdon 2005, p. 173.

106. As Renouard (1964) has maintained.

107. Robinson 1995, p. 38, quoted in Matheus 2003, p. 119. The "technical" explanation that is commonly given of this phenomenon is the wide use, during the Middle Ages, of the barrel as a means of transportation instead of the Roman amphora (which, because it was sealed, enabled long-term conservation of wine). Another consideration is that the wines of northern Europe, which had gained considerable importance in the Middle Ages, were generally lighter than Mediterranean wines.

108. Devroey 1989, p. 117.

109. Van Uyten 2003, pp. 119–120. This was repeated by the agronomist Piero de'Crescenzi in the fourteenth century. Matheus 2003, p. 119.

110. *Historia Francorum,* VII, 29.

111. *Consuetudines Floriacenses antiquiores:* "*pigmentatum quod clarum dicitur*"; *Conseutudines Hirsaugienses:* "*portionis pigmentatae, quae claretum, id est liitranch dicitur a pluribus.*" The quotations appear in Archetti 2003, p. 312 (n. 311). Even in Innocent III, *De contemptu mundi,* II, 19, PL 217, c. 724, *claretum* seems to be synonymous with spiced or treated wine: "*non sufficit vinum, non sicera, non cervisia, sed studiose conficitur mulsum, syropos, claretum.*"

112. Andreolli 2000.

113. For example. Diodorus Siculus wrote that "the Gauls are given to the use of wine and drink the one brought to their region by merchants without mixing it," and lacking self-control, they regularly get drunk. See Unwin 1993, p. 124.

114. According to Andreolli (2000), in the history of the relation between water and wine, it is possible to see four successive phases, roughly coinciding with the

ancient, medieval, modern, and contemporary periods. After the two phases mentioned in the text, in the modern era the recommendation of mixing and the "proper use" of wine seems to have come back into fashion, as opposed to excessive drinking and inebriation—no longer, however, in cultural terms, as in antiquity, but in social terms. Today, at last, the triumphal success of drinking uncut wine (wine, a work of art, cannot be modified and is more likely to determine what one eats with it) finds its new priest in the figure of the sommelier.

115. The *Regula Magistri* (27, 3) states that as soon as the brothers are seated for the meal, "*antequam comedant, singulos meros accipiant*"; four services of *mixtum* will follow the goblet of pure wine during the meal (three in the winter), diluted with warm water and mixed *in ragione* of a third: "*tertius impleat mixtus*" (ibid., 27, 39). See Archetti 2003, pp. 223–226. For references to *merum* in the lives of the saints during the high Middle Ages, see Tomea 2003, pp. 342–343.

116. *Vita et Regula Benedicti una cum expositione Regulae ab Hildemaro tradita*, Ratisbonae, Neo-Eboraci et Cincinnati, 1880, p. 107, quoted by Archetti 2003, p. 243.

117. See chapter 11 this volume.

118. Tombeur 1989, pp. 254–257.

119. Cyprian, *Epistlulae*, 63, 13, quoted in Tombeur 1989, p. 261.

120. Honoré of Autun, *Gemma animae*, i, 158: "*Per vinum divinitas, per aquam intelligitur humanitas*," quoted in Tombeur 1989, p. 262.

121. *De clericorum institutione*, I, 31, PL 107, c. 320: "*neuter horum sine altero in in sacrificio debet offerri, nec vinum sine aqua, nec aqua sine vino.*"

122. *De corpore et sanuine Domini*, 11, 42–45, quoted in Tombeur 1989, p. 263.

123. Rouche 1973; Hocquet 1985; Devroey 1987.

124. The discussion among scholars about the size of an *emina* (ranging from a quarter to a half of a liter, and even more according to the calculations proposed) is summarized by Archetti 2003, pp. 234ff.

125. One sees this in the 789 *Admonitio generalis*, MGH, *Leges*, CRF, I (n. 22), p. 55: "*ut monachi et clerici tabernas non ingrediantur edendi vel bibendi causa.*" See Theodolf of Orléans, *Capitula ad presbyteros*, PL 105, c. 13: "*ab ebrietate abstinieatis . . . neque per tabernas eatis bibendo aut comendendo.*" The quotations could easily be multiplied.

126. See Montanari 1979, p. 459, with reference again to the *Admonitio generalis*, p. 58: "*honestum nobis videtur ut ijudices eiuni causes audiant et discernant.*"

127. Odon of Cluny, *Vita Geraldi Auriliacensis comitis*, PL 133, c. 650.

128. *Vita Genovefae viriginis Parisiensis*, 15, MGH, SRM, III, pp. 220–221: the saint never drank in her entire life; "*vinum vel quicquid inebriare hominem potest.*"

129. *Epistulae*, 22, 1, 1, 3 and 5.

130. Bellini 2003, p. 416. According to Thomas Aquinas, drunkenness is an extenuating circumstance compared with the sins it provokes "because of the ignorance that accompanies it." Verdon 2005, p. 181.

131. Motta 2003, p. 200.

132. Gregory 1989, p. 153.

133. *Sermones*, 126, 3, 4. The same appears in Gregory the Great, *Moralia in Job*, 6, 15, 22–24: "*Aqua semel in vinum permutatam videntes cuncti mirati sunt: cotidie humor terrae in radicem vitis attractus per botrum in vinum veritur et nemo miratur.*" See Tombeur 1989, p. 252.

13. RICH FOOD, POOR FOOD

1. See chapter 2 of this volume.
2. Capatti and Montanari 1999.
3. Montanari 2002b, lesson 30 (The Invention of the Middle Ages).
4. Montanari 1993, pp. 57–62.
5. Grieco 1987, pp. 159ff.
6. Sabadino degli Arienti, *Le Porretane*, XXXVII, ed. G. Gambarin, Bari, Laterza, 1914, pp. 227–229. See Montanari 1993, pp. 114–115; Montanari 2008, pp. 110–113.
7. For everything that follows concerning the presence of vegetables in the cooking of the upper classes, see Capatti and Montanari 1999, pp. 41–44.
8. Ibid., pp. 52–58 (for all documented and bibliographical references).
9. Messedaglia 1974, I, pp. 175ff.
10. Montanari 1993, pp. 166–170.
11. Capatti and Montanari 1999, p. 69.
12. Ibid., p. 86 (as well as the quotations that follow).
13. See chapter 8 of this volume. On the medieval "ennoblement" of cheese, see Montanari 2008.
14. See chapter 2 of this volume.
15. See chapter 3 of this volume.
16. Capatti and Montanari 1999, pp. x–xi.
17. This topic was developed in Montanari 2010.

14. MONASTIC COOKING

1. Montanari 1988a, pp. 63ff (monastic diets).
2. François Rabelais, *Gargantua et Pantagruel*.
3. Montanari 1988a, p. 92. The text is in *Vie du bienheureux Pacôme*.
4. See chapter 6 this volume.
5. See chapter 6 this volume.
6. Rousselle 1974.
7. See Montanari 1999.
8. Montanari 1988a, p. 69.
9. Ibid., p. 70.
10. Montanari 1999.
11. Montanari 1988a, p. 71.
12. Ibid.
13. Ibid., p. 81.
14. Montanari 1979, p. 286.
15. Ibid.
16. Ibid.
17. Ibid., p. 287.
18. Ibid., p. 288 (for).
19. See chapter 7 this volume.

20. Moulin 1988. See chapter 8 this volume.
21. Montanari 1988a, p. 82.
22. Ibid., p. 83.
23. Montanari 1979, p. 157.
24. On *pulmentaria*, see chapter 3 this volume.
25. On the use of fats in the Middle Ages, see chapter 9 this volume.
26. Montanari 1988a, p. 86.
27. Ibid., p. 88.
28. See chapter 11 this volume.
29. De Vogüé (1964) stresses this.
30. Montanari 1988a, p. 72.
31. Ibid., pp. 76–77.
32. Rouche 1973.
33. Hocquet 1985.
34. Devroey 1987.
35. Montanari 1993, p. 33.
36. Ibid., p. 29. See chapter 16 this volume.
37. See chapter 16 of this volume.
38. On the monastic "language of silence" (and information that follows), see D'Haenens 1985; Tugnoli 1988–89.
39. Montanari 1988a, pp. 81ff, for the information that follows.
40. Carnevale Schianca 2011, pp. 231–232.

15. THE PILGRIM'S FOOD

1. Giovanni Italico, *Vita Sancti Odonis*, PL 133, c. 64.
2. On the qualities of bread, see chapter 5 of this volume.
3. See chapter 11 of this volume.
4. On this subject see Peyer 1990.
5. J. Vielliard, *Le guide du pèlerin de Saint-Jacques de Compostelle*, Macon, Protat Frères, 1969.
6. *Statuti dell'arte degli albergatori della città di Firenze*, 1324–42, ed. F. Sartini, Florence, Olschki, 1953.
7. *Il libro della cucina del sec. XIV*, ed. F. Zambrini, Bologna, Romagnoli, 1863, p. 75.
8. Ibid., p. 96 (n. 37).
9. Capatti and Montanari 1999, p. 94.
10. The cookbook was published in Laurioux 2005, pp. 57–109. The recipe in question is in note 84.
11. *Liber eremutucae Regulae*, XXIII, in *Les Consititutiones e la Regulae de vita eremitica del B. Rodolfo*, ed. F. Crosara, Rome, 1970, p. 57. On this, the *Book of hermitic regulations* decidedly echoes the Benedictine Rule.
12. Ibid.: "*Denique si corruptum, acidum macidumve fuerit inventum, aliis poterit ministrari, pro eremitis alius congruum inveniatur.*"

16. THE TABLE AS A REPRESENTATION OF THE WORLD

1. Barthes 1961.
2. Plutarch, *Moralia*, Book VIII, *Questiones conviviales* [Table talk].
3. Montanari 1989, pp. VIIff.
4. Amato di Montecassino, *Storia de' Normanni volgarizzata in antico francese*, ed. V. De Bertholomaeis, Rome, 1935, p. 343.
5. Montanari 1988a, p. 29.
6. Ibid.
7. Ibid., pp. 29–31, and text following.
8. Montanari 1989, p. ix.
9. Sahlins 1972, pp. 130–133.
10. This number is deduced from a document that details the daily supply of almonds necessary for the entire court; see Tramontana 1993, p. 183.
11. The expression is hyperbolic: "*numeri nulla lege coacta fuit.*" *De rebus siculis carmen*, RIS, XXI, ed. E. Rota, Città di Castello, 1904–1910, p. 40 (vols. 252–253).
12. Q. Sella, *Codex Astensis*, IV, Rome, 1880, pp. 43–44.
13. Montanari 1988a, p. 135.
14. Ibid., pp. 101ff.
15. Ibid., p. 120 (with a reference to Ambrosioni 1972, pp. 83–84).
16. *Le pergamene di S. Nicola di Bari, Periodo svevo*, 1195–1266, *Codice diplomatico barese*, VI (n. 93) [year 1254], ed. F. Nitti, Mari, 1906, p. 147: "*convivium in sala ipsius ecclesie, in quo accedebant omnes.*"
17. Montanari 1988a, p. 29.
18. Montanari 1989, p. ix (and the text reprinted on pp. 248–249, from *Libri delle cerimonie* of Emperor Constantine VII Porfirogenito, ed. A. Vogt, Paris, 1967, II, pp. 102–104).
19. Liudprandi, "Relatio de legatione constantinopolitana," XI, in *Opera*, ed. J. Becker, Hanover, 1915, p. 181. See Montanari 1988a, p. 28.
20. G. Sercambi, *Novelle*, ed. G. Sinicropi, Bari, Laterza, 1972, pp. 314–315 (novella LI).
21. Fossati and Mannoni 1981; Alexandre-Bidon 2005.
22. Alexandri Telesini, "De rebus gestis Rogerii Siciliaw regis," II, VI, a. 1130, in G. Del Re, *Cronisti e scritori sincroni napoletani*, I, Naples, 1845, p. 103. The same reference applies to what follows. See Tramontana 1993, p. 182.
23. *Liber qui dicitus Flores historiarum*, MGH, SS, XXVIII, ed. F. Libermann and R. Pauli, Hanover, 1888, p. 71.
24. Creating important controversies about who had precedence: one example (taken from the *Vita Martini* by Sulpicio Secero) is found in Montanari 1989, pp. 191–192.
25. Montanari 1989, pp. 401–402: an example taken from a novella by Franco Sacchetti, with Noddo d'Andrea as protagonist, whom we have already mentioned in chapter 3 of this volume.
26. Elias 1982; also Bertelli and Crifò 1985; Romagnoli 1997.
27. On the "satire of the rustic," see also Merlini 1894. See Montanari 2000.
28. Montanari 1991, p. viii (the text reprinted on pp. 247–249). See chapter 17 of this volume.

29. On the subject of "the rustic piggishness" to which peasants were given at the table, see novella XXV by Gentile Sermini, in *Le novelle*, ed. G. Vettori, Rome, Avanzini and Toraca, 1968, I, pp. 442–443.

30. *Regola Benedicti*, VI, in *La Régie de Saint Benoît*, ed. A. De Vogüé and J. Neufville, Paris, Le Cerf, 1972.

31. See Ugo Falcando, *Historia a Liber de Regno Siciliae*, ed. G. B. Siragusa, Rome, 1897: Gentile, the bishop of Agrigento, after the death of Ruggero II abandons himself to a life of dissolution, frequenting lavish and boisterous banquets (*"crebra convivia splendidissime celebrare . . . inter epulas loqui plurimum"*).

32. Eginardo, *Vita KaroliMagni*, 24, ed. G. H. Pertz, Hanover, 1863.

33. See Montanari 1989, p. xxiv.

34. See chapter 14 of this volume.

35. Ibn ak Athir, "Kamil 'at tawarib [Complete chronicle]," in F. Gabrieli, *Viaggi e viaggiatori arabi*, Florence, Sansoni, 1975, pp. 479–480.

36. Cassiodoro, *Variae*, XII, 4, CC, *Series latina*, 96, p. 467. This is a text we have already discussed (see chapter 4 of the present volume).

37. John of Salisbury, *Policraticus sive de nugis curialium et vestigiis philosophorum*, VIII, 7, ed. C. Webb, Oxford, 1909, pp. 270–271.

38. On the cuisine of ostentation, see Montanari 1993, pp. 115–118.

39. Anonimo Meridionale, *Due libri di cucina*, Book A, CXXXIV, ed. I. Boström, Stockholm, Almqvist & Wiksell, 1985, pp. 28–29.

40. Ibid., Book A, XXXVII, XXXVIII, XXXXII, CXXXVII; Book B, XV.

41. Ibid., Book A, III.

42. Ibid., Book A, LVIII.

43. Ibid., Book A, LXXVI.

44. Ibid., Book A, CXXX.

45. Ibid., Book B, XXXV.

46. Montanari 1990a.

47. See Bolens 1980.

48. A few important examples can be found in Camporesi 1993, pp. 75ff.

49. On the symbolic meanings of colors, see first of all Pastoureau 1989.

50. Anonimo Meridionale, *Due libri di cucina*, Book B, XXVII.

51. On the history of the tomato, see Gentilcore 2010; Montanari 2004, p. 150.

52. John of Salisbury, *Policraticus*, VIII, 7, pp. 271–272.

53. See Grottanelli and Parise 1988.

54. For example, in the Celtic poem "Scéla Mucce Meic Datho," which places at the center of the story the "pig of MacDatho"; see Sayers 1990). See also Montanari 1989, pp. 125ff (the Irish saga of Cu Chulainn and the attribution of the "hero's portion").

55. Montanari 1993, p. 31.

56. Ibid., p. 32.

57. Ibid., pp. 75–76.

58. Bread, wine, meat, and spices are the four principal items in food provisions for elegant houses. For some bishops' tables in twelfth-century Lazio, see "Chronicon Fossae Novae," in Del Re, *Chronisti e scrittori sincroni napoletani*, I, pp. 524–525 (*Annales Ceccanenses*). On the wide use of spices at the table of Frederick II, see Tramontana 1993, p. 184.

59. Johann von Winterthur, *Chronica*, ed. F. Baethgen, Munich, 1982, pp. 9–10: "*non intuitu divine retribuciones sed corporalis conservande causa sanitatus.*" See Tramontana 1993, p. 184.

60. Montanari 1993, pp. 35–36.

61. Bloch 1949.

62. Montanari 1993, pp. 155ff.

63. I used the translation by O. Schena, *Le leggi palatine di Pietro IV d'Aragona*, Cagliari, Edizioni della Torre, 1983, IV, 5, p. 247. See ibid., p. 29, for the derivation of this text from *Leges Palatinae* of the kingdom of Maiorca, issued by Giacomo III in 1337. For other analogous examples, where the amount of food was determined with mathematical precision according to social rank, see Laurioux 1992.

64. See Alberini 1969, pp. 21–22.

65. Montanari 1993, pp. 104–105; Redon 1992; Campanini 2006.

66. "Ordinationes generales et speciales editae per Serenissimum D. nostrum Regem Federicum tertium in Colloquio generalo Messanae celebrato," in F. Testa, *Capitula Regni Sicilae, quae ad odiernum diem lata sunt*, Palermo, 1741–42, I, pp. 99ff. See also Del Giudice 1887; Meldolesi 1973, p. 67.

67. Meldolesi 1973, p. 70.

68. Montanari 1979, pp. 453–456.

69. Riccardo di San Germano, *Chronica*, RIS, VII, ed. C. A. Garufi, Bologna, 1937, pp. 186–187: "*ita quod pauperes ultra guingentos manducaverunt, et saturati sunt nimis pane, vino et carnibus.*"

70. Lombardi, Satriani, and Meligrana 1982, pp. 99ff.

71. An example appears in Montanari 1989, pp. 302–303.

72. Schena, *Le leggi palatine*, I, 3, p. 89.

73. Ibid., I, 6, p. 95.

74. Ibid., I, 13, p. 159.

75. See chapter 15 of this volume.

76. Montanari 1993, pp. 118–121.

77. Montanari 1988a, p. 78.

78. Tommaso da Celano, *Vita seconda di San Francesco d'Assisi*, CLI, *Fonti francescane, Editio minor*, Assisi, 1986, pp. 487–488.

17. THE FORK AND THE HANDS

1. The miniature is in a codex preserved in the archive of the abbey of Montecassino, ms. 132. Dated in the eleventh century, like the codex, it illustrates the chapter "De cibo" in the work *De universo* by Rabano Mauro. See the reproduction in Montanari 1989, in the table between pages 200 and 201.

2. Pertusi 1983, p. 5.

3. Elias 1982, pp. 197–201.

4. This work by Bonvesin was published in *Poeti del Duecento, Poesia didattica del Nord*, ed. G. Contini, Turin, Einaudi, 1978, pp. 191–200.

5. Elias 1982, p. 198.

6. Capatti and Montanari 1999, pp. 59ff.

7. Franco Sacchetti, *Il Trecentonovelle*, cxxiv, ed. A. Borlenghi, Milan, Rizzoli, 1957, pp. 387–390. Whether the *maccheroni* in question might be gnocchi (this was the most common meaning of the term in the Middle Ages) or "modern" macaroni (as it began to be called in those very centuries) matters little from our viewpoint.

8. "Itinerario di Guglielmo di Rubruk," in *I precursori di Marco Polo*, ed. A. T'Serstevens, Milan, Garzanti, 1982, p. 230. See Montanari 1989, p. 349.

9. Elias 1982, pp. 203–204.

10. Ibid., pp. 204–206.

11. Michel de Montaigne, *Journal de Voyage*, ed. François Rigolot, Paris, Presses Universitaires de France, 1992, p. 96.

12. Elias 1982, p. 206.

13. Ausonio, "Efemeride, ossia le occupazioni di tutta la giornata," 5–6, in *Opere*, ed. A. Pastorino, Turin, Utet, 1971, p. 271. See also Montanari 1989, pp. 184–185.

14. Vincenzo Nolfi, "Ginipedia, ovvero avertimenti oer la donna nobile," in *La gentildonna italiana a convito*, Pisa, Mariotti, 1898; see the passage in Montanari 1991, pp. 247–249.

15. Elias 1982, pp. 210–211.

16. Capatti and Montanari 1999, pp. 171–174.

17. Filippo Tommaso Marinetti e Filìa, *La cucina futurista*, Milan, Sonzogno, 1932 (reprint, Milan, Longanesi, 1986), p. 32.

18. THE TASTE OF KNOWLEDGE

1. The codification of the four flavors goes back to 1864 through the work of the anatomist Fick, based on the research of Chevreul (1824) on the distinctions among tactile, olfactory, and gustatory sensations. See Faurion 1996, 1999.

2. See Montanari 2004, pp. 73ff.

3. For this and what follows, I refer to Prosperi 2007.

4. Augustine, *De libero arbitrio*, II, 3, 82; II, 7, 15.

5. This idea would be taken up by Gregory the Great, *Moralia in Job*, XI, 4.

6. Augustine, *Genesis ad litteram libri duodecim*, XII, 20, 42.

7. Ibid., VII, 17, 23.

8. Gregory the Great, *Moralia in Job*, XI, 6, 5.

9. Gregory the Great, *Omelie su Ezechiele*, II, 5, 9.

10. An indispensable reference is volume 10 of the revue *Micrologus*, 2002, entirely devoted to the theme of "The Five Senses."

11. Montanari 1988a, pp. 3ff (the sin of Adam), for what follows.

12. Ibid., pp. 63ff.

13. Ibid., p. 5.

14. The text was published in Burnett 1991, pp. 236–238.

15. See, in regard to the question of sound as "accident," the entertaining and instructive tale included in "Novellino, IX," in *Prosatori del Duecento, Trattati morali e allegorici, Novelle*, ed. C. Segre, Turin, Einaudi, 1976, pp. 72–73. See Montanari 1989, pp. 361–362.

16. I owe this information to Gabriella Morini, docent of chemistry at the University of Gastronomic Sciences in Pollenzo.

17. *Umami* was identified as a fundamental flavor in 1908 by the Japanese chemist Kikunae Ikeda.

18. See chapter 11 this volume.

19. Burnett 2002.

20. See chapter 11 this volume.

21. "Regimen sanitatis," in *Flos medicinae Scholae Salerni*, ed. A. Sinno, Milan, Mursia, 1987, pp. 96ff (VII, 1–3).

22. In this connotation, I coined the expression "Galenic cook": see Capatti and Montanari 1999, pp. 145ff.

23. Pucci Donati 2006, p. 120; Grappe 2006, pp. 78–82.

24. Aldobrandino of Siena, *Le régime du corps*, I, 2, ed. L. Landouzy and R. Pépin, Paris, Champion, 1911 (and Slatkine Reprint, Geneva, 1978), p. 14: *"car si com dist Avicennes, se li cors de l'oume est sains, totes les coses ki li ont milior savour à la bouche, mieux le nourissent."*

25. Maynis de' Mayneriis, *Regimen sanitatis*, Lugduni, Jacobum Myt, 1517, III, XX, f. 44v: *"Ea enim ex quibus cibaria condiuntur sunt in sanitatis regimine non modicum utilia, tamen quia per condimenta gustui efficiuntur* delectabiliora, et per consequens digestibiliora. *Nam quod est delectabilius est ad digestionem melius, tum quia per condimenta additur bonitas et corrigitur malicia."* A similar concept appears in *Opusculum de saporibus* by the same Maineri (an extract from *Regimen sanitatis*); see Thorndike 1934, p. 186.

26. "Regimen sanitatis," chapter VI.

27. Augustine, *Ennarationes in psalmos*, 51, 18.

28. Gregory the Great, *Moralia in Job*, XI, VI, 9.

29. Ibid., IX, XXXI, 47.

30. Montanari 1993, p. 109.

31. Vercelloni 2005, pp. 20–25, 56–59.

32. Flandrin 1987, pp. 230–238.

33. François-Marie Voltaire, "Goût," in *Encyclopédie ou dictionnaire raisonné des sciences, des arts et des métiers*, VII, Leghorn, 1778, pp. 746–747. See Vercelloni 2005, pp. 20–21.

34. Hauser 1998, p. 49.

35. D'Angelo 2000, pp. 11–34; see Perullo 2006, pp. 16–17.

36. Gentile Sermini, *Les novelle*, ed. G. Vettori, Rome, Avanzini and Torraca, 1968, vol. 2, p. 600.

37. Montanari 2008 [English translation: 2010, *Cheese, Pears, and History*, New York, Columbia University Press].

Bibliography

Adamson, Melitta Weiss. 2004. *Food in Medieval Times*, Westport, Greenwood.

Alberini, Massimo. 1969. *Ippolito Cavalcanti duca di Buonvicino e la cucina napoletana del suo tempo*, Milan, Franco Angeli.

Alexandre-Bidon, Danièle. 2005. *Une archéologie du goût: Céramique et consommation*, Paris, Picard.

Ambrosioni, Annamaria. 1972. "Contributo alla storia della festa di San Satiro a Milano," *Archivio Ambrosiano*, 23, pp. 71–96.

André, Jacques. 1981. *L'alimentation et la cuisine à Rome*, Paris, Les Belles Lettres.

Andreolli, Bruno. 1994. "La terminologia vitivinicola nei lessici medievali italiani," in *Dalla vite al vino: Fonti e problemi della vitivinicoltura italiana medievale*, ed. J.-L. Gaulin and A. Grieco, Bologna, Clueb, pp. 15–37.

——. 2000. "Un contrastato connubio: Acqua e vino dal Medioevo all'età moderna," in *La vite e il vino: Storia e diritto (secoli XI–XIX)*, ed. M. Da Passano, A. Mattone, F. Mele, and P. Simbula, Rome, Carocci, 2, pp. 1031–1051.

Antoniazzi, Lucia, and Citti, Licia, eds. 1988. *I detti del mangiare: 1738 proverbi segnalati da 1853 medici commentati in chiave nutrizionale da Bruna Lancia*, Milan, Editiemme.

Arcari, Paola Maria. 1968. *Idee e sentimenti politici dell'alto Medioevo*, Milan, Giuffrè.

Archetti, Gabriele. 1998. *Tempus vindemie: Per la storia delle vigne e del vino nell'Europa medievale*, Brescia, Fondazione Civiltà Bresciana.

——. 2003. "De mensura potus: Il vino dei monaci nel Medioevo," in *La civiltà del vino: Fonti, temi e produzioni vitivinicole dal Medioevo al Novecento*, ed. G. Archetti, Brescia, Centro Culturale Artistico di Franciacorta e del Sebino, pp. 205–326.

Arnaldi, Girolamo. 1986. "Preparazione delle lampade e tutela del Signore: Alle origini del papato temporale," *La Cultura*, 24, pp. 38–63.

Aymard, Maurice, Grignon, Claude, and Sabban, Françoise, eds. 1993. *Le temps de manger: Alimentation, emploi du temps et rythmes sociaux*, Paris, Maison des Sciences de L'homme.

Ballerini, Luigi, and Parzen, Jeremy, eds. 2001. *Maestro Martino, Libro de arte coquinaria*, Milan, Guido Tommasi. [Ballerini and Parzen, eds. 2005. *The Art of Cooking: The First Modern Cookery Book*, Berkeley, University of California Press.]

Barthes, Roland. 1961. "Pour une psycho-sociologie de l'alimentation contemporaine," *Annales ESC*, 16/5, pp. 977–986. [Barthes. 2012. "Toward a Psychosociology of

Contemporary Food Consumption," in *Food and Culture: A Reader*, ed. Carole Couni-
han and Penny Van Esterik, New York, Routledge, pp. 23–30.]

Baruzzi, Marina, and Montanari, Massimo. 1981. *Porci e porcari nel Medioevo*, Bologna,
Clueb.

Basini, Gian Luigi. 1970. *L'uomo e il pane: Risorse, consumi e carenze alimentari della popolazione
modenese nel Cinque e Seicento*, Milan, Giuffrè.

Bautier, Anne-Marie. 1984. "Pain et pâtisserie dans les texts médiévaux antérieurs au
XIIIe siècle," in *Manger et boire au Moyen Âge*, Nice, Les Belles Lettres, 1, pp. 33–65.

Beck Bossard, Corinne. 1981. "L'alimentazione in un villaggio siciliano del XIV secolo:
Sulla scorta delle fonti archeologiche," *Archeologia medievale*, 8, pp. 311–319.

Bellini, Roberto. 2003. "Il vino nelle leggi della Chiesa," in *La civiltà del vino: Fonti, temi e
produzioni vitivinicole dal Medioevo al Novecento*, ed. G. Archetti, Brescia, Centro Culturale
Artistico di Franciacorta e del Sebino, pp. 365–420.

Benporat, Claudio. 1990. *Storia della gastronomia italiana*, Milan, Mursia.

——. 1996. *Cucina italiana del Quattrocento*, Florence, Olschki.

Bertelli, Sergio, and Crifo, Giuliano, eds. 1985. *Rituale cerimoniale etichetta*, Milan, Bompiani.

Bertolini, Lucia. 1998. "Fra pratica e scrittura: La cucina nell'Europa del tardo Medioevo," in *Archivio storico italiano*, 156, disp. IV, Florence, Olschki, pp. 737–743.

Bertolotti, Maurizio. 1991. *Carnevale di massa, 1950*, Turin, Einaudi.

Bianchi, Enzo, ed. 2001. *Regole monastiche d'Occidente*, Turin, Einaudi.

Bloch, Marc. 1949. *La società feudale*, Turin, Einaudi (ed. orig. Paris, Albin Michel, 1939).
[Bloch. 1961. *Feudal Society*, Chicago, University of Chicago Press.]

Bolens, Lucie. 1980. *Pain quotidien et pains de disette dans l'Espagne musulmane*, Paris, Armand
Colin.

Bonnassie, Pierre. 1989. "Consommation d'aliments immondes et cannibalisme de
survie dans l'Occident du haut Moyen Âge," *Annales ESC*, 44/5, pp. 1035–1056.

Branca, Paolo. 2003. "Il vino nella cultura arabo-musulmana," in *La civiltà del vino: Fonti,
temi e produzioni vitivinicole dal Medioevo al Novecento*, ed. G. Archetti, Brescia, Centro
Culturale Artistico di Franciacorta e del Sebino, pp. 165–191.

Braudel, Fernand. 1982. *Civiltà materiale, economia e capitalismo*, Vol. 1, *Le strutture del quotidi-
ano*, Turin, Einaudi (ed. orig. Paris, Armand Colin, 1979). [Braudel. 1983. *Civilization
and Capitalism, 15th–18th Century*, Vol. 1, *The Structures of Everyday Life*, London, Collins.]

Brugnoli, Andrea, Rigoli, Paolo, and Varanini, Gian Maria. 1994. *Olio ed olivi del Garda
veronese: Le vie dell'olio gardesano dal medioevo ai primi del Novecento*, Cavaion Veronese, Turri.

Brun, Jean-Pierre. 2003. *Le vin et l'huile dans la Méditerranée antique: Viticulture, oléiculture et
procédés de fabrication*, Paris, Editions Errance.

Bruneton-Governatori, Ariane. 1984. *Le pain de bois: Ethnohistoire de la châtaigne et du
châtaigner*, Toulouse, Éché.

Burnett, Charles. 1991. "The Superiority of Taste," *Journal of the Warburg and Courtauld
Institutes*, 54, pp. 230–238.

——. 2002. "*Sapores sunt octo*: The Medieval Latin Terminology for the Eight Flavours,"
Micrologus, 10, pp. 99–112.

Cagnin, Giampaolo. 1988. "La presenza ed il ruolo delle castagne nell'alimentazione
a Treviso nel secolo XIV," in *La civiltà del castagno*, Combai, Pro Loco di Combai, 3,
pp. 37–55.

Campanini, Antonella. 2006. "La table sous contrôle: Les banquets et l'excès alimentaire dans le cadre des lois somptuaires en Italie entre le Moyen Âge et la Renaissance," *Food and History*, 4/2, pp. 131–150.

Camporesi, Piero. 1970. "Introduzione a P. Artusi," in *La scienza in cucina e l'arte di mangiar bene*, Turin, Einaudi, pp. ix–lxx.

——. 1980. *Il pane selvaggio*, Bologna, Il Mulino. [Camporesi. 1989. *Bread of Dreams: Food and Fantasy in Early Modern Europe*, Chicago, University of Chicago Press.]

——. 1985. "Il formaggio maledetto," in Piero Camporesi, *Le officine dei sensi*, Milan, Garzanti, pp. 47–77.

——. 1990. "Certosini e marzolini: 'Liter casearium' di Pantaleone da Confienza nell'Europa dei latticini," in Piero Camporesi, *La miniera del mondo: Artieri inventori impostori*, Milan, Il Saggiatore.

——. 1993. *Le vie del latte*, Milan, Garzanti.

Capatti, Alberto, De Bernardi, Alberto, and Varni, Angelo, eds. 1998. "L'alimentazione," in *Storia d'Italia*, "Annali," 13, Turin, Einaudi.

Capatti, Alberto, and Montanari, Massimo. 1999. *La cucina italiana: Storia di una cultura*, Rome-Bari, Laterza. [Capatti and Montanari. 2003. *Italian Cuisine: A Cultural History*, New York, Columbia University Press.]

Carnevale Schianca, Enrico. 2011. *La cucina medievale: Lessico, storia, preparazioni*, Florence, Olschki.

Cherubini, Giovanni. 1984a. "La 'civiltà' del castagno alla fine del Medioevo," in Giovanni Cherubini, *L'Italia rurale del basso Medioevo*, Rome-Bari, Laterza, pp. 149–171.

——. 1984b. "Olio, olivi, olivicoltori," in Giovanni Cherubini, *L'Italia rurale del basso Medioevo*, Rome-Bari, Laterza, pp. 173–194.

Ciappelli, Giovanni. 1997. *Carnevale e Quaresima: Comportamenti sociali e cultura a Firenze nel Rinascimento*, Rome, Edizioni di Storia e Letteratura.

Cogrossi, Cornelia. 2003. "Il vino nel 'Corpus iuris' e nei glossatori," in *La civiltà del vino: Fonti, temi e produzioni vitivinicole dal Medioevo al Novecento*, ed. G. Archetti, Brescia, Centro Culturale Artistico di Franciacorta e del Sebino, pp. 499–531.

Comba, Rinaldo. 1983. "'Stirpere nemus et colere terram': Espansione dei coltivi e ristrutturazioni insediative fra X e XIII secolo," in Rinaldo Comba, *Metamorfosi di un paesaggio rurale: Uomini e luoghi del Piemonte sud-occidentale fra X e XVI secolo*, Turin, Celid, pp. 25–102.

Corbier, Mireille. 1989. "Le statut ambigu de la viande à Rome," *Dialogues d'Histoire ancienne*, 15/2, pp. 107–158. [Corbier. 1989. "The Ambiguous Status of Meat in Ancient Rome," *Food and Foodways*, 3/3, pp. 223–264.]

Cremaschi, Lisa, ed. 2003. *Regole monastiche femminili*, Turin, Einaudi.

Cunsolo, Felice. 1970. *La gastronomia nei proverbi*, Milan, Novedit.

D'Angelo, Paolo. 2000. "Il gusto in Italia e Spagna dal Quattrocento al Settecento," in *Il gusto: Storia di un'idea estetica*, ed. L. Russo, Palermo, Aesthetica, pp. 11–34.

D'Haenens, Albert. 1985. "Quotidianità e contesto: Per un modello di interpretazione della realtà monastica medievale nei secoli XI e XII," in *Monachesimo e ordini religiosi del Medioevo subalpino*, ed. Centro Ricerche e Studi Storici, Turin, Assessorato alla Cultura Regione Piemonte, pp. 38–40.

Davies, Roy William. 1971. "The Roman Military Diet," *Britannia*, 2, pp. 122–142.

Del Giudice, Giuseppe. 1887. *Una legge suntuaria inedita del 1290*, Naples, Tipografia della Regia Università.

Dell'Oro, Ferdinando. 2003. "Il vino nella liturgia latina del Medioevo," in *La civiltà del vino: Fonti, temi e produzioni vitivinicole dal Medioevo al Novecento*, ed. G. Archetti, Brescia, Centro Culturale Artistico di Franciacorta e del Sebino, pp. 421–456.

Deroux, Carl. 1998. "Anthime et les tourterelles: Un cas d'intoxication alimentaire au très haut Moyen Âge," in *Maladie et maladies dans les textes latins antiques et médiévaux*, ed. C. Deroux, Brussels, Latomus, pp. 366–381.

De Vogüé, Adalbert. 1964. "Travail et alimentation dans les règles de Saint Benoît et du Maître," *Revue Bénédictine*, 74, pp. 242–251.

Devroey, Jean-Pierre. 1987. "Units of Measurement in the Early Medieval Economy: The Example of Carolingian Food Rations," *French History*, 1/1, pp. 68–72.

——. 1989. *L'éclair d'un bonheur: Une histoire de la vigne en Champagne*, Paris, La Manufacture.

Dion, Roger. 1959. *Histoire de la vigne et du vin en France des origines au XIXe siècle*, Paris, Clavreuil.

Dufourcq, Charles-Emmanuel, and Gautier-Dalché, Jean. 1983. *Historia económica y social de la España cristiana en la Edad Media*, Barcelona, El Albir.

Elias, Norbert. 1982. *La civiltà delle buone maniere*, Bologna, Il Mulino (ed. orig. Frankfurt, Suhrkamp, 1936). [Elias. 1982. *The History of Manners*, New York, Pantheon Books.]

Ermini Pani, Letizia. 2008. "Condurre, conservare e distribuire l'acqua," in *L'acqua nei secoli altomedievali*, Spoleto, Fondazione Centro Italiano di Studi sull'Alto Medioevo, pp. 389–428.

Faccioli, Emilio, ed. 1985. *Platina, Il piacere onesto e la buona salute*, Turin, Einaudi.

——, ed. 1987. *L'arte della cucina in Italia*, Turin, Einaudi.

Faurion, Annick. 1996. "Le goût: Un défi scientifique et intellectuel," *Psychologie française*, 41/3, pp. 217–225.

——. 1999. "I sapori sono quattro," in *Gli spinaci sono ricchi di ferro*, ed. J.-F. Bouvet, Milan, Raffaello Cortina, pp. 53–59.

Febvre, Lucien. 1938. "Répartition géographique des fonds de cuisine en France," in *Travaux du Ier Congrès International de Folklore*, atti del convegno (Paris, 23–28 août 1937), Paris-Tours, Arrault, pp. 123–130 (ripreso in *Annales ESC*, 16/4, 1961, pp. 749–756).

Firpo, Luigi, ed. 1971. *Medicina medievale*, Turin, Utet.

Flandrin, Jean-Louis. 1984. "Internationalisme, nationalisme et régionalisme dans la cuisine des XIVe et XVe siècles: Le témoignage des livres de cuisine," in *Manger et boire au Moyen Âge*, Nice, Les Belles Lettres, 2, pp. 75–91.

——. 1987. "La distinzione attraverso il gusto," in *La vita privata*, Vol. 3, *Dal Rinascimento all'Illuminismo*, ed. P. Ariès and R. Chartier, Rome-Bari, Laterza, pp. 205–240. [Flandrin. 1989. "Distinction Through Taste," in *A History of Private Life*, 3, pp. 265–307.]

——. 1989. "Vigne, vin et société," in *Image et réalité du vin en Europe*, Colloque pluridisciplinaire Vin et Sciences (Louvain-la-Neuve, 28 septembre–1 octobre 1988), Paris, Éditions Sider, pp. 295–301.

——. 1990. "Le goût de l'eau: Anciens discours diététiques et culinaires," in *Le grand livre de l'eau*, ed. M. A. Bernardis and A. Nesteroff, Paris, La Manufacture, pp. 161–169.

——. 1992. *Chronique de Platine*, Paris, Odile Jacob.

——. 1993. "Les heures des repas en France avant le XIXe siècle," in *Le temps de manger: Alimentation, emploi du temps et rythmes sociaux*, ed. M. Aymard, C. Grignon, and F. Sabban,

Paris, Maison des Sciences de L'homme, pp. 197–226. [Flandrin. 1996. "Mealtimes in France Before the Nineteenth Century," *Food and Foodways*, 6/3–4, pp. 261–282.]

——. 1994. *Il gusto e la necessità*, Milan, Il Saggiatore (ed. orig. "Le goût et la nécéssité: Sur l'usage des graisses dans les cuisines d'Europe occidentale," *Annales ESC*, 38/2, 1983, pp. 369–401).

——. 1997a. "Condimenti, cucina e dietetica tra XIV e XVI secolo," in *Storia dell'alimentazione*, ed. J.-L. Flandrin and M. Montanari, Rome-Bari, Laterza, pp. 381–395. [Flandrin. 1999. "Seasoning, Cooking, and Dietetics in the Late Middle Ages," in *Food: A Culinary History from Antiquity to the Present*, New York, Columbia University Press, pp. 313–327.]

——. 1997b. "Dalla dietetica alla gastronomia o la liberazione della gola," in *Storia dell'alimentazione*, ed. J.-L. Flandrin and M. Montanari, Rome-Bari, Laterza, pp. 534–551. [Flandrin. 1999. "From Dietetics to Gastronomy: The Liberation of the Gourmet," in *Food: A Culinary History from Antiquity to the Present*, New York, Columbia University Press, pp. 418–433.]

Flandrin, Jean-Louis, and Montanari, Massimo, eds. 1997. *Storia dell'alimentazione*, Rome-Bari, Laterza. [Flandrin and Montanari. 1999. *Food: A Culinary History from Antiquity to the Present*, New York, Columbia University Press.]

Flandrin, Jean-Louis, and Redon, Odile. 1981. "Les livres de cuisine italiens des XIVe et XVe siècles," *Archeologia Medievale*, 8, pp. 393–408.

Fossati, Silvana, and Mannoni, Tiziano. 1981. "Gli strumenti della cucina e della mensa in base ai reperti archeologici," *Archeologia Medievale*, 8, pp. 409–419.

Frosini, Giovanna. 1993. *Il cibo e i signori: La Mensa dei Priori di Firenze nel quinto decennio del secolo XIV*, Florence, Accademia della Crusca.

Fumagalli, Vito. 1970. "Colonizzazione e insediamenti agricoli nell'Occidente altomedievale: La Valle Padana," *Quaderni Storici*, 14, pp. 319–338.

——. 1976. *Terra e società nell'Italia padana*, Turin, Einaudi.

Galloni, Paolo. 1993. *Il cervo e il lupo: Caccia e cultura nobiliare nel Medioevo*, Rome-Bari, Laterza.

Gasparini, Danilo. 1988. "Il castagno a Combai e nella Valmareno in età moderna e contemporanea," in *La civiltà del castagno*, Combai, Pro Loco di Combai, 3, pp. 7–36.

Gautier, Alban. 2004. "Alcuin, la bière et le vin: Comportements alimentaires et choix identitaires dans la correspondance d'Alcuin," in *Alcuin, de York à Tours: Écriture, pouvoir et réseaux dans l'Europe du haut Moyen Âge*, ed. P. Depreux and B. Judic, *Annales de Bretagne et des Pays de l'Ouest*, 111/3, pp. 431–441.

Gentilcore, David. 2010. *La purpurea meraviglia: Storia del pomodoro in Italia*, Milan, Garzanti. [Gentilcore. 2010. *Pomodoro!: A History of the Tomato in Italy*, New York, Columbia University Press.]

Giagnacovo, Maria. 1997. "Due 'alimentazioni' del basso Medioevo: La tavola dei mercanti e la tavola dei ceti subalterni," in *Alimentazione e nutrizione secc. XIII–XVIII*, ed. S. Cavaciocchi, Florence, Le Monnier, pp. 821–829.

Gillet, Philippe. 1985. *Par mets et par vins: Voyages et gastronomie en Europe (16e–18e siècles)*, Paris, Editions Payot.

Ginzburg, Carlo. 2000. *Rapporti di forza: Storia, retorica, prova*, Milan, Feltrinelli. [Ginzburg. 1999. *History, Rhetoric, and Proof*, Hanover, University Press of New England.]

Goubert, Jean-Pierre. 1986. *La conquête de l'eau: L'avènement de la santé à l'âge industriel*, Paris, Robert Laffont. [Goubert. 1989. *The Conquest of Water: The Advent of Health in the Industrial Age*, Princeton, Princeton University Press.]

Grant, Mark. 2005. *La dieta di Galeno: L'alimentazione degli antichi romani*, Rome, Edizioni Mediterranee. [Grant. 2000. *Galen on Food and Diet*, London, Routledge.]

Grappe, Yann. 2006. *Sulle tracce del gusto: Storia e cultura del vino nel Medioevo*, Rome-Bari, Laterza.

Gregory, Tullio. 1989. "Sémantique," in *Image et réalité du vin en Europe*, Colloque Pluridisciplinaire Vin et Sciences (Louvain-la-Neuve, 28 septembre–1 octobre 1988), Paris, Éditions Sider, pp. 151–154.

——. 2008. "Le acque sopra il firmamento: 'Genesi' e tradizione esegetica," in *L'acqua nei secoli altomedievali*, Spoleto, Fondazione Centro Italiano di Studi sull'Alto Medioevo, pp. 1–41.

Grieco, Allen J. 1987. *Classes sociales, nourriture et imaginaire alimentaire en Italie (XIVᵉ–XVᵉ siècles)*, Paris, Ehess. [Grieco. 1999. "Food and Social Classes in Late Medieval and Renaissance Italy," in *Food: A Culinary History from Antiquity to the Present*, New York, Columbia University Press, pp. 302–312.]

——. 1994. "I sapori del vino: Gusto e criteri di scelta fra Trecento e Cinquecento," in *Dalla vite al vino: Fonti e problemi della vitivinicoltura italiana medievale*, ed. J.-L. Gaulin and A. Grieco, Bologna, Clueb, pp. 163–186.

Grottanelli, Cristiano, and Parise, Nicola, eds. 1988. *Sacrificio e società nel mondo antico*, Rome-Bari, Laterza.

Hagen, Ann. 1995. *A Second Handbook of Anglo-Saxon Food and Drink: Production and Distribution*, Hockwold-cum-Wilton, Anglo-Saxon Books.

Harris, Marvin. 1990. *Buono da mangiare: Enigmi del gusto e consuetudini alimentari*, Turin, Einaudi. [Harris. 1985. *Good to Eat: Riddles of Food and Culture*, New York, Simon and Schuster.]

Hauser, Arnold. 1998. *Storia sociale dell'arte*, Turin, Einaudi. [Hauser. 1951. *The Social History of Art*, New York, Knopf.]

Haussleiter, Johannes. 1935. *Der Vegetarismus in der Antike*, Berlin, Alfred Täpelmann.

Hémardinquer, Jean-Jacques. 1970a. "Les graisses de cuisine en France: Essai de cartes," in *Pour une histoire de l'alimentation*, ed. J.-J. Hémardinquer, Paris, Ehess, pp. 254–271.

Hémardinquer, Jean-Jacques, ed. 1970b. *Pour une histoire de l'alimentation*, Paris, Ehess.

Hilton, Rodney. 1973. *Bond Men Made Free: Medieval Peasant Movements and the English Rising of 1381*, London, Temple Smith.

Hocquet, Jean-Claude. 1985. "Le pain, le vin et la juste mesure à la table des moines carolingiens," *Annales ESC*, 40/3, pp. 668–670.

Iorio, Raffaele. 1985. "Olivo e olio in Terra di Bari in età normanno-sveva," *Quaderni medievali*, 20, pp. 67–102.

Kaplan, Steven. 1976. *Bread: Politics and Political Economy in the Reign of Louis XV*, The Hague, Martinus Nijoff.

Kislinger, Ewald. 2003. "Dall'ubriacone al krasopateras: Il consumo di vino a Bisanzio," in *La civiltà del vino: Fonti, temi e produzioni vitivinicole dal Medioevo al Novecento*, ed. G. Archetti, Brescia, Centro Culturale Artistico di Franciacorta e del Sebino, pp. 139–163.

Knibiehler, Yvonne. 1981. "Essai sur l'histoire de la cuisine provençale," in *National and Regional Styles of Cookery*, Oxford Symposium on Food and Cookery, London, Prospect Books, pp. 184–190.

Koder, Johannes, and Weber, Thomas. 1980. *Liutprand von Cremona in Konstantinopel*, Vienna, Verlag der Osterreichischen Akademie der Wissenschaften.

Lachiver, Michel. 1988. *Vins, vignes et vignerons: Histoire du vignoble français*, Paris, Fayard.

Lambert, Carole, ed. 1992. *Du manuscrit à la table: Essais sur la cuisine au Moyen Âge et répertoire des manuscrits médiévaux contenant des recettes culinaires*, Montréal, Presses de l'Université de Montreal/Paris, Champion-Slatkine.

Laurioux, Bruno. 1983. "De l'usage des épices dans l'alimentation médiévale," *Médiévales*, 5, pp. 15–31. [Laurioux. 1985. "Spices in the Medieval Diet: A New Approach," *Food and Foodways*, 1/1–2, pp. 43–75.]

——. 1988. "Le 'Registre de cuisine' de Giovanni Bockenheym, cuisinier du pape Martin V," *Mélanges de l'École Française de Rome*, 100, pp. 709–760.

——. 1992. "Table et hiérarchie sociale à la fin du Moyen Âge," in *Du manuscrit à la table: Essais sur la cuisine au Moyen Âge et répertoire des manuscrits médiévaux contenant des recettes culinaires*, ed. C. Lambert, Montreal, Presses de l'Université de Montréal/Paris, Champion-Slatkine, pp. 87–108.

——. 1996. "I libri di cucina italiani alla fine del medioevo: Un nuovo bilancio," *Archivio Storico Italiano*, 154, pp. 33–58.

——. 1997a. "Cucine medievali (secoli XIV e XV)," in *Storia dell'alimentazione*, ed. J.-L. Flandrin and M. Montanari, Rome-Bari, Laterza, pp. 356–370. [Laurioux. 1999. "Medieval Cooking," in *Food: A Culinary History from Antiquity to the Present*, New York, Columbia University Press, pp. 295–301.]

——. 1997b. *Le règne de Taillevent. Livres et pratiques culinaires à la fin du Moyen Âge*, Paris, Publications de la Sorbonne.

——. 1997c. *Les livres de cuisine médiévaux*, Turnhout, Brepols (Typologie des sources du Moyen Âge Occidental, fasc. 77).

——. 2005. *Une histoire culinaire du Moyen Âge*, Paris, Champion.

——. 2006. *Gastronomie, humanisme et société à Rome au milieu du XVᵉ siècle*, Florence, Sismel/ Edizioni del Galluzzo.

Le Goff, Jacques. 1977. *Tempo della Chiesa e tempo del mercante*, Turin, Einaudi. [Le Goff. 1980. *Time, Work and Culture in the Middle Ages*, Chicago, University of Chicago Press.]

Lévi-Strauss, Claude. 1958. *Anthropologie structurale*, Paris, Plon. [Lévi-Strauss. 1963–76. *Structural Anthropology*, New York, Basic Books.]

——. 1964. *Le cru et le cuit*, Paris, Plon. [Lévi-Strauss. 1969. *The Raw and the Cooked*, New York, Harper & Row.]

——. 1965. "Le triangle culinaire," in *L'Arc*, 26, pp. 19–29 (riproposto in *Food And History*, 2/1, 2004, pp. 9–19). [Lévi-Strauss. 1997. "The Culinary Triangle," in *Food and Culture: A Reader*, London, Routledge, pp. 28–35.]

——. 1966. *Du miel aux cendres*, Paris, Plon. [Lévi-Strauss. 1973. *From Honey to Ashes*, New York, Harper & Row.]

——. 1968. *L'origine des manières de table*, Paris, Plon. [Lévi-Strauss. 1978. *The Origin of Table Manners*, New York, Harper & Row.]

Lombardi Satriani, Luigi M., and Meligrana, Marinella. 1982. *Il ponte di San Giacomo: L'ideologia della morte nella società contadina del Sud*, Milan, Rizzoli.

Lorcin, Marie-Therèse. 1985. "Humeurs, bains et tisanes: L'eau dans la médecine médiévale," in *L'eau au Moyen Âge*, Aix-en-Provence, Publications du CUER MA—Université de Provence, pp. 259–273.

Lubello, Sergio. 2002. "I ricettari italiani di cucina dei secoli XIV–XVI," in *Saperi e sapori del Mediterraneo: La cultura dell'alimentazione e i suoi riflessi linguistici*, ed. A. Marra, I. Pinto, and D. Silvestri, Naples, Istituto Universitario Orientale, pp. 1141–1154.

Mane, Perrine. 1983. *Calendriers et techniques agricoles (France-Italie, XIIe–XIIIe siècles)*, Paris, Le Sycomore.

Marchese, Pasquale. 1989. *L'invenzione della forchetta*, Soveria Mannelli, Rubbettino.

Martellotti, Anna. 2005. *I ricettari di Federico II: Dal "Meridionale" al "Liber de coquina*," Florence, Olschki.

Matheus, Michael. 2003. "La viticoltura medievale nelle regioni transalpine dell'Impero," in *La civiltà del vino: Fonti, temi e produzioni vitivinicole dal Medioevo al Novecento*, ed. G. Archetti, Brescia, Centro Culturale Artistico di Franciacorta e del Sebino, pp. 91–121.

Mazzarino, Angelo. 1951. *Aspetti sociali del quarto secolo: Ricerche sulla società tardo-romana*, Rome, L'"Erma" di Bretschneider.

Mazzetti di Pietralata, Mario, ed. 2006. *Prima colazione: Come & perché: Storia, scienza e cultura*, Rome, Agra.

Meldolesi, Claudio. 1973. *Spettacolo feudale in Sicilia: Testi e documenti*, Palermo, S. F. Flaccovio.

Melis, Federigo. 1984. "Note sulle vicende storiche dell'olio d'oliva (secoli XIV–XVI)," in Federigo Melis, *I vini italiani nel Medioevo*, Florence, Le Monnier, pp. 127–134.

Merlini, Domenico. 1894. *Saggio di ricerche sulla satira contro il villano*, Turin, Loescher.

Messedaglia, Luigi. 1941–42. "Schienale e morona: Storia di due vocaboli e contributo allo studio degli usi alimentari e dei traffici veneti con il Levante," *Atti del Reale Istituto Veneto di scienze, lettere ed arti*, 101/2, pp. 1–58.

——. 1943–44. "Leggendo la Cronica di frate Salimbene da Parma: Note per la storia della vita economica e del costume nel secolo XIII," *Atti dell'Istituto veneto di scienze, lettere ed arti*, 103/2, pp. 351–426.

——. 1974. *Vita e costume della Rinascenza in Merlin Cocai*, Padua, Antenore.

Montanari, Massimo. 1979. *L'alimentazione contadina nell'alto Medioevo*, Naples, Liguori.

——. 1984. *Campagne medievali: Strutture produttive, rapporti di lavoro, sistemi alimentari*, Turin, Einaudi.

——. 1988a. *Alimentazione e cultura nel Medioevo*, Rome-Bari, Laterza.

——. 1988b. "Uomini e orsi nelle fonti agiografiche dell'alto Medioevo," in *Il bosco nel Medioevo*, ed. B. Andreolli and M. Montanari, Bologna, Clueb, pp. 55–72.

——. 1989. *Convivio: Storia e cultura dei piaceri della tavola dall'Antichità al Medioevo*, Rome-Bari, Laterza.

——. 1990a. "Alimentazione e cultura tra Medioevo ed Età moderna," in *Maestro Martino da Como e la cultura gastronomica del Rinascimento*, Milan, Terziaria, pp. 39–43.

——. 1990b. "Vegetazione e alimentazione," in *L'ambiente vegetale nell'alto Medioevo*, Spoleto, Fondazione Centro Italiano di Studi sull'Alto Medioevo, pp. 281–322.

——. 1991. *Nuovo Convivio: Storia e cultura dei piaceri della tavola nell'Età moderna*, Rome-Bari, Laterza.

——. 1993. *La fame e l'abbondanza: Storia dell'alimentazione in Europa*, Rome-Bari, Laterza. [Montanari. 1994. *The Culture of Food*, Cambridge, Mass., Blackwell.]

———. 1997a. "Condimento, fondamento: Le materie grasse nella tradizione alimentare europea," in *Alimentazione e nutrizione: Secc. XIII–XVIII*, ed. S. Cavaciocchi, Florence, Le Monnier, pp. 27–51.

———. 1997b. "Strutture di produzione e sistemi alimentari nell'alto Medioevo," in *Storia dell'alimentazione*, ed. J.-L. Flandrin and M. Montanari, Rome-Bari, Laterza, pp. 217–225. [Montanari. 2013. "Production Structures and Food Systems in the Early Middle Ages," in *Food: A Culinary History*, New York, Columbia University Press, pp. 168–177.]

———. 1999. "Il messaggio tradito: Perfezione cristiana e rifiuto della carne," in *La sacra mensa: Condotte alimentari e pasti rituali nella definizione dell'identità religiosa*, ed. R. Alessandrini and M. Borsari, Modena, Fondazione Collegio S. Carlo—Banca Popolare dell'Emilia Romagna, pp. 99–130.

———. 2000. "Immagine del contadino e codici di comportamento alimentare," in *Per Vito Fumagalli: Terra, uomini, istituzioni medievali*, ed. M. Montanari and A. Vasina, Bologna, Clueb, pp. 199–213.

———. 2002a. "Bologna grassa: La costruzione di un mito," in *Il mondo in cucina: Storia, identità, scambi*, ed. M. Montanari, Rome-Bari, Laterza, pp. 177–196.

——— (with G. Albertoni, T. Lazzari, and G. Milani). 2002b. *Storia medievale*, Rome-Bari, Laterza.

———. 2003. "Acqua e vino nel Medioevo cristiano," in *Storia dell'acqua: Mondi materiali e universi simbolici*, ed. V. Teti, Rome, Donzelli, pp. 225–236.

———. 2004. *Il cibo come cultura*, Rome-Bari, Laterza. [Montanari. 2010. *Food Is Culture*, New York, Columbia University Press.]

———. 2005a. "Maometto, Carlo Magno e lo storico dell'alimentazione," *Quaderni medievali*, 40, pp. 64–71.

———. 2005b. "Un historien gourmand," in *Le désir et le goût: Une autre histoire (XIIIe– XVIIIe siècles)*, ed. O. Redon, L. Sallmann, and S. Steinberg, Saint-Denis, Presses Universitaires de Vincennes, pp. 371–381.

———. 2008. *Il formaggio con le pere: La storia in un proverbio*, Rome-Bari, Laterza. [Montanari. 2010. *Cheese, Pears, and History: In a Proverb*, New York, Columbia University Press.]

———. 2010. *L'identità italiana in cucina*, Rome-Bari, Laterza. [Montanari. 2013. *Italian Identity in the Kitchen, or Food and the Nation*, New York, Columbia University Press.]

Montanari, Massimo, and Sabban, Françoise, eds. 2002. *Atlante dell'alimentazione e della gastronomia*, Turin, Utet.

Motta, Giuseppe. 2003. "Il vino nei Padri: Ambrogio, Gaudenzio e Zeno," in *La civiltà del vino: Fonti, temi e produzioni vitivinicole dal Medioevo al Novecento*, ed. G. Archetti, Brescia, Centro Culturale Artistico di Franciacorta e del Sebino, pp. 195–204.

Moulin, Léo. 1988. *La vita quotidiana dei monaci nel Medioevo*, Milan, Mondadori (ed. orig. Paris, Hachette, 1978).

Mulon, Marianne. 1970. "Les premières recettes médiévales," in *Pour une histoire de l'alimentation*, Paris, École Pratique des Hautes Études, pp. 236–240.

———. 1971. "Deux traités inédits d'art culinaire médiévale," in *Actes du 93e Congrès National des Sociétés Savantes*, Vol. I, *Les problèmes de l'alimentation*, Paris, Editions de la Bibliothèque Nationale, pp. 369–435.

Muzzarelli, Maria Giuseppina. 1982. "Norme di comportamento alimentare nei libri penitenziali," *Quaderni medievali*, 13, pp. 45–80.

Naso, Irma. 1990a. *Formaggi nel Medioevo: La "Summa lacticiniorum" di Pantaleone da Confienza*, Turin, Il Segnalibro.

——. 1990b. "L'alimentation à la cour de Savoie (XIIIe–XVe siècles)," in *La Maison de Savoie en Pays de Vaud*, ed. B. Andenmatten and D. De Raemy, Lausanne, Payot.

Parenti, Stefano. 2003. "Il vino nella liturgia bizantina," in *La civiltà del vino: Fonti, temi e produzioni vitivinicole dal Medioevo al Novecento*, ed. G. Archetti, Brescia, Centro Culturale Artistico di Franciacorta e del Sebino, pp. 457–475.

Pasquali, Gianfranco. 1972. "Olivi e olio nella Lombardia prealpina," *Studi medievali*, s. 3, 13, pp. 257–265.

——. 1974. "La vitivinicoltura in Romagna nell'alto Medioevo (secoli IX–X)," *Studi Romagnoli*, 25, pp. 215–233.

Pastoureau, Michel. 1989. *Couleurs, images, symboles: Études d'histoire et d'anthropologie*, Paris, Le Léopard d'or.

Pérez Samper, Maria de los Angeles. 1998. *La alimentación en la España del Siglo de Oro: Domingo Hernández de Maceras, Libro del arte de cocina*, Huesca, La Val de Onsera.

Pertusi, Agostino. 1983. "Civiltà della tavola a Bisanzio e a Venezia," in A. Pertusi, G. Ortalli, and I. Paccagnella, *Civiltà della tavola dal Medioevo al Rinascimento*, Vicenza, Neri Pozza, pp. 3–13.

Perullo, Nicola. 2006. "Per un'estetica del cibo," *Aesthetica Preprint*, 78, pp. 16–17.

Peyer, Hans Conrad. 1990. *Viaggiare nel Medioevo: Dall'ospitalità alla locanda*, Rome-Bari, Laterza (ed. orig. Hanover, Hahnsche Buchhandlung, 1987).

Pini, Antonio Ivan. 1990. "Vite e olivo nell'alto Medioevo," in *Il mondo vegetale nell'alto Medioevo*, Spoleto, Fondazione Centro Italiano di Studi sull'Alto Medioevo, pp. 329–380.

——. 2000. "Miracoli del vino e santi bevitori nell'Italia d'età comunale," in *La vite e il vino: Storia e diritto (secoli XI–XIX)*, ed. M. Da Passano, A. Mattone, F. Mele, and P. Simbula, Rome, Carocci, I, pp. 367–382.

Pinkard, Susan. 2009. *A Revolution in Taste: The Rise of French Cuisine*, New York, Cambridge University Press.

Prosperi, Ilaria. 2007. "Gnoseologia e fisiologia del gusto nella tradizione neoplatonica-agostiniana e in quella aristotelica-tomista, tesi di dottorato" in *Storia medievale*, relatore M. Montanari, Bologna, Università di Bologna.

Pucci Donati, Francesca. 2006. "Dietetica e cucina nel 'Regimen sanitatis' di Maino de' Maineri," *Food and History*, 4/1, pp. 107–131.

——. 2007. *Dieta, salute, calendari: Dal regime stagionale antico ai "regimina mensium" medievali: Origine di un genere nella letteratura medica occidentale*, Spoleto, Fondazione Centro Italiano di Studi sull'Alto Medioevo.

——. 2012. "Frammenti di cultura alimentare nella tradizione proverbiale italiana dei secoli XIII–XV," *Studi medievali*, s. 3, 53/1.

Rebora, Giovanni. 1996. *La cucina medievale italiana tra Oriente ed Occidente*, Genoa, Università di Genova.

Redon, Odile. 1992. "La réglementation des banquets par les lois somptuaires dans les villes d'Italie (XIIIe–XVe siècles)," in *Du manuscrit à la table: Essais sur la cuisine au Moyen Âge et répertoire des manuscrits medievaux contenant des recettes culinaires*, ed. C. Lambert, Montreal, Presses de l'Université de Montréal/Paris, Champion-Slatkine, pp. 109–119.

Redon, Odile, Sabban, Françoise, and Serventi, Silvano. 1994. *A tavola nel Medioevo*, Rome-Bari, Laterza (ed. orig. Paris, Stock, 1993). [Redon et al. 1998. *The Medieval Kitchen: Recipes from France and Italy*, Chicago, University of Chicago Press.]

Renouard, Yves. 1964. "Le vin vieux au Moyen Âge," *Annales du Midi*, 76, pp. 447–455.

Robinson, Jancis. 1995. *Das Oxford Weinlexikon*, Bern-Stuttgart, Hallwag. [Robinson. 1994. *The Oxford Companion to Wine*, Oxford, Oxford University Press.]

Roche, Daniel. 1984. "Le temps de l'eau rare du Moyen Âge à l'Epoque Moderne," *Annales ESC*, 39/2, pp. 383–399.

Romagnoli, Daniela, ed. 1991. *La città e la corte: Buone e cattive maniere tra Medioevo ed Età Moderna*, Milan, Guerini.

——. 1997. "'Guarda no sii vilan': Le buone maniere a tavola," in *Storia dell'alimentazione*, ed. J.-L. Flandrin and M. Montanari, Rome-Bari, Laterza, pp. 396–407. [Romagnoli. 1999. "'Mind Your Manners': Etiquette at the Table," in *Food: A Culinary History from Antiquity to the Present*, New York, Columbia University Press, pp. 328–337.]

Rouche, Michel. 1973. "La faim à l'époque carolingienne: Essai sur quelques types de rations alimentaires," *Revue Historique*, 250/I, pp. 295–320.

——. 1984. "Les repas de fête à l'époque carolingienne," in *Manger et boire au Moyen Âge*, Nice, Les Belles Lettres, I, pp. 265–296.

Rousselle, Aline. 1974. "Abstinence et continence dans les monastères de la Gaule méridionale à la fin de l'Antiquité et au début du Moyen Âge: Étude d'un régime alimentaire et de sa fonction," in *Hommage à André Dupont*, Montpellier, Fédération Historique du Languedoc Méditerranéen et du Roussillon, pp. 239–254.

Sada, Luigi, and Valente, Vincenzo. 1995. *Liber de coquina: Libro della cucina del XIII secolo: Il capostipite meridionale della cucina italiana*, Bari, Puglia Grafica Sud.

Sahlins, Marshall. 1972. "La sociologia dello scambio primitivo," in *L'antropologia economica*, ed. E. Grendi, Turin, Einaudi, pp. 95–146. [Sahlins. 1965. "On the Sociology of Primitive Exchange," in *The Relevance of Models for Social Anthropology*, ed. M. Banton, London, Tavistock Publications.]

Salvatico, Antonella. 1999. *Il principe e il cuoco: Costume e gastronomia alla corte sabauda nel Quattrocento*, Turin, Paravia.

Sayers, William. 1990. "A Cut Above: Ration and Station in an Irish King's Hall," *Food and Foodways*, 4/2, pp. 89–110.

Scully, Terence. 1997. *L'arte della cucina nel Medioevo*, Casale Monferrato, Piemme. [Scully. 1995. *The Art of Cookery in the Middle Ages*, Rochester, Boydell Press.]

Sergi, Giuseppe. 1970. "La produzione storiografica di S. Michele della Chiusa, II," *Bullettino dell'Istituto Storico Italiano per il Medio Evo*, 82, pp. 173–242.

Soler, Jean. 1973. "Sémiotique de la nourriture dans la Bible," *Annales ESC*, 28/4, pp. 943–955.

Sorcinelli, Paolo. 1998. *Storia sociale dell'acqua: Riti e culture*, Milan, Bruno Mondadori.

——. 1999. *Gli italiani e il cibo: Dalla polenta ai cracker*, Milan, Bruno Mondadori.

Squatriti, Paolo. 2008. "I pericoli dell'acqua nell'alto Medioevo italiano," in *L'acqua nei secoli altomedievali*, Spoleto, Fondazione Centro Italiano di Studi sull'Alto Medioevo, pp. 583–618.

Stouff, Louis. 1970. *Ravitaillement et alimentation en Provence aux XIVᵉ et XVᵉ siècles*, Paris, La Haye, Mouton.

Thorndike, Lynn. 1934. "A Medieval Sauce-book," *Speculum*, 9, pp. 183–190.

Tombeur, Paul. 1989. "L'allégorie de la vigne et du vin dans la tradition occidentale," in *Image et réalité du vin en Europe*, Paris, Éditions Sider, pp. 181–273.

Tomea, Paolo. 2003. "Il vino nell'agiografia: elementi topici e aspetti sociali," in *La civiltà del vino: Fonti, temi e produzioni vitivinicole dal Medioevo al Novecento*, ed. G. Archetti, Brescia, Centro Culturale Artistico di Franciacorta e del Sebino, pp. 341–364.

Tramontana, Salvatore. 1993. *Vestirsi e travestirsi in Sicilia*, Palermo, Sellerio.

Tugnoli, Maria Bernadetta. 1988–89. *I segni del cibo: Alimentazione e linguaggio silenzioso nelle Consuetudini cluniacensi dei secoli X–XIII, tesi di laurea*, relatore M. Montanari, Bologna, Facoltà di Lettere e Filosofia, Università di Bologna.

Unwin, Tim. 1993. *Storia del vino: Geografie, culture e miti dall'antichità ai giorni nostri*, Rome, Donzelli. [Unwin. 1992. *Wine and the Vine: An Historical Geography of Viticulture and the Wine Trade*, London, Routledge.]

Van Uyten, Raymond. 2003. "Der Geschmack am Wein im Mittelalter," in *Weinproduktion und Weinkonsum im Mittelalter*, ed. M. Matheus, Stuttgart, Franz Steiner Verlag, pp. 119–132.

Varanini, Gian Maria. 1983. "L'olivicoltura e l'olio gardesano nel Medioevo," in *Un lago, una civiltà: Il Garda*, ed. G. Borelli, Verona, Banca Popolare di Verona, I, pp. 115–158.

Vercelloni, Luca. 2005. *Viaggio intorno al gusto: L'odissea della sensibilità occidentale dalla società di corte all'edonismo di massa*, Milan, Mimesis.

Verdon, Jean. 2005. *Bere nel Medioevo: Bisogno, piacere o cura*, Bari, Dedalo.

Visser, Margaret. 1991. *The Rituals of Dinner: The Origins, Evolution, Eccentricities, and Meaning of Table Manners*, New York, Penguin Books.

Vogel, Cyril. 1976. "Symboles cultuels chrétiens: Les aliments sacrés: Poisson et refrigeria," in *Simboli e simbologia nell'alto Medioevo*, Spoleto, Fondazione Centro Italiano di Studi sull'Alto Medioevo, pp. 197–252.

Younger, William. 1966. *Gods, Men and Wine*, Cleveland, The Wine and Food Society.

Zagnoni, Renzo. 1997. "La coltivazione del castagno nella montagna fra Bologna e Pistoia nei secoli XI–XIII," in *Villaggi, boschi e campi dell'Appennino dal Medioevo all'età contemporanea*, Porretta Terme, Gruppo di Studi Alta Valle del Reno/Pistoia, Società Pistoiese di Storia Patria, pp. 41–57.

Zug Tucci, Hannelore. 1985. "Il mondo medievale dei pesci tra realtà e immaginazione," in *L'uomo di fronte al mondo animale nell'alto Medioevo*, Spoleto, Fondazione Centro Italiano di Studi sull'Alto Medioevo, pp. 291–360.

Index

Abelard, Peter, 75, 219*n*10
abstinence: animal product, during Lent, 93; during Lent, 66, 74; from meat, in monastic diet, 73, 74, 75, 160, 161, 184; sexual, during Lent, 66; sexual, in monastic culture, 161; from wine and oil, in monastic diet, 222*n*34, 235*n*95. *See also* renunciation
adults, milk consumption and, 79–80
Aelfric, 29
aged cheese, 81–82, 86
aged wine, 145–46, 236*n*107
agriculture, 62
agronomy treatise, of Tanara, 104–5
Alcuin, on wine, 134–36, 140
Aldobrandino of Siena: on meat as nourishing food, 64, 65; on pleasurable food as guide to health, 205; on wine, 143
alimentary system: external projection of, 26; grammar of food and, 26; internal structure, 26; peasant culture, 26–27, 30–31
Alpine regions, 87, 100, 101
ambiguous status, of fish, 72–78
Ambrose, 126, 132, 142, 148, 235*n*73
Antimo, 28, 92–93
Antimus, 58, 229*n*44
Apicius, 24, 92
appearance, of cheese, 82
Appenine region, 108, 113
appetite, Salerno "regimen" on, 206

Appolinare, Sidonio, 75
Aquinas, Thomas: on drunkenness, 237*n*130; on flavor of water, 123–24, 128; herring eaten by, 76
Arabs, food grammar influence, 28
archeology, 8–9
aristocracy, 208; bread, 59; cheese consumption, 83; food of, 149–57; fresh food consumption, 156, 184; fresh meat consumption, 68; gout from meat of, 67; marketplace use of, 46–47; mealtimes of, 49; meat in dominant place, 36, 39, 100; military, 160; taste and customs convergence with peasantry, 150–51, 157, 208; wedding banquets duration, 50; wine served by, 136. *See also* nobility
Aristotle, on flavor of water, 123, 127, 128
artificial cooking, 17
artificial seasonality, 52
astringent properties, of chestnut, 116
Augustine, 124, 183; on drunkenness, 148; on five senses, 199–200; on sweetness of God and food, 207; on taste, 199–200; on water, 120–21, 126; on wine, 132, 136, 142, 233*n*45; on work, 130
auxiliary food, bread as, 57

baking, of bread, 59–60
banquet table. *See convivio*